FAIRY TALES 101

AN ACCESSIBLE INTRODUCTION TO FAIRY TALES

DR. JEANA JORGENSEN

CONTENTS

ACADEMIC ARTICLES

RESOURCES & RECOMMENDATIONS

Once again, I must thank my family for being endlessly supportive of my writing endeavors…this book, too, is for you!

This book is also dedicated to my folklore and fairy-tale colleagues. Our conversations at conferences, over emails, and in all manner of unexpected venues have provided so much fuel and inspiration for me!

Finally, this book is for fairy-tale lovers everywhere.

INTRODUCTION

WELCOME TO FAIRY TALES 101! This book is a collection of essays—some short, some long, some new, some old—meant to provide an accessible, fun introduction to the academic study of fairy tales. I'll explain a bit about how the book is structured here in the Introduction, but if you want to dive in and flip around, feel free! There's a glossary at the end for any jargon you might not know yet.

Whether you're a fairy-tale fan, a writer, a teacher, or any other kind of person who has fairy tales on the brain, this book will teach you the basics of what fairy tales are, how they work, and how they relate to other areas of society, like folklore, gender, and identity. So let's get started with some basic definitions here!

Oh, but you might be asking, who's your guide on this quest? I'm a folklore scholar with 20+ years in the field and an actual PhD in folklore (yes, this is a thing you can do) who's written over 20 academic articles and book chapters on fairy tales, along with encyclopedia articles on them. I've loved fairy tales since I was a kid and you better believe I freaked out (in a good way) when I got to college and learned that you could study folklore and fairy tales from an academic perspective. I wrote my first book, *Folklore 101*, as a general guide to folklore studies, and this book is a kinda-sorta sequel in the sense that it's meant to give an introduction to studying fairy tales, but it's also organized a bit differently (which I'll get to shortly). Really this book is more of a chimera, a wondrous sort of misshapen beast, than its predecessor. I also read and watch fairy-tale retellings constantly, and I may have written a few of my own...which you're not supposed to admit when you're a serious scholar, but whatever.

Anyway, moving on.

The way I'm defining fairy tales in this book is as fictional, formulaic narratives involving transformations, magic, and quests. Fairy tales shapeshift their way through folklore and literature, elite and pop cultures, oral and literary traditions, and multiple time periods and regions of the world. If you're sitting here going, "what's a narrative?", don't worry, I unpack all these terms in more detail in the next chapter.

The section immediately following this introduction will give you a handle on the basics: how we define fairy tales, what makes a folktale and a fairy tale overlap or not, a super brief history of fairy tales, and a guide on how to study fairy tales. There are some chapters in that section devoted to scholarly terminology too, like motifs and tale types, along with tale structure.

If you're intrigued by fairy tales but don't know much about them beyond what your faves are, I'd start with this next section. It will give you a good grounding in basic concepts and scholarly stuff. There's way more to fairy tales than meets the eye (or, ahem, the Disney versions), and I am always excited to start from the ground up to help build a working knowledge of these topics.

The next section contains some of my short essays and blog posts on fairy tales. Having studied them for over 20 years I have a lot of opinions, you know? In these essays, I connect fairy tales to current day events, weigh in on weird historical facts, and so on. There *might* be one or two of my signature rants in there as well.

The following section contains some of my scholarly work on fairy tales, in case you're wondering what academic writing on fairy tales looks like. I got permission from two academic presses to reprint published articles of mine that aren't generally available to the public. I dislike the fact that so much scholarly writing lives behind paywalls, so this is my attempt to set information free (in a legal way). I retained their original citation formats, so while the bulk of the book uses MLA style for citations, one of the essays utilizes Chicago style. Thank you to the folks at Wayne State University Press and the University of Illinois Press for permission.

The final section contains resources and recommendations. Of note is the glossary, since yes, unfortunately there is some jargon in this book. I try to briefly define new words the first time they appear in the book, but, well, that doesn't help much if you're reading the book out of order. I'm a big believer in making knowledge accessible, but I believe scholarly language evolved for a reason: to help us have highly specific intellectual conversations with precision. I promise that fairy-tale studies jargon isn't that bad, so if you encounter a word you don't know in this book, please flip to the glossary and look it up, then continue on your merry way. I also tried to pack in some goodies to this final section, like lists of classic fairy-tale works you should read (and which translator! Because that matters too!), favorite modern-day fairy-tale retellings, and other scholarly works to get you started. I annotate all these lists so you can get a sense of what will work best for you and your preferences. Oh, and there's an index at the end, since my scholarly training insists on needing one even if many people read on e-books these days anyway.

Also, just to get us on the same page real quick, here are some stylistic conventions you'll note throughout the book:

- When it's a noun, fairy tale is two words (as in this sentence).
- When it's an adjective, we hyphenate it (for example, we might speak of fairy-tale retellings).
- When referring to the title of a short standalone text, like the Grimms' version of "Little Red Riding Hood," it goes in quotation marks, and the same goes for literary renditions like short stories and poems; if it's a novel-length version or a film, like Disney's *Sleeping Beauty*, it goes in italics. Just referring to the tale type, like the generally well-known plot of something like "Cinderella," I tend to put it in quotation marks still, but other folklorists leave those out.
- Since fairy tales are a type of folklore, we'll also talk about folklore a bit in this book. Folklore is the noun version, and it doesn't get pluralized (so don't say "folklores," that just sounds weird; if you need to refer to plural something you can say "folklore text" or "folklore items" or "folk narratives" or something like that). As an adjective we might say folkloric, whereas if we're specifically in the realm of scholarship, we might say folkloristic (bit of a

mouthful, I know, but it's a parallel to how linguistic scholarship is the study of languages, so folkloristic scholarship is the study of folklore).

Unlike *Folklore 101*, which is primarily a series of short, interconnected book chapters teaching basic folklore topics, *Fairy Tales 101* goes a bit above and beyond the basics. We start with the basics, yes, like definitions, terminology, and history...but then I include academic articles, which are not necessarily beginner-friendly. If those aren't your cup of tea, feel free to ignore them; I just figured I would toss them in since they're already written and they're pretty representative of my scholarship. The recommendation and resources lists, too, are a new feature of this book, since I wanted to jam everything fairy-tale-related in as much as possible.

If you've gotten this far in the introduction, hopefully you know what to expect as you read. And hopefully you enjoy it!

BASIC CONCEPTS & HISTORY

MAKING PEACE WITH THE DEFINITION BEAST

WHAT THE HECK is a fairy tale?! Scholars are debating the specifics of our definitions, like, constantly. I'll share some of my faves below, so you can see how they compare to my preferred definition.

Here's what I tend to go with: fairy tales are fictional, formulaic narratives involving transformations, magic, and quests. Fairy tales shapeshift their way through folklore and literature, elite and pop cultures, oral and literary traditions, and multiple time periods and regions of the world.

Let's unpack all that!

A narrative is essentially a story (and you can use the terms interchangeably, though narrative is the more technical term in my mind). But not everything is a story, despite how the word gets tossed around to mean almost anything these days. Don't get me wrong, I love Instagram as much as the next person, but I don't think Instagram "stories" actually...tell a story. I think of a narrative/story as a framed recounting of events, usually with some intention and/or artistry behind it.

The example I give when teaching this concept in my college classes is that if I read you my grocery list aloud—green beans, almond milk, and so on—that's not a story. Nothing happens in it. It's just a list. I can think of some very clever storytellers who have made a list into a story (and here I am swooning in the general direction of Carmen Maria Machado; I highly recommend her story collection *Her Body and Other Parties*), but a list is not inherently a story. It's just a grouping of items.

In contrast, if I tell you: "OMG, the wildest thing happened to me while I was on my way to the market! There I was, when suddenly..." then that is the start of a story. It sets up something as having happened, which I shall recount to you. I'm framing the event, rather than assuming you were there as a witness, and so there is some artistic interpretation involved.

Classifying something as a narrative does not inherently weigh in on its truth value, which is something that is true of all folklore, really. Some narratives are closely based on truth, others have a looser relationship to it, and some narratives fly right by truth value on their way to more interesting things. A narrator might make truth claims about what they're telling or writing, but those claims will have more to do with what genre of narrative it is than whether it's a narrative or not.

In Western storytelling, it's common to think about stories as all having a beginning, a middle, and an end, though of course they don't have to be narrated in that order. We'll discuss fairy-tale structure later on, but in brief, I think the main takeaway here is that something has to happen or change within a story for it to be considered a story.

Fairy tales are narratives, as in stories, as in artistically framed recountings of events, yes? But since not all narratives are fairy tales, we need to narrow it down further. That's where the concept of genre comes in. A genre is a classification of similar items, so if you're perusing a movie theater or bookstore's selection, you'll see stuff classified as science fiction, romantic comedies, and so on.

Fairy tales are their own genre of folklore. They're narratives, but specifically those narratives that are fictional and formulaic, belonging to the larger genre umbrella of folktales (we'll get into that more too in the next section). Other narrative genres that are similar to fairy tales are myths and legends, in that they're all folk narratives (narratives found in folklore, hence, informally transmitted traditional culture). But these genres also have features that distinguish them from fairy tales. Myths are sacred narratives about the origins of the world and the people in it; they are told as true, at least for believers of that religion/spirituality. Legends are belief tales, also told as true, but they tend to take place more in recent/historical time rather than mythic/cosmic time. Fairy tales, being defined as fictional right off the bat, are thus inherently different from myths and legends.

To give a few brief examples so you can see what I'm talking about, we can look at these genres on the level of motif (that is, a recurring detail). Character motifs in myths are often gods, demons, and the first humans. Character motifs in legends are often ghosts, teenagers, and serial killers (especially if we're talking urban legends!). Character motifs in fairy tales are royalty, peasants, talking animals, and so on.

Now, you may get overlap in motifs between genres. The myth of the Garden of Eden in the Bible—and note, myth is not a derogatory term, it just means it's a sacred narrative to its believers—features an apple. The fairy tale "Snow White" also features an apple. But the stories are told/written in different contexts, for different audiences, and for different purposes. So don't be waylaid by superficial similarities between stories in genres that might be completely different!

As another way of understanding what it means that fairy tales are fictional, we can consider that no one thinks a fairy tale is recounting anyone's biography. No one thinks Cinderella is/was a real person. Lots of fairy tales have talking animal characters in them too…last I checked, those don't exist in the real world. Nor do magical items like magic rings or carpet exist.

Are fairy tales totally untrue? Ehh, not quite. While fairy tales weave a web of magical fantasy, they also revolve around real relationships: parents and children, lovers and spouses, rivals and helpers. Their emotional core resonates even if the surface layer of magical stuff is utterly fantastical and unreal.

Fairy tales are fictional narratives: check. But their definition also includes the phrase "formulaic," which I use to mean that they are highly patterned and repetitive. Sooo many things come in threes, for instance: the three little pigs, three nights at the ball, three tests of a protagonist's character, and so on. The plot structures of fairy tales are also pretty patterned. Most of them follow the downturn and uptick of a person's fate with a happily-ever-after to cap it off. There are exceptions, of course, but this kind of upwards-rising plot structure is the norm.

The second half of my definition sentence specifies that fairy tales revolve around transformations, quests, and magic. This is because fairy tales are generally considered to be a subset of the folktale genre, folktales being those folk narratives that are fictional and formulaic but don't necessarily involve tons of magic and fantastical motifs. But there's also some weird overlap and ambiguity between folktale and fairy tale, which I discuss in a few chapters. Classic fairy tales, though, almost always have magic in them, and they almost always showcase transformations: youthful protagonists mature, low-status people attain or regain higher social and/or economic standing, and single people often end up paired off and married. Quests are a little more hit-or-miss, since not every classic fairy tale sends people on quests, but some sort of journey is usually central to the plot.

Everything mentioned so far is about what's inside the fairy tale text, which I call its content. The motifs (like typical characters and magical objects) all live within the text, as do the themes (such as transformation). The fact that these stories are made-up rather than closely tracking to reality also relates to their content.

While the content of fairy tales tends to be pretty unique and easily identifiable, the context is also worth mentioning. That's what my second defining sentence covers: Fairy tales shapeshift their way through folklore and literature, elite and pop cultures, oral and literary traditions, and multiple time periods and regions of the world.

Fairy tales are natural shapeshifters; that's why we see them in written literature, in oral tradition (a.k.a. folklore), in film, in poetry, in graphic novels, in fashion, in children's toys, in costumes, and more. But as fairy tales move through the world, we would do well to observe the world in which they move…which is basically context.

Context is everything that surrounds a text and makes it meaningful. Who told the story? Who happened to write it down? In which language? In which region/country? In which time period? Context answers "who/when/where" questions, whereas content tends to answer "what" questions (as in, what is this story about, what do the characters in it do, and so on).

Fairy tales occupy numerous contexts. We have story texts from ancient Egypt and Greece and Rome that most people would read and be like, "That's basically a fairy tale, yep" and if you want to look those up yourself, I recommend finding translations of, in the order I described them, "The Tale of the Two Brothers," "Rhodopis" by Strabo, and "Cupid and Psyche" from Ovid's *Metamorphoses*. Mostly, though, the fairy tale as a recognizable genre crystallized in the Mediterranean in the 16th and 17th centuries, at a place and time where cultures collided in trade and print was beginning to flourish alongside oral tradition. I'll get into the debates about the potential origins of fairy tales in the history chapter, but most scholars agree on at least this much.

With a few solid centuries of documented fairy-tale history, plus numerous threads pointing at older origins, we can thus think of fairy tales as a somewhat recent phenomenon with way old roots. Additionally, fairy tales are constantly being updated to suit the beliefs and values of their tellers/writers/directors, since, unlike most written literature, there's not necessarily a single "correct" version of them.

Which brings us to the folklore vs. literature aspect of fairy tales. I hope your brain is ready to accommodate some ambiguity, because the answer is really "both/and." In fact, it's been argued that the various formats they appear in are interdependent on one another: "oral and literary tales form one immense and complex genre because they are inextricably dependent on one another" (Zipes 3). Fairy tales have their roots in oral tradition *and* they are transmitted through literature. Fairy tales are told among peasants and people tied to agriculture *and* they are transmitted by the cultural elite. Fairy tales are part of folklore, subject to endless revisions with not a single "original" or "right" version in sight *and* they are incorporated in pop culture, mass produced as movies and dolls and whatever the latest Disney or Pixar thing is.

You can hear a masterful rendition of a fairy tale from an illiterate woman on a farm *and* you can read the literary fairy tales of French aristocrats from the 1690s.

You can see a fairy tale on the big screen *and* read fanfiction of that same fairy tale on the internet.

You get the idea: fairy tales are told and retold in multiple registers of culture, from the rich and fancy and moneyed to the everyday folk. Fairy tales exist in places with little technology, and have leapt onto just about every digital platform there is. Just because a fairy tale (or folklore more generally) is technologically mediated doesn't mean it's not a fairy tale anymore, though of course earlier fairy tales, often those labeled "classical" or "canonical," come from time periods where all these forms of media didn't exist yet.

Their very mutability makes fairy tales difficult to define, but hey, it's also part of the fun.

In addition to content (what's in the stories) and context (what surrounds the stories), when working to define fairy tales, it's also worth touching on style and function.

The style of fairy tales is often distinct, but also somewhat variable. Swiss theorist Max Lüthi did some pioneering work on fairy-tale style, and his observations generally hold up: fairy tales have an abstract style, often focusing on surfaces rather than depths, and metallic colors rather than every spectrum of the rainbow. Just think of all the descriptions you've probably read of golden hair, a dress as bright as the moon or stars, and so on. The classic color trio of red, black, and white is an example of this too, as in Snow White's coloring in many versions. But then, the style might change depending on whether you're engaging with a tale from oral tradition or literature, and if you're reading it in translation, the translator's biases may have made an impact on the language too.

Finally, function is the purpose, meaning, or general "why" of a fairy tale (or any other narrative genre, really). Why do people want to tell or write this stuff? Why do audiences want to listen to or read it? What larger social role does it serve?

I rant about this a lot in *Folklore 101* (and to my college students...sorry if you've been on the receiving end of this particular diatribe in person), but basically, with anything that's folklore or folklore-adjacent, since we define it as informally-transmitted traditional culture, there's no law making it happen. Since folklore is not institutionalized the same way education, laws, medicine, and the economy are, it is not upheld by rules and the criminal justice system but rather by everyday people who *choose* to engage in it. There are social consequences for doing folklore badly, but no legal consequences.

With folklore and fairy tales, entertainment is an assumed function. Like duh, people tell fairy tales to entertain their audience, just like they tell jokes to make them laugh or sing laments while mourning. The artistic, creative, entertaining value of fairy tales is baked into their definition, so it's only noteworthy as a first step to getting to the real meaty stuff.

Underneath the sparkly fairy dust, fairy tales actually do a lot of heavy lifting: they educate about gender roles and what's considered "proper" behavior, they uphold social norms around monogamy and marriage, they showcase values such as "might makes right" and the importance of material wealth, they offer wish fulfillment to marginalized people, and then they also subvert all of the above to various degrees. While lots of tales idealize marriage, some say "nope, bad idea, run away from that serial killer before you're next" (here I'm thinking of the Grimms' tales "The Robber Bridegroom" and "Bluebeard"). While tons more tales idealize kindness and passivity and especially seem to encourage these traits in young girls, others show us female giant-killers like Molly Whuppie who remorselessly tricks the giant into killing his own children.

Basically, I don't think we'd be this culturally obsessed with fairy tales—and for centuries!—if they didn't play a serious function in our society. They enchant and entertain us, yes, but they also hold up a funhouse mirror that distorts our social norms and values, reflecting back both idealized and villainous versions of ourselves for us to ponder. While their glossy trappings and persistent (and inaccurate!) association with children may seem to trivialize their importance, trust me, fairy tales serve a variety of functions for people both past and present. I don't believe Disney would have been able to build their empire on anything less (not that Disney is the full extent of what fairy tales are or can be).

So: fairy tales are a distinct narrative genre, or form of storytelling, in terms of their content, context, style, and function. However, all the stuff we just covered is about what fairy tales *are*. Not to be too negative, but I also want to talk briefly about what fairy tales are *not*. This will hopefully help dispel some prevalent misconceptions about the genre.

Fairy tales are not universal, timeless, or ageless. I know they can seem that way, and there's at least one fairy-tale animated motion picture with a song containing the line "Tale as old as time" in it. But that's simply not accurate.

Fairy tales aren't universal because folklore (of which fairy tales are a subset) isn't universal. Since folklore is constantly changing and adapting to meet the needs of its tellers, there's not going to be any single piece of folklore that meets everyone's needs all at once. I'm not a big fan of the concepts of universals in the first place, and when we do see things that seem universal, they're usually so general as to be useless. Pretty much every culture has a star-crossed lovers story... okay, and? Every single culture has some form of storytelling, yes, but those genres vary according to the specific values of that culture. I'd feel safe saying that every culture distinguishes between true and less-true narrative genres, but even so, we don't find things that look like fairy tales in every single culture documented around the world. The main exception is that through cultural exchange and contact—and, some would say, cultural exports from those with the most clout—fairy tales have *become* darn near universal. Disney is a household name. But I don't believe that fairy tales *started* out as a universal folk narrative genre.

Fairy tales are also not timeless or ageless; again, because they're folklore (except for when they're more literary, sigh, I know) they're tied to specific people in specific times and places. Charles Perrault's version of "Little Red Riding Hood" looks very different from the Grimm brothers' version because late 17th century France was a very different place than early-to-mid-19th century not-yet-Germany. Erasing the specificity of the times, places, and people connected to fairy tales means we don't get the benefit of the context helping us interpret the stuff inside the tale.

Put another way, it totally matters that Hans Christian Andersen was writing in 19th-century Denmark, which was a highly class stratified society. That's part of why we see so many underdogs in his tales, from "The Ugly Duckling" to

"The Brave Tin Soldier" to "The Little Mermaid." If you pluck Andersen's tales out of his social context, you can still read and enjoy them, but you might be missing important information.

On a related note, fairy tales are not anonymous. At least most of the time. We have a lot of named writers/collectors— like Perrault, Jacob and Wilhelm Grimm, and Andersen as mentioned above—but even in an oral tradition situation, the people in the village *know each other*. They know who's a good storyteller and who's not quite there yet. When folklorists and anthropologists go out to collect fairy tales or any other kind of folklore, current best practice is to provide biographical information about the teller/performer/whomever.

Granted, some of these tales have been around for so long, we don't know who first created them. That's okay. We can still learn about whose hands have shaped the tales in the long chain of oral and literary transmission. Though, a time machine is still on my wish-list, so I can maybe eventually answer some of those pesky origin questions! The point is, fairy tales come from people, so assuming they're anonymous is false and also a tad insulting to the folks who've come up with highly artistic and well-thought-out versions of the tales, whether in oral or print tradition.

Finally, onto my biggest pet peeve: the assumption that fairy tales are for children. This assumption has been around for at least 200 years and I'll talk about it more in the history chapter, but basically, since the time of the Grimm brothers (early 1800s), fairy tales were slowly becoming entwined with the nascent genre of children's literature, to the point where people assumed they'd always gone hand-in-hand.

But no, fairy tales have always been by and for adults. Kids are a frequent audience, and goodness knows there are plenty of fairy tales as well as animal folktales (like Aesop's fables) with simplistic morals and saccharine messages intended to educate. But it's inaccurate to assume that fairy tales are primarily for children. Some of the earliest written collections, including those by the subversive French women writers of the late 17th century salon vogue, are clearly aimed at fellow adults, with lots of witty takes on society, gender, and power.

The sheer presence of so much sex and violence in fairy tales should be a clue that they haven't always been aimed at kids. Disney wasn't the first sanitizing presence in the genre, but their impact has been lasting. And this association of fairy tales with children (and women, and the domestic sphere) has in turn contributed to their marginalization and trivialization as compared to more "serious" forms of art and literature.

Now that we've covered all the facets of my preferred definition of fairy tales, I'd like to turn to some of my colleagues' definitions. This will also serve to introduce you to some of the big names in the field, though you'll also get a sense of who they are in the recommendations section at the end of the book.

Maria Tatar, known for her pioneering work on the Grimms' tales, writes:

There is magic in fairy tales, and the presence of enchantment is perhaps the defining feature of the genre... Rumpelstiltskin spins straw to gold; Hansel and Gretel discover a woodland cottage with a roof made of bread and windows of spun sugar; a skull lying on the forest floor begins to talk; a boy sails down the river in a peach. Again and again we witness transformations that create a crisis, breaking down the divide between life and death, nature and culture, animal and human, or self and other. Magic implies metamorphosis, and presto! we can see the clear link between these two defining features of the fairy tale. (xii)

What I like about Tatar's definition is that her emphasis on magic and metamorphosis parallels my insistence on the presence of magic, quests, and transformation in fairy tales. You'll find a scant few fairy tales without much magic in them, but some kind of transformation or change always occurs.

Kate Koppy, in *Fairy Tales in Contemporary American Culture*, writes:

I describe fairy tales as fictional narratives that simultaneously transmit cultural values and offer the audience discursive space to imagine "a future that differs from what now exists" as they observe the main character's struggle to ameliorate the lack that was the impetus to action. (45)

Once again, we see the emphasis on these stories being fictional, and some kind of change or progress, as the characters strive to better their lives.

This notion of progress is essential to the way that Jack Zipes, one of the most prolific fairy-tale scholars of our era, perceives the genre. Zipes is known for applying Marxist and feminist theories to fairy tales, as well as a foray into memetics. Like in my definition, Zipes makes it clear that "fairy tales tend to be secular" (2) even if they do contain magic; that magic is based less on prescriptive religious interpretations of the world, even if we do get characters like the Devil sometimes waltzing into fairy tales as either the helper figure or the villain (or sometimes both at once). Zipes continues:

the focus of fairy tales, whether oral, written, or cinematic, has always been on finding magical instruments, extraordinary technologies, or powerful people and animals that will enable protagonists to transform themselves along with their environment, making it more suitable for living in peace and contentment...Fairy tales begin with conflict because we all begin our lives with conflict. (2)

As we'll see in the chapter on structure, conflict and its resolution are needed for fairy-tale plots to happen.

I could pull books off my shelves and keep typing up definitions for hours, but I think you get the point: fairy tale scholars largely agree on how to define fairy tales and which aspects to highlight (their fictional nature; their inclusion of magic; their tendency to highlight progress, change, and transformation) even if we choose to emphasize different details about the genre.

References:

Bascom, William. "Four Functions of Folklore." *The Journal of American Folklore* vol. 67, no. 266, 1954, pp. 333-349.

Koppy, Kate. *Fairy Tales in Contemporary American Culture: How We Hate to Love Them.* Lexington Books, 2021.

Tatar, Maria, ed. *The Classic Fairy Tales. Second Norton Critical Edition.* W. W. Norton & Company, 2017, 1999.

Zipes, Jack. *The Irresistible Fairy Tale: The Cultural and Social History of a Genre.* Princeton University Press, 2012.

HOW DID FAIRY TALES GET THEIR NAME?

How many fairy tales can you think of that actually have fairies in them?

I'm guessing we've got a few classics: some versions of "Cinderella" that have a fairy godmother, the kind/unkind girls story in Charles Perrault's "The Fairies," the Disney version of "Sleeping Beauty" with the three fairies in it, and...hmm...

Hmm...plenty of fairy tales don't actually have fairies in them. I'm thinking about stories like "Little Red Riding Hood," "Jack and the Beanstalk," "Rumpelstiltskin," "Snow White," "Bluebeard," "Hansel and Gretel," "The Juniper Tree," "The Dragon-slayer," and...you get the point.

If fairy tales aren't technically defined by the presence of fairies in them, why is the word "fairy" in the bloody title?! This is due to a weird quirk of history and translation.

First off, different languages have different names for things (duh). What this means in our case is that "fairy tales" get called different things in different places: we have in

German the word märchen which basically means fairy tale, but there are a few distinct registers. To refer to something more from oral tradition we have volksmärchen or folktale, and to refer to something more from literature we have kunstmärchen or art tale. In Russian, the word for tale is skazka (plural: skazki) and so a fairy tale is called a volshebnoya skazka (wonder tale). And so on through a variety of languages that all have their own nuance.

Even in English, fairy tales get called different things sometimes. In Northern Ireland, they might be called fireside tales (Glassie 230) and would consist of traditional stories scholars classify as fairy tales, down to the exact tale types found in other regions of Europe. Migrant Traveller communities in Scotland simply use the word story to mean "narratives that both teller and audience recognize as fictional in content... Animals may speak, witches may cast spells, horses may fly, and cooking pots may walk of their own accord" (Braid 52).

The English-language term "fairy tale" specifically comes from French, where the term for these sorts of stories is contes de fées, which translates to tales of the fairies. This is specifically due to the influence of Marie-Catherine d'Aulnoy, a disgraced baroness who published Les Contes des fées in 1697. The works of d'Aulnoy became quite popular in English translation (Jones and Schacker 185), and so in translation, the phrase contes de fees became fairy tales, and it stuck.

Why fairies instead of any other supernatural creature? Well, it turns out that in early modern French storytelling, fairies played an important role. According to some important (and in my opinion, under-cited) scholarship by Holly Tucker, fairies were conflated with midwives in French society at the time. Just as midwives presided over pretty much all births (this was before "doctor" became the profession it is today), in

25

fairy tales fairies attend births and "determine the circum-stances and outcome of pregnancy by providing—or with-holding—aid to the mother-to-be" (56). Both midwives and fairies expected compensation for their assistance (62) and could turn nasty if it was not given. To sum up, in France from the 1600s onwards, fairy tales address "cultural concerns about the fairy-midwife's ability to baptize the newborn—for good or for evil" (70). So fairies played a really serious, really pervasive role in French fairy tales, and when those tales were brought over to England and translated, the name stuck even when the magical figure du jour got swapped out.

Also, not to make things more confusing, it's important to note that not every narrative with a fairy in it counts as a fairy tale. British and Irish legends (stories told as though they could have really happened) feature tons of fairies, but these aren't the nice Disney version with wands, wings, and a cheery demeanor. In County Fermanaugh in Northern Ireland, for example, folklorist Henry Glassie documented fairy beliefs about these "wee small people" who are well-dressed and live in castles, often accompanied by lovely lights and music (302). But humans must beware crossing the fairies, for they might steal a human child and leave a deformed changeling in its place, or strike a greedy man deaf, or rain misfortune on someone who dared to build on a fairy pad or a fairy pass, which are "rights of way, routes of travel they will alter for no man" (Glassie 305).

The fairies of legends can be quite dangerous; the fairies of fairy tales are primarily dangerous if you're mean to them or somehow cross them. They can serve the narrative role of donor figures, magic helpers, or villains...but those roles can just as easily be served by any other magical critter specific to the region where the fairy tale is being told.

Recently, some scholars have come to prefer the term wonder tale, as it's not quite as Eurocentric. Noted feminist scholar Cristina Bacchilega, for instance, observes:

> The genre of the "fairy tale" is still generally understood as European and North American; the Middle East constructed as the Orient has produced *The Thousand and One Nights*, wonder tales that have become identified with exotic magic and fantasy; most of the rest of the world has or had "folktales" that can become "fairy tales" but are not yet. (21)

Wonder tale is a bit more of a catch-all term, the same way that folktale is: a larger denomination of a fictional, formulaic narrative genre that may include references to magic and the supernatural. Calling something a wonder tale or a folktale doesn't lay a claim to the historic (mostly European) legacy of fairy tales the same way that, well, "fairy tale" signals that lineage.

I've chosen to use fairy tale in this book for the most part, because even though it's not even all that accurate—as you'll see, many of the tales discussed in this book don't feature fairies, like, at all—it's still the best way to signal this genre that we all know and love. Just be prepared to find other words occasionally mixed in, and if you read or speak other languages, get ready to encounter those words too! Fairy tales are a heady mixture of the transnational and the local, and our language reflects that.

REFERENCES:

Bacchilega, Cristina. *Fairy Tales Transformed?: Twenty-First-Century Adaptations & the Politics of Wonder*. Wayne State University Press, 2013.

Braid, Donald. *Scottish Traveller Tales: Lives Shaped through Stories*. University Press of Mississippi, 2002.

Glassie, Henry: *The Stars of Ballymenone*. Indiana University Press, 2006.

Jones, Christine A., and Jennifer Schacker, eds. *Marvelous Transformations: An Anthology of Fairy Tales and Contemporary Critical Perspectives*. Broadview Press, 2013.

Tucker, Holly. *Pregnant Fictions: Childbirth and the Fairy Tale in Early-Modern France*. Wayne State University Press, 2003.

FOLKTALE VS. FAIRY TALE

Navigating the differences between folktales and fairy tales is a bit tricky, in part because there's going to be overlap and ambiguity no matter how we slice and dice our definitions, but in general, folktale is considered the larger umbrella under which fairy tales fall.

If you've ever taken a world literature course, chances are good you've read folktales such as *The Canterbury Tales* by Geoffrey Chaucer or the *Decameron* by Giovanni Boccaccio. A lot of Shakespeare's plays incorporate plots from folktales, such as "King Lear" being based on the tale "Love Like Salt" (Aarne-Thompson-Uther tale type number or ATU 923, tale types being a plot classification system I'll talk about a bit in this chapter, and extensively in their own chapter).

Folklorist JoAnn Conrad defines folktale as such: "a form of traditional, fictional, prose narrative that is said to circulate orally" (363). Folktales are told worldwide, and they do not necessarily have magic and transformations as part of their definition the same way fairy tales do. If we drew a Venn diagram, folktale would be a big circle containing the smaller circle of fairy tales (since fairy tales are also traditional, fictional, prose narratives)...except for those fairy tales that generated outside of oral tradition, more in literary tradition. But even literary tales, created by a single person's brain (like Hans Christian Andersen's "The Little Mermaid") can flow back into oral tradition and become a part of a culture's folklore. So, again, these are not quite watertight categories since culture is messy and complicated.

Making things even more complicated, we *think* fairy tales evolved from folktales, but it's difficult to prove how the evolution happened. Regardless, they also exist contemporaneously. Conrad notes: "The folktale and the fairy tale continue to coexist in an uneasy balance" (366). Folklorists and anthropologists are still able to go out in certain communities and collect folktales and fairy tales that thrive in oral tradition. I regularly teach two of my favorite collections of this type in a course on global women's rights: *Speak, Bird, Speak Again: Palestinian Arab Folktales* by Ibrahim Muhawi and Sharif Kanaana and *Mondays on the Dark Night of the Moon: Himalayan Foothill Folktales* by Kirin Narayan. Both were based on fieldwork done in the 1980s and 1990s, with both folktales and fairy tales populating the books.

Some scholars base the folktale/fairy tale distinction more on how the tales function in a given society. Jack Zipes asserts:

Originally the folk tale was (and still is) an oral narrative form cultivated by non-literate and literate people to express the manner in which they perceived and perceive nature and their social order and their wish to satisfy their needs and wants. Historical, sociological, and anthropological studies have shown that the folk tale originated as far back as the Megalithic period and that both non-literate and literate people have been the carriers and transformers of the tales. (7)

In contrast, fairy tales arose as a specific response to the early modern era (roughly 1500-1800) and its shift in values, literacy, and economies. Zipes classifies the "rise of the fairy tale in the Western world as the mass-mediated cultural form of the folktale" (15) and goes on to argue that fairy tales became incorporated into various culture industries—children's literature, Disney, and so on—as a way of passing on bourgeois morals to children.

One useful distinction here, the "how much magic is in the story" metric, bears out when we look at how folklorists have classified folktales for over a century now. The tale type system is our way of categorizing folktale and fairy-tale plots based on their structure, and so we group together animal tales (like Aesop's fables), fairy tales proper, and then a whole host of folktales that have to do with (non-magical or less-magical) tricksters, scorned lovers, stupid monsters, and so on.

Example time. One of the oldest recorded folktales is in *The Odyssey*. While the overall text comes across as belonging to the genre of epic—tales of heroes and warriors, often set in semi-mythic time since there are also gods and supernatural critters running around—we also have the episode where Odysseus faces down the Cyclops Polyphemus. What does Odysseus do? He fakes an identity ("I'm Nobody"), blinds Polyphemus, and then runs away, leaving Polyphemus to make a fool of himself while bellowing, "Nobody did this to me!" That is classic trickster folktale territory: it's a fictional prose narrative that's passed on traditionally. We've documented its existence (tale type 1137 if you're curious) told among speakers of Russian, Lithuanian, Turkish, Greek, Catalan, Icelandic, and more.

The prophesized patricide and incest of Oedipus? Also a tale type (number 931). It's found in the West Indies, Ireland, Hungary, Spain, and more. While the plot in its ancient Greek form is unmistakably a Greek tragedy, it also shapeshifts to fit different contexts. And in fact, the surrounding tale types in the 930 numbers are all about predestination and prophecy, explored in folktale form (I guess it's a popular topic?).

When I teach a first-year seminar on fairy tales, in recent years I've taken to opening the class with some snippets from the *Decameron*. This is both to teach my students about how people have always turned to stories during times of pandemic (Boccaccio is thought to have written the *Decameron* after the Black Death rolled through Europe in 1348, and the frame tale contains references to the plague as well) and to demonstrate the inherent linkages between folktales and fairy tales.

The gist of the *Decameron* is that seven women and three men meet up in church while the Black Death is ravaging Florence, and so they do the olden-times version of quarantine by holing up in a villa and telling each other stories to pass the time. This is the frame tale: the external narrative that contains the internal stories, the ones they tell each other. It's called a "Proem" in the text though, if you want to find one of the multiple free public domain copies circulating online (I went with Project Gutenberg for this one). One of the tales I assign is the third story of the second day, where this dude named Alessandro has three uncles that spend all their money, so

Alessandro is kicking it in England trying to manage their affairs when a war breaks out and so he flees. He takes up with an abbot who, bizarrely, comes onto Alessandro after inviting him to share his bed in an inn (is this the origin of the "only one bed" trope?!)...but the abbot turns out to be the cross-dressed daughter of the King of England who wants to marry Alessandro, and so saves him and his uncles from ruin.

It's not *quite* a fairy tale. There's no magic in it, just bizarrely good fortune. But there's also a sudden rise in status, marrying royalty, cross-dressing, and the number three. Those are classic fairy-tale motifs. So to my eye, this tale looks a lot like a proto-fairy tale: almost there but not quite, a predecessor that helps lay the groundwork for the genre to crystalize in the 1500s or 1600s or so.

We call these texts—these portions of Greek mythology and of the *Decameron*—folktales because if you look at them and squint, you can be like, "Yes, this is a traditional story that no one actually believes is true. Kinda like fairy tales, but different." They are distinct from myths (sacred origin narratives about the very beginning of the world) and legends (belief tales set in more recent times, which can have more secular or more supernatural elements, but in theory could have happened).

So, once again, I'm sorry: I wish I could simplify this into nice, clear-cut categories that never overlap and never get muddy. In general, you're safe to assume that folktales exist globally as part of oral tradition (though they're sometimes written down), and that they're generally regarded as a fictional repertoire of storytelling, with their truth existing more in their commentary on the human condition than in their literal details. As such, fairy tales tend to be a subset of folktales. So far, at least.

REFERENCES:

Boccaccio, Giovanni. *The Decameron of Giovanni Boccaccio.* Translated by John Payne. Project Gutenberg. https://www. gutenberg.org/files/23700/23700-h/23700-h.htm Accessed 8 June 2022.

Conrad, JoAnn. "Folktale." In *The Greenwood Encyclopedia of Folktales & Fairy Tales,* ed. Donald Haase. Greenwood Press, 2008. 363-366.

Zipes, Jack. *Breaking the Magic Spell: Radical Theories of Folk & Fairy Tales.* Revised and expanded edition. The University Press of Kentucky. 2002 [1979].

A SUPER BRIEF HISTORY OF FAIRY TALES

THIS CHAPTER, y'all...writing it was no easy feat. I once witnessed a conference panel on the origins of fairy tales devolve into a shouting match that then migrated to the hotel bar with continuing raised voices.

I don't actually believe that we will ever know the full story of the origin of fairy tales. There are too many missing links: things from oral tradition that nobody wrote down, destroyed manuscripts, cases where some kind of transmission or innovation happened but the details were lost to the sands of time. But fairy-tale scholars have pieced together a lot of the story, and that is what I'm presenting here, with an attempt to make note of what the evidence is, where it came from, and when certain claims are regarded as controversial or not 100% true.

I also think that we risk getting distracted by flashy claims about the "true" origins of fairy tales. Assuming we ever manage to recover that much information, yeah, that would be super fascinating to know...but I worry that the hankering for origins distracts us from more pressing issues, like whether the gender politics in fairy tales actually instill conformist gender stereotypes in us all or not.

I'm going to make three (because of course) brief interrelated points about the history of fairy tales before diving into the details. First, while fairy tales as a coherent genre more or less evolved out of folktales in the 16th and 17th centuries in Europe, their history is far more global than that.

Second, fairy tales are primarily regarded as secular stories, but they do have some connection to religion and to religious history. In texts where characters like the Devil and Virgin Mary appear, they're there as stand-ins for a donor figure or villain, not as actual tell-you-what's-true-and-holy religious figures. This happened a lot in the Grimms' collection (early 1800s), so look up texts like "The Virgin Mary's Child" if you want to see what I'm talking about. It's to the point where you can almost expect references to the god/gods of a given religion, plus local ideas about angels or demons, to show up in fairy tales at least semi-regularly.

Third, while the full history of fairy tales is still a bit murky, it has always included multiple voices from different levels of society. In scholarly jargon, we'd say they're polyvocal or multivalent, speaking with more than one voice on more than one register. For all that a lot of dudes have been central to the history of fairy tales—to the point where scholars sometimes jokingly refer to the holy trinity of Perrault, the Grimms, and Andersen—new scholarship is uncovering women's contributions on a regular basis. Same with those of non-Westerners, social outsiders, and so on. And this work on fairy tales, both old and new, canonical and variant? It demonstrates that fairy tales have always been political, despite the sanitized versions for kids that many of us have become accustomed to.

The development of the fairy tale can be roughly divided into the following time periods: ancient times, the European *and* global Middle Ages, the early modern period (1500s-1800s), the 1800s, the 1900s, and the present. Some of these time periods overlap and intermingle, so I'll do my best to point out their distinctive traits.

As far as we can tell, something like folktales existed in ancient times, and some of them closely resemble fairy tales and were preserved in writing. Two examples stand out. "The Tale of Two Brothers" (from 13th-12th century BCE Egypt) features brothers whose fates are linked and multiple transformations. It is bizarrely similar to the Grimms' tale "The Two Brothers," as both feature animal helpers and a magical sign of life (as well as two brothers whose fates are linked, as the title indicates). As Andrew Teverson notes, these comparisons "cannot be seen as evidence of an unbroken line of transmission between the fictions of ancient Egypt and Modern Germany," but they do, "however, furnish evidence that tales of magic with resemblances to those fictions we now call fairy tales were in circulation in Ancient Egypt three millennia before the genre-defining collections of the modern era" (3). Next, North African writer Lucius Apuleius's 2nd century CE novel *Metamorphoses* contains the tale "Cupid and Psyche," which is an early beastly bridegroom tale, thought to be a forerunner of "Beauty and the Beast." Texts of both these tales are available in the Jones and Schacker volume in the works cited list below.

Early texts of "Cinderella" similarly ask us to consider the potential links and sources of fairy-tale history. The oldest recorded version of the tale dates back to 9th century China, featuring a young woman mistreated by her stepmother, granted the ability to go to a gathering where she'll be selected for marriage by a king...by a magic fish, rather than a fairy godmother. Titled "Yeh Hsien," this text was likely brought to Europe via trade routes. Alternatively, the 1st century BCE tale "Rhodopis" by Strabo has been posited as a precursor to Cinderella, since it involves an eagle bringing a maiden's shoe to a king, who then wishes to marry her (Teverson 4). My go-to book on fairy tales in the ancient world is Graham Anderson's book of that name.

Going farther abroad, there are multiple other folktale and/or fairy-tale sources worth noting. For instance, the *Panchatantra* is a collection from 3rd century BCE India, written in Sanskrit, which contains a number of folktales within a frame tale. Many of the tales are fables or animal tales, with speaking animal protagonists that convey wise and moral messages. It's thought to have reached Europe via Arabic translations (Belcher), pointing at an important chain of transmission for folk narratives in the past.

During the Middle Ages, we also have some evidence of fairy-tale-like things in circulation. Jan Ziolkowski has a whole book on the influence of medieval Latin poetry on fairy tales, *Fairy Tales from Before Fairy Tales*. Among other things, he found evidence that "the Brothers Grimm drew directly on narratives they encountered in Medieval Latin manuscripts" (4). And while the first published version of "Little Red Riding Hood" is Charles Perrault's 1697 text, Ziolkowski analyzes an 11th century Latin verse titled "A Girl Saved from Wolf Cubs." This poem tells of a little girl in a red baptismal garment kidnapped by a wolf to feed to its cubs, but the cubs cannot harm the girl (103; 116-117). Whether or not this text was a direct source for more modern versions of "Little Red Riding

Hood" that are only 300 years old instead of 1,000 years old, the similarity is uncanny, and it tells us that these motifs are all likely interlinked somehow. This is also an indication about how religion can play a role in fairy tales even when the tales themselves are not explicitly religious; "A Girl Saved from Wolf Cubs" likely riffs on Christian beliefs of the day, from the importance of baptism to the godfather figure who is named in the text.

The other interesting thing happening in the Middle Ages was a phenomenon called the lays (or lais) of Marie de France. She lived during the 12th century in, you guessed it, France, and that's most of what we know about her. She wrote fables as well as lays (which are short narrative romances, but in verse rather than prose), and those lays contained some classic fairy-tale elements: not just fairies, but courtly love and social unions. Her lays "preserve the enchantment and magic of the original folk narratives" (Neeman 605), thereby presenting yet another potential precursor for modern fairy tales. In the Jones and Schacker volume, they print one of the lays titled "La Fresne" (translated as the ash tree), about twin girls separated at birth, one raised in an abbey with a rich recognition token, which is later the key to being with her fellow high-born lover. Sounds very fairy-tale-esque to me.

In less-Eurocentric contributions from the Middle Ages, we can't not mention *The Arabian Nights*, which is also called *The Thousand and One Nights*. Framed by a brutal tale about wife-killer King Shahrayar, who marries the vizier's daughter Scheherazade, who tells him tales with cliff-hangers night after night in order to save her life, the collection contains hundreds of tales. Some of the tales therein are fables or animal tales, others are less-magical folktales, and still others are fairy tales proper.

39

The earliest manuscript of the *Nights* dates back to the fifteenth century, but scholars believe its origins to be much older: "The frame tale partly derives from Indian models, was constituted in Persian in the pre-Muslim or early Muslim period, and is first attested in tenth-century Arabic sources" (Marzolph 47). So, it's probably older than our oldest recorded version, since stuff tends to circulate in oral tradition for a while before someone thinks to write it down.

The *Nights* makes for an interesting case study, though, because while we can place its origins in the global Middle Ages (or earlier?!), it transformed yet again into a very different iteration in the early 1700s. French dude Antoine Galland decided to do a translation from Arabic, and he also decided to include some new tales, those he'd heard from Syrian taleteller Hanna Diab. Those tales include "Aladdin and the Magic Lamp" and "Ali Baba and the Forty Thieves" (Marzolph 49), which a lot of Westerners associate with the *Nights* today but were not in fact in the original manuscript (as far as we know, anyway). Galland's publisher apparently added in some Turkish tales just for kicks too (Marzolph 47), making this a truly multicultural, syncretic masterpiece. It's an amazing, multifaceted work that I don't have the space to truly get into here, so I recommend, if you're interested, checking out scholarship by Ulrich Marzolph on the topic as well as the new, beautiful annotated edition of the *Nights* translated by Yasmine Seale.

On to the early modern period. As a history nerd, this is a really fascinating time: it includes the transition from the European Middle Ages to the Renaissance, the Reformation and the Counter-Reformation, and—unfortunately for most of the global population—the beginning of European colonization of much of the rest of the world. Europeans were *hyped* about trade, scientific discovery, and literacy. We also see the last gasps of many monarchies, and the beginnings of phenomena like modern-day democracy and nationalism.

This is also when the fairy tale really came together as a recognizable genre on its own merit.

Scholars debate how much emphasis to place on this date, but I'll lead with it anyway: in the 1550s, Giovan Francesco Straparola published *Le Piacevoli Notti* (*The Pleasant Nights*), which, like classic texts that preceded it (Chaucer's *Canterbury Tales* and Boccaccio's *Decameron*) utilize a frame tale to give people an excuse to get together and tell stories, which are all written down and presented to the reader. But unlike the earlier collections, which are mostly folktales with a few hints of things that are kinda fairy-tale-like, Straparola's collection is saturated with fairy tales. Like whoa. This cannot be understated. One of the great scholars of the early modern Italian tale tradition, Nancy Canepa, writes: "it is not until Straparola, and especially Basile, that the types of what would become the Western fairy-tale tradition assume their wholly recognizable form" (59).

Straparola was a dude from Caravaggio who moved to Venice, where he did his work, and he published *Pleasant Nights* around the premise that fancy rich people go to the island of Murano to share tales (this is the frame tale). The tales told include fifteen fairy tales, including ones we know today like "King Pig" (a beastly bridegroom tale), "Constantino Fortunato" (an early version of "Puss in Boots"), and "Tebaldo and Doraclice" (my favorite relative of "Cinderella" that features, instead of a wicked stepmother driving the girl away, an incestuous father).

Working not quite one century later, Basile was middle-class and Neapolitan. His dialect shone in his posthumously

41

published 1630s work *Lo Cunto de li Cunti* (*The Tale of Tales, or Entertainment for Little Ones*), which surpasses Straparola's collection in that it not only contains a frame tale to organize the collection, but its frame tale *is* a fairy tale. An unlaughing princess, Zoza, is cursed to love an enchanted prince, but just as she's close to filling a pitcher with her tears in order to disenchant him, a treacherous slave takes her place. Zoza gets her comeuppance by casting a spell to attract the now-pregnant usurper's attention and make her crave fairy tales. Zoza disguises herself as one of the storytellers, they tell a bunch of stories (the tales contained in the volume), and then Zoza gets her man back.

The Tale of Tales, like *Pleasant Nights*, contains a bunch of recognizable fairy tales: versions of stories like "Cinderella" and "Rapunzel" plus "Sun, Moon, and Talia" (a "Sleeping Beauty" that definitely needs a trigger warning or three). The "murky moral world" of these tales is alternately enchanting and grotesque (Canepa 65), which is also a good way to describe the 2015 film, *Tale of Tales* (it's weird and gory, but I liked it).

Back to Straparola. This many fairy tales in one place was groundbreaking. It also created a fair bit of dissent among modern-day scholars.

Yeah, remember that conference panel fight I mentioned earlier? We're gonna get into it now.

In 2009, scholar Ruth Bottigheimer (who had up til that point done some very respectable studies of the Grimms) published a book called *Fairy Tales: A New History*. She criticizes fairy-tale scholars for accepting as an "unquestioned proposition" that "the folk invented and disseminated fairy tales" (1). Instead, Bottigheimer traces the generation of the entire fairy-tale genre to Straparola's mid-1500s publication.

One useful distinction Bottigheimer provides is between restoration tales and rise tales: whether the plot follows a rich/royal protagonist who falls in status and must endure trials and tasks to be restored to their original status, or whether the plot follows an impoverished protagonist who through the acquisition of magic and money, ends up in a well-off happily-ever-after. Restoration tales have clear links to "their medieval precursors" as "they begin with a royal personage—usually a prince or princess, but sometimes a king or queen—who is driven away from home and heritage" (10). In contrast, the characters in rise tales begin dirt-poor and must claw their way up the hierarchy. This is an interesting way to think about classifying fairy tales, though of course, the tales themselves are too malleable to make this simple; early versions of "Cinderella," like Basile's, have her coming from a noble family (hence it's a restoration tale) whereas other versions of "Cinderella," like one of the texts from Russia featuring Baba Yaga as a donor figure, have her starting out in a hut in the forest. Which one's the "right" version of the fairy tale? Trick question, there is no right version, just endless variability.

This is one of the critiques of Bottigheimer's ideas: her assumption that Straparola invented the rise tale, at precisely a time in social history when it would've been super relevant hence appealing. Bottigheimer writes: "As they were composed in the 1500s…rise tales are brief, secular narratives, with a plotline altogether new…they were quintessentially for and about people living in cities" (24). Does this mean that fairy tales for and about rural people are less valid?

Bottigheimer had long been a Straparola fan prior to the publication of *Fairy Tales: A New History* in 2009. In 2005, she presented her assertions about the origins of fairy tales at the

Congress of the International Society for Folk Narrative Research in Tartu, Estonia, with a follow-up roundtable in 2006 at the Annual Meeting of the American Folklore Society in Milwaukee, Wisconsin, USA. I attended both; the second one contained much more shouting. As a result, a bunch of the attending folklorists published a special issue of the *Journal of American Folklore* in 2010, including Bottigheimer's voice as well as contrasting perspectives. If you want to get deep into these debates, I'd suggest tracking down this issue of *JAF*.

I'll end this section with the perspective of Cristina Bacchilega, who ultimately disagrees with Bottigheimer not as a matter of historical record (because that, sadly, will always be incomplete hence inconclusive) but as a matter of identity and power. Bacchilega casts suspicion on Bottigheimer's account because it suggests that preliterate populations were not capable of coming up with their own wonder tales—they needed literate elites to come along and do it for them. In other words:

The poor, and by extension other subaltern groups, from women to colonized peoples, were—and are, is the implication—helpless to effect change, hopelessly dependent, apparently unable to narrate their own desires— and furthermore duped by entrepreneurial authors to buy this story and its magic as placebo and then reproduce it as their own. (Bacchilega 198-199)

Advocating for this kind of restrictive view of the agency people hold over their own lives and stories is not a great look. Further, saying the entire history of fairy tales began with print books kinda misses the point: freakin' long narratives *do* exist in oral tradition. I mean look at the Homeric epics for goodness' sake, so it's not as though the rural folk are incapable of spinning marvelous tales.

This scholarly conflict was quite tense at times, and for good reasons: it called into question the stakes of why we do what we do. One more quote from Bacchilega: "many of us in folktale and fairy-tale studies are aware of how buying into a European books-only history of the fairy tale means giving up on the social dynamics that keep people from all walks of life telling and retelling wonder tales across media, locations, and cultures" (201). Again, it's pretty Eurocentric to assume that only European people could've invented the fairy tale.

So, I'd recommend that you engage with this debate by following up on some of the sources I mention here if you're really curious about the nuances. For our purposes, though, we can reiterate the importance of the contributions of Straparola and Basile in Italy (hopefully without overstating it?!) and then move on to France.

France in the late 17th century had a lot of social conditions that led to it being the perfect petri dish for not one but two major styles of fairy tale. Let's dive into that context.

Christine A. Jones writes, in the introduction to her wonderful translation of Charles Perrault's tales:

In the seventeenth century, when Perrault wrote the story of Cendrillon, kings ruled all of Europe, an absolute monarch ruled France, and women had limited social and scant political influence. Stories of girls and their princes were not fantasy, they were the inexorable fate of any high-ranking member of society. In that world, writers of fairy tales did not so much project a dream about larger-than-life success—the way we tend to read these plots today—as draw on the material conditions of court life in France. (22)

This is a reminder that we modern-day readers benefit from: King Louis XIV was an absolutist ruler, with strict social etiquette and censorship in his court. Art was political back then (well, it always is), but it was specifically intended to promote the king's vision of a glorious unified France: "Literature and politics were not distinct enterprises in the mid-seventeenth century; on the contrary, the literati supplied the eloquence necessary to depict France's glory" (Jones 45).

Amidst all the fancy stuff happening at Versailles and around Paris meant to commemorate the Sun King's victorious reign...people were writing fairy tales. Why? This brings us to the two main strands of French fairy tales: the compact tales of Charles Perrault and the sophisticated complex tales of his female colleagues, the *conteuses*.

Perrault (1628-1703) was an important guy in his day: an academician and writer who served in the court of the Sun King. He participated in an important debate over women's worth, ultimately defending women's right to participate in public life, though he comes across as a bit conservative based on modern values. And the dude wrote fairy tales.

In 1697, Perrault published *Histoires ou Contes du temps passé* (*Stories or Tales of the Past*), now dubbed the Mother Goose tales. They include "Sleeping Beauty," "Little Red Riding Hood" (one in which she simply dies at the end, no rescue), "Bluebeard," "The Master Cat; or, Puss in Boots,"

"The Fairies," "Cinderella; or, the Little Glass Slipper," "Ricky with the Tuft," and "Hop o' my Thumb." The new translation by Jones in *Mother Goose Refigured* is excellent, but you can find public domain translations of Perrault all over the place because his work was just that popular. His "Cinderella" provides many of the details in the Disney version—glass slipper, fairy godmother, pumpkin carriage—while his narrative style, sometimes witty and dry, sometimes saccharine, also gave way to the appending of morals to the ends of tales. You know, for the children.

In short, Perrault's eight tales have become iconic. The *conteuses* wrote over a hundred tales during this first fairy-tale vogue from 1690 until 1715 (Jones 2) and yet they're barely known.

Fortunately, many feminist scholars today are on a mission to fix this lapse. In fact, the beginning date of this fairy-tale trend in France, 1690, is directly thanks to the work of one woman: Madame d'Aulnoy (1650/51?-1705).

I'll write a bit about d'Aulnoy's life and work, and just mention a handful of her peers due to not wanting this chapter to get too long, but trust me, they're all fascinating and worth looking up. In 1690, Marie-Catherine d'Aulnoy published "L'Ile de la Félicité" ("The Island of Happiness"), an early literary fairyland tale that, ironically, does not end happily (sorry, spoilers). It's also a noteworthy work since it's embedded in a larger frame tale, and as we saw above, frame tales and fairy tales have gone together for a long time.

D'Aulnoy led a tumultuous life. I go with Madame as her title, since she was technically a baroness whose mom led a plot to get d'Aulnoy's husband (who was thirty years older than her) accused of treason but it backfired, and the mom got exiled while d'Aulnoy was locked up (possibly in a convent?)

and...you can see where it gets a little convoluted. Anyway, d'Aulnoy was back on the scene in Paris by 1690 where she started publishing fairy tales and hanging out with her salon buddies. D'Aulnoy's tales don't always end happily, but they give us wondrously bizarre images of transformation (as in "The White Cat") and one of the better cross-dressing stories out there (a story called "Belle-Belle," think "Mulan" but more love triangles and general weirdness).

Some of d'Aulnoy's contemporaries include Catherine Bernard, Henriette-Julie de Murat, and Marie-Jeanne L'Héritier. A later addition to the French lady writer crew is Jeanne-Marie LePrince de Beaumont, who worked as a governess (in France and in in England) and who in 1756 published the version of "Beauty and the Beast" (based on the 1740 much longer version of Madame de Villeneuve) that would become canonical. Er, mostly (Disney still changed a fair bit).

Oh, and people weren't just writing fairy tales—they were reading them aloud, performing them in salons (kinda like the TED talks of their day), and then publishing them. This is a great reminder that fairy tales have always traversed the oral/literary divide in complicated ways. The women of fairy-tale salons were essentially like a girl gang who looked out for each other and helped one another promote their works. Plus it's another chance to make a point about identity and power; a lot of these women were ridiculously well-educated, but barred from participation in academic and medical societies because of their gender. So they came up with salons, "a setting for literary exchanges among brilliant and witty society women" (Jasmin 43), where *they* made the rules and *they* got to tell their own stories about gender. Holly Tucker goes so far as to suggest that the *conteuses* were "more than familiar with well-known medical and lay 'recipes' for conception and sex selection" (13) and thus inserted medical theories into their tales, not just for fun, but also to thumb their noses at the all-male establishment that locked them out of its halls.

Women who don't just write fairy tales, but also pack them full of sophisticated medical references out of spite? Those sound like my people.

The key takeaways from France in the late 1600s and early 1700s are: fairy tales were by and for adults (even ones with very grown-up serious jobs like Perrault), fairy tales were totally informed by debates about gender and sexuality in the time period, and they were incredibly sophisticated for the most part. Now read that sentence again and notice how many of those points run counter to the modern American under-standing of fairy tales (for kids; simplistic morals/meanings).

The next main development in fairy tales came in the early 1800s in Germany, except it wasn't Germany yet.

This is a point I stress in the classroom: "Germany" didn't exist yet. It was a collection of principalities, duchies, and the like, not a country.

The Grimm brothers, Jacob and Wilhelm, weren't collecting fairy tales just for kicks, or to show off their mad editing skills. They were collecting fairy tales in part to demonstrate that hey, Germans not only share a language, they share a common cultural heritage. And if the Grimms could prove that, with folktales and fairy tales as the evidence of common cultural heritage, then just maaaaybe they deserved to be a country. So nationalism played a role in shaping the Grimms' collection, even if fairy tales and politics don't seem obviously linked to everyone.

The backdrop for all this, too, was the Napoleonic wars and the rise of Romanticism. As a response to the Enlighten-ment's emphasis on logic and rationality, Romanticism attempted to nope out of modernity and hark back to a time when humans lived more in tune with nature. This is a bit of an oversimplification, but you get the drift. Folktales and fairy tales seemed to come from a more innocent time, so they were super appealing to all the Romantics.

It was a tumultuous time for German people as well as for the Grimms personally. As Jack Zipes notes, the Grimms and their work were influenced by a ton of major events: "the constant wars on German soil; the introduction and enforcement of the Napoleonic code in the Rhineland; the continual censorship of the arts, journals, newspapers, etc.; the changing loyalties of the German state" (*Breaking the Magic Spell* 65) and more. And they were bummed both at the prospect of continued French rule and the prospect of "oppressive German princes" being restored; they felt "a deep longing to have the German people united in one nation through customs and laws of their own making" (Zipes "Introduction" xxvi).

On the personal front, the Grimms didn't have easy lives. Jacob Grimm (1785-1863) and Wilhelm Grimm (1786-1859) were the two eldest children of Philipp and Dorothea Grimm (there were nine births total; only six survived childhood). When their dad died, the family was plunged into precarity, but when Wilhelm and Jacob rocked out at school, they went on to study at university and become scholars of law, linguistics, literature, and folklore (Zipes "Introduction" xxiii-xxv). Like, NBD, if you've studied historical linguistics, you'll know about Grimm's law, which is about phonetic change in Indo-European language. It was named after Jacob Grimm.

They were serious scholars, in short, contrary to the image of them in that movie directed by Terry Gilliam that always makes me shudder. And in their social circles, fellow Romantic writers Clemens Brentano and Achim von Arnim were already collecting and publishing folk songs, and started to nudge the Grimms to do the same. So they did.

Between 1807 and 1812 they started collecting tales. They didn't roam the countryside and visit peasants, but rather invited taletellers to come to them (Wilhelm even married one of them, Dortchen Wild). Some of these women were middle class or had aristocratic roots, and so some of the tales the Grimms recorded came from literary and even French (gasp!) sources. The Grimms also took some tales straight from books, and then heavily edited them. (Zipes "Introduction" xxix). The whole enterprise opened a can of worms about whether the tales are authentic (and heck, what does that even mean?!) and in fact whether fairy tales should be judged by their supposed authenticity or not. Since most fairy tales have transnational plots that happen to get their window-dressing by whichever local details are most interesting/relevant, this remains a compelling question in the scholarship.

Starting in 1812, the Grimms published seven main editions of their fairy tales, *Kinder- und Hausmärchen* (*Childhood and Household Tales*). The first edition, published in two volumes (one in 1812, one in 1815) contained 156 tales, while the final edition in 1857 had 211 tales (Zipes "Introduction" xxx-xxxi). Wilhelm made some serious alterations to them over time, taking out sexy stuff and adding Christian references. They also took out stuff that sounded too French— remember, their focus was on German folklore and heritage. The brothers extensively annotated the tales in early editions too, which helped found the study of fairy tales as we know it.

Another super important point about the progression of the editions is that they started out scholarly, but became more geared towards children as an audience. As you'll recall, I've been emphasizing that fairy tales have, for much of their history, been by and for adults. The Grimms were one of the early factors in changing this up. Zipes breaks this down for us:

Moreover, though the collection was not originally printed with children in mind as the primary audience—the first two volumes had scholarly annotations, which were later published separately—Wilhelm made all the editions from 1819 on more appropriate for children, or rather, to what he thought would be proper for children to learn. ("Introduction" xxxiii)

Some of the tales might seem harsh to modern readers, with disobedient children being turned into logs to toss on a witch's fire (as in "Frau Trude" for example), but still, this is where the trend started of associating fairy tales with being educational for children.

Technically the collection (which we often abbreviate to KHM in scholarly works) contains some folktales, fables, and legends alongside the fairy tales. Like, props if you can figure out how to classify "The Golden Key," a tale that often is last in the collection, as it's puzzled and intrigued scholars for centuries. Regardless, it's one of the most important fairy-tale collections out there. But buyer beware, it really matters not only which edition you read, but also which translation. Victorian-era British translators were prone to editing out any violent or racy bits, so while you can definitely find tons of editions of the Grimms' work in public domain for free on the internet, it might be worth looking up a decent translation.

Jack Zipes is my go-to guy for this; you can always have fun comparing his translation of the 1812 edition to the 1857 edition.

Some of the most famous of the Grimms' tales have become enshrined in Disney films, like their version of "Sleeping Beauty," which is "Briar Rose." Their "Little Red Riding Hood" introduces the woodcutter who saves the girl and grandmother, whereas Perrault's version lets them stay dead. Their "The Frog King, or Iron Heinrich" and "Rapunzel" provided part of the basis for *The Princess and the Frog* and *Tangled*. Their "Hansel and Gretel" is *chef's kiss* iconic with the house made of cake and candy. Lots of their tales aren't as well known, though; 21st century audiences don't seem too into stories about incest, *Game of Thrones* aside, so I haven't seen many adaptations of their "All Kinds of Fur." I'm into weird hedgehog dudes so I like their tale "Hans My Hedgehog" and I especially like Jim Henson's adaptation of the tale on his late 1980s show *The Storyteller*, but it also creeps out my students. It just gets weirder from there!

Other German romantic-era tales are worth checking out (E.T.A Hoffman is one of the big names), but we're going to move on, having emphasized the connections of fairy tales to things like nationalism, which will become important soon.

Another major figure in fairy-tale history, operating around the time of the Grimms, was Hans Christian Andersen (1805-1875). Andersen wrote 156 tales in the mid-1800s, and while not all of them are technically fairy tales, this was still a major contribution. Ironically, while he's mostly remembered for his fairy tales, he wrote tons of other genres like autobiographies, novels, poetry, drama, and more (Høyrup 32).

Andersen's life provides a useful case study for why we scholars treat fairy tales as embedded in society (in the lives of their narrators/writers, in the time period and region they're told/written in) rather than free-floating texts that are universal. Andersen was born to a cobbler and a washerwoman, but was lucky enough to attract the attention of a patron, Jonas Collin, who helped pay for his schooling and promote his work (Zipes *Fairy Tales* 82-85). We believe that Andersen remained deeply ashamed of his low-class origins and always felt kinda awkward in high society, as much as he craved their approval.

We see these themes in Andersen's tales, such as "The Ugly Duckling," which is one of the literary tales he invented (as opposed to a fairy tale from existing tradition that he retold, like "The Wild Swans" or "The Traveling Companion"). Andersen was also deeply Christian, and so we see spiritual themes in tales like "The Little Mermaid," which was another of his literary inventions...and it looks pretty different from what Disney envisioned for it. Themes of salvation and judgment appear in some of Andersen's grislier tales, wherein he also seems to really enjoy punishing audacious girls: "The Red Shoes" and "The Girl Who Trod on a Loaf" especially come to mind. There's a lot of religious stuff in "The Snow Queen" too, which again, became something quite distinct when Disney based *Frozen* on it.

Andersen pushed the artistic evolution of the literary fairy tale by writing tales that didn't end with "and they lived happily ever after," such as "The Little Mermaid" and "The Little Match Girl." Maybe this was autobiographical, maybe it wasn't. There is plenty of speculation that Andersen never married because he was into men, at a time when that was utterly prohibited. This is corroborated by some of his letters to his adoptive brother, Edvard Collin, wherein Andersen basically confessed his love and his frustration that they would always be kept apart (Zipes *Fairy Tales* 85). So we could also possibly read "The Little Mermaid" as a queer love story.

Some of Andersen's tales are overly sentimental and flowery...literally, like the guy had a thing for fairy tales about talking flowers. But Andersen also was keenly observant, and had a lot of deep thoughts to share about art and life, as in "The Nightingale." And he occasionally delivered cutting social critique, as in "The Emperor's New Clothes." So it's a mixed bag with the consistency of his tales, and he definitely continued the trend of associating fairy tales with children and the emerging genre of children's literature.

Other writers continued this trend. Yes, there were always fairy-tale haters, those who disliked flights of fancy and declared that they'd rot kids' brains (or something like that). But from the mid-1800s onward, fairy tales were picked up by more and more serious authors, and their place in the children's literature canon was solidified. Zipes chronicles this shift in *Fairy Tales and the Art of Subversion*, describing the contributions of authors like George MacDonald, Oscar Wilde, and L. Frank Baum in particular. Other authors worth mentioning, whose literary fairy tales became cemented in popular culture, include Italian author Carlo Collodi, who wrote the novel *The Adventures of Pinocchio*, and Lewis Carroll (who was actually named Charles Dodgson), who wrote the *Alice in Wonderland* books.

And here we reach a hard truth in fairy-tale history: a lot of beloved fairy tales today don't come from oral tradition, they come from literary invention. As far as scholars can tell, Andersen's "The Little Mermaid" is the first of its kind. Sure, there were legends about mermaid encounters, but there wasn't a fairy tale quite like it. With *Pinocchio*, yeah, there have been myths like the story of Galatea being sculpted as well as legends about golems and other nonhuman constructs...but Collodi's novel was the first to put that motif into a fairy-tale format. In my view, this doesn't make these creations any less valid as fairy tales; goodness knows they've become a part of pop culture and passed into folklore as well, with plenty of parents retelling these stories from memory to their kids. It's just helpful, if you're concerned with origins, to know the ins and outs of which tales are firmly rooted in oral tradition and which are newer to the scene.

Remember I went on about nationalism and fairy tales earlier? Now we get to the nationalism. See, post-Grimms, a bunch of people were like, "If they did it, so can we." This is why you find tale collections from the mid-to-late 19th century and early 20th century from countries all over the world...but especially countries that were colonized or otherwise power-less. These ideas spread from Europe worldwide, to the point where "the collection and study of folktales became a strategy to assert national identity and establish or reestablish a basis of nationhood" (Haase 663). We see an especially strong emphasis on collecting folklore—and subsequent folklore programs and archives within universities—in countries like Ireland, Estonia, and India, all countries that have been colonized. As a result, you can find tons of folktale and fairy-tale collections with the title "Folktales and/or Fairy Tales from [insert country name here]." It's a massive phenomenon, and a fun deep dive, though you do have to watch out for fabrications and alterations, where collectors or editors want to spruce things up for a public audience. Donald Haase characterizes this as such: "the occurrence of fakelore has been attributed to the nationalistic agenda of the collector or editor who reshapes texts to fit a cultural ideal or create texts to supply a cultural need" (663). Fairy tales are so popular they can make great propaganda (and in fact the Nazis took advantage of this), so it's something to keep an eye out for.

Getting into the 20th century, there's a lot of Disney to talk about, but thankfully that's not the whole story of fairy tales. Disney wasn't the first to put fairy tales on film—look up French director George Méliès for some earlier groundbreaking stuff—but Disney was among the earliest to stake a claim and dominate the field.

Walt Disney started producing animated fairy-tale adaptations working with Ub Iwerks in the early 1920s, including versions of "Little Red Riding Hood," "Puss in Boots," "Jack and the Beanstalk," and more (Zipes *Fairy Tales* 196-197). The "Little Red Riding Hood" video is actually available on YouTube, and I like to shock my students with it: some parts seem nonsensical to the modern eye, and the plot is also super rapey, with a rich gentleman filling in for the wolf and trying to trap Little Red. More films came in the 1930s, and then in 1937, Disney released *Snow White and the Seven Dwarfs*, which really kicked off the modern-day fairy-tale animated film era. Further, this film "played a crucial role in the re-imagining of the American Dream in the midst of the Great Depression in the 1930s" (Mollet 222).

With subsequent films—*Cinderella* (1950), *Sleeping Beauty* (1959), *The Little Mermaid* (1989), and so on—Disney solidified the intertwining of the fairy tale with American ideologies (gender and capitalist especially) and the spectacle of flashy songs and revolutionary animation. Their domination of the market is not "uncontested" but rather has "set a worldwide standard in the twentieth century against which all fairy-tale films, whether animated or live action, are measured" (Zipes *Fairy Tales* 211).

It's fine to like Disney fairy tales. It's fine to dislike Disney fairy tales. The important thing is to understand how they evolved, and how the conversation is much more complicated than "Disney made the original/dark versions fluffy and sanitized so they'd sell better." I mean, yeah, kinda, but as we've established in this chapter, it's damn near impossible to determine when and where the "original" version of a tale first popped up, and I've got a chapter later on critiquing the whole obsession with supposedly "dark" fairy tales.

Do Disney films promote girl power, or offer a shallow vision of feminism? Has Disney irrevocably changed how copyright and intellectual property work? These are great questions, which unfortunately I don't have the space to address here. But for the purposes of giving a general history of fairy tales, we had to at least touch on Disney.

While fairy tales were gracing the silver screen, they continued to develop in new ways in literature. Firmly established as children's literature, the stuff of picture books, by the 20th century, fairy tales weren't considered a very adult-y thing to do until the 1970s and 1980s, what scholars refer to as the Carter generation (okay, there's an important predecessor from the 1950s: Italo Calvino's 1956 book *Italian Folktales*, which experimented with narrative form in the nationalistic tradition).

Named for English author Angela Carter, the Carter generation bears her name for her "extensive work on the traditions of the fairy tale—as author, editor, and critic" which was "preeminently influential in establishing a late-twentieth-century conception of the tales" (Benson 2). This generation also includes Robert Coover, A. S. Byatt, Margaret Atwood, and Salmon Rushdie (Benson 2), give or take some other authors. I would definitely include poets Anne Sexton and Olga

Broumas in the category, given that their poetry does ground-breaking things with gender and sexuality in the Grimms' (and other) fairy tales.

Angela Carter's collection of adapted fairy tales, *The Bloody Chamber* (1979), is generally considered a seminal text here. She retells classics like "Bluebeard," "Beauty and the Beast" (twice), "Puss in Boots," "Sleeping Beauty," and "Little Red Riding Hood" (thrice) with a focus on Gothic settings, gender politics, and overt displays of sexuality, all cloaked in lush, seductive prose. Not all of her tales end happily, and the same can be said of Anne Sexton's poems in *Transformations* (1971), which I adore, but let me put it this way: I once taught one of her poems without a trigger warning, and that was a mistake (it's her version of "Sleeping Beauty," titled "Briar Rose," look it up, it's hauntingly beautiful, but it definitely needs a content note for abuse).

The Carter generation made a bold move by essentially saying through their writing: "Hold up, fairy tales are for adults again..." with a vengeance! (Sometimes literally, since a lot of these tales are very murder-y) As Benson notes "the Carter generation changed fairy-tale fiction and its potential for magic and wonder" (14).

As we move into the 1980s and 1990s, we get more texts by and for adults: the musical *Into The Woods*, the fiction of Jeanette Winterson and Robin McKinley, TV shows like Jim Henson's *The Storyteller* and *Beauty and the Beast* (the old one, not the CW one). A lot of these texts question the fairy tale genre's supposed promise of a happily ever after.

One of the notable features of these more recent fairy tales is that while "Disney is key to the image of the fairy tale in popular cultural memory," such as the parodies in the *Shrek* films, people are also "questioning the authority (on their lives) of the Disneyfied fairy tales that sugarcoated the Brothers Grimm's and Charles Perrault's tales to produce a romantically enchanting happily ever after" (Bacchilega 11). Further, a lot of people, regardless of whether they identify as feminist, are displaying "widespread sensibility to issues of gender in fairy tales, and we see this on and off the Internet" (Bacchilega 12).

Starting in the 1990s, we see fairy tales that don't simply play with gender roles, but also explore alternative sexualities. Emma Donoghue's retold tale collection *Kissing the Witch* (1997) was among the first to explicitly reject heterosexual pairings in fairy tales, often leaving the female main characters choosing the company of other women, whether romantic or platonic. Novels like *Ash* by Malinda Lo (2009) and *Cinderella Is Dead* by Kalynn Bayron (2020) both retell "Cinderella" but from a queer perspective (and let's face it, for all that they promote a lot of heterosexual marriages, fairy tales aren't the straightest genre out there). While queer fairy tales have taken off recently, I have noticed that we see more representations of characters with same-gender desires than those who are transgender or genderqueer. It's slowly changing, though, as with examples like S. T. Lynn's Black trans "Cinderella" retelling, *Cinder Ella* (2016). Some of the examples in this paragraph also show that fairy tales aren't just the domain of white people; we see some neat interventions that challenge white supremacy, and I don't just mean Disney giving us one Black princess, Tiana.

Nowadays? Fairy tales are literally everywhere. There are literally too many to mention in one chapter (or one book). National archives are still collecting and analyzing fairy tales, while writers, artists, and creatives of all types are refashioning them in a myriad of ways. I'll recommend some classics and faves in the last section of this book, but for now I'll note that this is a totally global phenomenon, so you can read Caribbean Canadian author Nalo Hopkinson's tale collection *Skin Folk* or watch Japanese director Hayao Miyazaki's ecologically-oriented take on "The Little Mermaid," *Ponyo*, among a zillion other options.

Well, this was my attempt at constructing a super brief history of fairy tales. I don't think this chapter was actually that brief, but given that multiple books have been written on this topic, I think it managed to be reasonably concise. The neat thing, too, is that this is a topic that is constantly evolving. Sometimes we find cool stuff in archives, or "discover" writers that are relatively unknown today but had a real impact in their own time period.

Two quick examples: first, in 2009, a German teacher, Erika Eichenseer, discovered five hundred tales collected in the 1850s by Franz Xaver von Schönwerth. Schönwerth was inspired by the Grimms and undertook his own collection efforts...but only published a fraction of them. Thanks to this lucky find, which has now been translated into English by Maria Tatar, we've got *The Turnip Princess and Other Newly Discovered Fairy Tales* 2015), which is a real treat, including twists on classics like "Cinderella" and some very threatening merfolk stories. Second, there's a great new book that provides a missing link between some of the classic tales of women writers (like the French *conteuses*) and the Carter generation: *Women Writing Wonder: An Anthology of Subversive Nineteenth-Century British, French, and German Fairy Tales*, edited and translated by Julie L. J. Kohler, Shandi Lynne Wagner, Anne E. Duggan, and Adrion Dula (who also happen to be some of my conference buddies). This collection contains such delights as German-Livonian Karoline Stahl's tale of a princess raised as a pauper with a kind heart, "Princess Elmina" and French woman Louise Michel's mash-up of the ogress in Perrault's "Sleeping Beauty" with the historical figure of Béatrix de Mauléon, who lived during the Crusades and was regarded as a cannibalistic ogress. Fun times.

In short, fairy tales are the gift that keep on giving. Their history is complicated and in some places uncertain, sure, but there's a treasure trove of information out there for those who want to understand the genre better!

REFERENCES:

Bacchilega, Cristina. *Fairy Tales Transformed?: Twenty-First-Century Adaptations & the Politics of Wonder*. Wayne State University Press, 2013.

Belcher, Stephen. *"Panchatantra."* In *The Greenwood Encyclopedia of Folktales & Fairy Tales*, edited by Donald Haase. Greenwood Press, 2008. 723-725.

Benson, Stephen. Introduction. *Contemporary Fiction and the Fairy Tale*, edited by Stephen Benson. Wayne State University Press, 2008. 1-19.

Bottigheimer, Ruth. *Fairy Tales: A New History*. State University of New York Press, 2009.

Canepa, Nancy. "The Formation of the Literary Fairy Tale in Early Modern Italy: 1550-1636." *The Fairy Tale World*, edited by Andrew Teverson. Routledge, 2019. 58-67.

Haase, Donald. "Nationalism." In *The Greenwood Encyclopedia of Folktales & Fairy Tales*, edited by Donald Haase. Greenwood Press, 2008. 662-663.

Høyrup, Helene. "Andersen, Hans Christian." In *The Greenwood Encyclopedia of Folktales & Fairy Tales*, edited by Donald Haase. Greenwood Press, 2008. 32-36.

Jones, Christine A., and Jennifer Schacker, editors. *Marvelous Transformations: An Anthology of Fairy Tales and Contemporary Critical Perspectives*. Broadview Press, 2013.

Jones, Christine A. *Mother Goose Refigured: A Critical Translation of Charles Perrault's Fairy Tales*. Wayne State University Press, 2016.

Marzolph, Ulrich. "The Middle Eastern World's Contribution to Fairy-Tale History." *The Fairy Tale World*, edited by Andrew Teverson. Routledge, 2019. 45-57.

Mollet, Tracey. "The American Dream: Walt Disney's Fairy Tales." *The Fairy Tale World*, edited by Andrew Teverson. Routledge, 2019. 221-231.

Neeman, Harold. "Marie de France." In *The Greenwood Encyclopedia of Folktales & Fairy Tales*, edited by Donald Haase. Greenwood Press, 2008. 605.

Teverson, Andrew. "Introduction: The Fairy Tale and the World." *The Fairy Tale World*, edited by Andrew Teverson. Routledge, 2019. 1-14.

Ziolkowski, Jan M. *Fairy Tales from Before Fairy Tales: The Medieval Latin Past of Wonderful Lies.* University of Michigan Press, 2007.

Zipes, Jack. *Breaking the Magic Spell: Radical Theories of Folk & Fairy Tales.* Revised and Expanded Edition. The University Press of Kentucky, 2002 [1979].

---. *Fairy Tales and the Art of Subversion.* Second Edition. Routledge, 2006.

---. Introduction. *The Complete Fairy Tales of the Brothers Grimm,* translated and introduced by Jack Zipes. Bantam Books, 2003. xxiii-xxxvii.

MOTIFS AND TALE TYPES

FAIRY TALES ARE A MULTICULTURAL PHENOMENON, which on the one hand is awesome, but on the other hand can make them a little challenging to study. That's where our concepts of motif and tale type, and the corresponding tools the Motif Index and the Tale Type Index, come in. First, I'll introduce the concepts and give examples, and second, I'll explain the resources that help us study them.

A motif is basically the smallest level of narrative detail that can be transferred from one story to another. We tend to think of motifs as being one of three types: an object, an event, or a character.

Examples of object motifs might include a magic ring or carpet (as in "Aladdin"), a poisoned apple (like in "Snow White"), or a glass slipper (like in Perrault's "Cinderella"). An event motif might be learning a secret formula by overhearing robbers, as in the "Open Sesame" tale, one of the better known versions being "Ali Baba and the Forty Thieves" in *The Thou-*

sand and One Nights. In case you're wondering, yes, these event motifs are often bizarrely specific.

Character motifs are, in my opinion, where fairy tales really shine (no shade to the many magic rings and talking horses, though). Few things conjure the image of fairy tale more than wicked stepmothers, witches, damsels in distress, and princes to the rescue. The big bad wolf, the little girl in red, the cannibalistic giant, the plucky giant-killer...the list of fairy-tale character motifs goes on and on.

Since motifs by definition are narrative details that can hop from story to story, we do see fairy-tale motifs showing up elsewhere. There are a lot of legends about witches, for example. And while giants and ogres are common fairy-tale villains, we also find them in Scandinavian legends, where giants who stay outside when the sun rises turn to stone and end up as notable landmarks.

Tale types, in contrast, are less about the superficial details (which are often motifs) and more about the underlying plot. At least, in theory. The idea behind tale types is that as folktales and fairy tales circulate through time and space, they often end up with different titles. So you can spot versions of "Cinderella" that are alternately titled "Cendrillon" (in French), "Aschenputtel," in German, and so on. The main story is still the same: downtrodden girl oppressed by stepfamily, magical helper gets her to a ball where she meets the prince, the recognition token is usually a shoe, etc. The window dressing might change, but the plot perseveres.

So instead of giving ourselves headaches over trying to keep track of all the local names of tales, folklorists use tale types, which essentially assigns a number to each distinct folktale and fairy-tale plot. "Cinderella" is 510A, "Little Red

Riding Hood" is 333, and so on. Once you know that tale type numbers exist, you're ahead of the curve.

Technically the Tale Type Index came first, but I'm going to talk about the Motif Index first. Also a brief typography note: you may have noticed that I'm pretty neurotic about consistently italicizing book titles. Here, I'm referring to the indices with capitalized but not italicized titles, because a) the titles are obnoxiously long and I want to refer to them shorthand, and b) the titles and editions have changed over time, at least for the Tale Type Index, so I'm giving it my own catch-all title to refer to the concept of the Tale Type Index. When I'm referring to a specific edition, I'll say so, and you'll see the title in italics then.

So, where can we find motifs? In the Motif Index, which in its full glory is the *Motif-Index of Folk-Literature*, published in six volumes from 1955-1958 by American folklorist Stith Thompson. Luckily it's been digitized, so you can find a couple versions online pretty easily. It's organized into alphabetical chapters, with each letter corresponding to a major theme: A is for motifs related to the gods and creation, B is for animals, C is for taboos, D is for magic (like transformations, disenchantment, etc.), E is for the dead (ghosts, resurrections, etc.), and on through the list. It's worth poking around to get a sense for all this. Why would you want to do this? Because it's one of the best ways (at least prior to the existence of Google Books) to find dang near every time a motif shows up in folk narrative. If you're on a kick about the grateful dead (helpful ghosts, not the band) or shoes as recognition tokens, this is the place for you.

Where can we find tale types? This one gets a little tricky. The first version of the tale type index was published in 1910 by Finnish scholar Antti Aarne, and then it was revised and updated by Thompson in 1961, and then it was revised and updated yet again by German scholar Hans-Jörg Uther (and his international team) in 2004. If referring to the second (and most widely available) edition, scholars will refer to the tale type as AT (Aarne-Thompson) numbers. If referring to the most recent version, scholars will refer to the tale type as ATU (Aarne-Thompson-Uther) numbers. This latter one is the gold standard of scholarship, but also, not everyone can afford to order the three volumes of the ATU index from the publisher in Finland sooo…yeah. Your best bet is probably a nearby university library, or bothering your folklorist friends who actually do have a copy.

When using the Tale Type Index, no matter which edition you've got, there are a few helpful things to know. First, it's organized according to folktale subgenre. Tale type numbers 1-299 are animal tales, a.k.a. fables; numbers 300-749 are fairy tales; numbers 750-849 are religious tales; numbers 850-999 are novelle or romantic tales (folktales that don't have much magic in them necessarily, but are still fictional and formulaic); and higher numbers, up through the 2000s, are narrative jokes like anecdotes, stories about people getting cuckolded, about priests who are dishonest, about marital disputes, and so on.

To drill a bit deeper into the fairy tales section, those are organized according to the main characters and what's going on with them. Tale types 300-399 feature supernatural adversaries (so, "Hansel and Gretel," type 327A, shows up there because of the witch); types 400-459 feature an enchanted spouse (so, "Sleeping Beauty" is type 410 for obvious reasons); types 460-499 feature supernatural tasks (one of the best known types in this section is 480, "The Kind and the Unkind Girls," which is the iconic tale where a good girl and a bad girl both encounter a magical figure who tests them and judges them accordingly); types 500-599 feature supernatural helpers (like "Rumpelstilskin," tale type 500, titled "The Name of the Helper" in the index); types 560-649 feature magic objects ("Aladdin" is type 561); types 650-699 feature supernatural power or knowledge (type 670 is "The Animal Languages," where a guy learns, you guessed it, animal languages, which shows up as a tale in *The Thousand and One Nights* and seems to condone domestic abuse); and types 700-749 are in the catch-all category for other tales of the supernatural (like type 706, "The Maiden Without Hands," which is creepy but a fave of mine).

A couple tale types outside the 300-749 range do somewhat resemble fairy tales though, which just complicates matters. In the 880s we have *Mulan*-style tales with women crossdressing in order to fight in wars, for example, which feel pretty darn fairy-tale to me. And while "Little Red Riding Hood" is type 333, in the 300s range with supernatural adversaries because what else do you call a talking wolf, there's also type 123, "The Wolf and the Kids," which has pretty much the exact same plot but the (talking) wolf is conniving to eat the (talking) goat's babies. Why is one tale in animal tales and the other in fairy tales? Who knows.

In my opinion, the Motif Index and the Tale Type Index work best when used in tandem, but their strengths lie in different areas. The Motif Index is global; the Tale Type Index started out mainly cataloging European folktales, and has slowly become more global over time. The Motif Index contains motifs from all narrative genres, not just folktales and fairy tales, whereas the Tale Type Index is tightly focused on folktales and fairy tales (but sometimes other genres creep in, especially where the boundaries blur, like with saints legends that can take on a fairy-tale tinge).

These are some of the most useful tools we have for folk narrative study, but they're also deeply flawed. For one thing, as Alan Dundes has observed, the "categories of motifs delineated by Thompson are...not all mutually exclusive and in fact are unavoidably overlapping" (102) because if we have the category of event motifs, those are meaningless without characters to be doing things in them, so it gets to be a bit confounded. As noted above, this is a problem with the tale type index too; if you put animal tales in their own category, but then you have basically the same plot with another actor instead, what's the right classification?

And while the Motif Index was notable for going beyond earlier methods of just, like, alphabetically listing stuff, rather than paying attention to how motifs are related to one another, it can lull us into a false sense of security. My colleague Mikel Koven, who does great work on film and folklore has, for instance, pointed out that mere "motif-spotting" is not a robust form of analysis; you have to do more than point at motifs in whatever text you're analyzing and then give yourself a pat on the back.

Further, the personal biases of the scholars involved in creating these tools emerged in a few ways. Dundes called out Thompson for intentionally omitting obscene folklore motifs from the Motif Index, in particular lambasting Thompson's "skewed logic in leaving only fifty numerical slots" (103) for what are likely hundreds or thousands of obscene motifs that emerge naturally in the folklore. And trust me, there's a lot of sketchy folklore out there, from bawdy jokes to racy versions of fairy tales.

Another useful critique of these tools come from a feminist perspective. Torborg Lundell, in a book chapter that blew my mind when I was in grad school, argues that both of the indexes "generally classify the female protagonist as passive and subordinate, supportive rather than full of initiative, weak rather than strong" (161) and that these biases are baked into the very organization of the indexes, in how they categorize and title whole tale types. Since then, the revision of the Tale Type Index by Uther and his team has helped fix some of this stuff, but it's still worth having on your radar.

I wish I could tell you these tools were perfect, but alas, they were made by humans and thus they're flawed. They are a necessary starting point, though, because folktales and fairy tales are so transnational that it doesn't make any sense to start your research assuming that you've found a completely unique specimen...cross-check it here first! Then you can move on to building accurate claims and doing some neat interpretive work.

REFERENCES:

Aarne, Antti. *The Types of the Folktale: A Classification and Bibliography.* Translated and enlarged by Stith Thompson. 2nd revision. Academia Scientiarium Fennica, 1961.

Dundes, Alan. "The Motif-Index and the Tale Type Index: A Critique." In *The Meaning of Folklore: The Analytical Essays of Alan Dundes,* edited and introduced by Simon J. Bronner. Utah State University Press, 2007. 101-106.

Lundell, Torborg. "Gender-Related Biases in the Type and Motif Indexes of Aarne and Thompson." In *Fairy Tales and Society: Illusion, Allusion, and Paradigm,* edited by Ruth Bottigheimer. University of Pennsylvania Press, 1986. 149-164.

Thompson, Stith. *Motif-Index of Folk-Literature.* 6 volumes. Indiana University Press, 1955-1958.

Uther, Hans-Jörg. *The Types of International Folktales: A Classification and Bibliography.* 3 volumes. Academia Scientiarum Fennica, 2004.

THE HISTORIC-GEOGRAPHIC METHOD (A.K.A. THE FINNISH METHOD OR THE COMPARATIVE METHOD)

I WAS partway through writing this book when I was like, wait a minute, I can't *not* talk about this stuff. The impulse behind this scholarly trend was majorly formative for how we study and talk about fairy tales today, even though we've ditched some of its implications.

First, a distinction using fancy language: in folklore scholarship, we sometimes talk about taking a diachronic vs. a synchronic approach to our materials. Folklorist Simon Bronner explains the distinction: "Diachronic approached the development of material historically, whereas synchronic analysis examined items contemporaneously" (88). So for example, if you want to look at how versions of "Sleeping Beauty" have evolved over time, from Basile to Perrault to the Grimms to Disney, that's a diachronic approach. But if you want to look at the theme of, say, gender in "Sleeping Beauty" texts, that's a synchronic approach, because you're approaching the works based more on their content than on their context. I'd say that a lot of my scholarship is synchronic, since I tend to draw out themes of gender and sexuality in fairy-tale texts, both old and new. And really, most scholarship these days ends up being both since obviously we need to pay attention to multiple dimensions of folklore in order to best analyze it.

But the diachronic approach actually dominated scholarship for a while, which is why I'm introducing the terms diachronic and synchronic now. Alan Dundes usefully summarizes how the major late 19th century schools of folk narrative scholarship were all diachronic: the solar mythology school, which "claimed that the bulk of folkloristic materials was primitive man's poetic translation of celestial phenomena such as the rising and setting of the sun"; the anthropological school, which was "convinced that folklore evolved from historical facts and primordial customs"; and the Finnish/historical-geographical method, which attempted to "determine the paths of dissemination and the process of development of folkloristic materials" (90). All three of these approaches are diachronic (interested in the study of materials over time), and they're also all comparative. Luckily we no longer imbue solar mythology origins into every single text, though.

The main comparative *and* diachronic approach I want to talk about in this chapter is the historic-geographic method, which is also called the Finnish method, which is also sometimes called the comparative method. The first title is easy to explain: the goal of this method of scholarship is to document the historical and geographic spread of a particular tale type. The second title is due to how the main scholars initially pioneering this method were Finnish, like Julius Krohn and his disciple Antti Aarne (who gave us the first version of the Tale Type Index, which is meant to facilitate this kind of work, among other aims). I'm one-quarter Finnish and so I am very proud of my heritage when it comes to discussing folklore scholarship!

There are a couple of assumptions that go into using this method. One is that "each narrative came to be viewed as having its own history," and over centuries would wander "from nation to nation assuming varying forms along the way" (Apo 452). Step one is you'd gather every version of the tale in existence, step two is you'd sort them by time and space (a tough task before computers existed!), and step three is you figure out where they cluster and maybe get some maps and diagrams involved.

The general goal was to determine a tale type's "urform" or its "basic or original form" (Apo 453), so that we could make educated statements about its origins and how it made its way through the world. But of course, determining the origin point for something that essentially began in oral tradition, and may have wandered and mutated a lot before anyone ever thought to write it down, is tricky, and maybe even impossible.

So why bother? Well, utilizing this method does give us some useful data. For example, Swedish scholar Anna Birgitta Rooth published in 1951 a sweeping study of "Cinderella" tales, documenting seven hundred versions of them, and concluded that in the "Cinderella" tale type (which includes the classic Western version, ATU 510A, as well as the lesser-known incest-y version, ATU 510B, and a couple other variants) generally spread from Asia to Europe, and from the Near East into nearby parts of Europe, before it arrived in Northern Europe. Good to know, right? And there are maps in Rooth's book!

To take the "Cinderella" example a bit farther, I have a particular fascination with the subtype 510B, generally known as "The Dress of Gold, or Silver, and or Stars" or "Donkeyskin" or "All Kinds of Fur." I wrote my master's thesis on it (which you can read for free since it's published in the open access academic journal *Cultural Analysis*)...but my work wouldn't have been possible without Rooth's work, and the subsequent scholarship by Christine Goldberg. Goldberg investigates some of the lesser-known variants of ATU 510B, which...actually, let me summarize the better-known versions first.

In most Western European versions of ATU 510B, there are a king and queen who have a daughter. The queen has something distinctive—golden hair, a golden star on her forehead, most beautiful woman in the world, whatever—and she gets sick and dies. Before dying, however, she makes her husband promise to only remarry someone who...fill in the blank: has the same golden hair, the same golden star on her forehead, who her ring fits, who her shoe fits, etc. Time passes and the person who fulfills these conditions turns out to be their daughter. She gets help and/or advice and asks for three marvelous dresses to buy some time (usually the titular dresses: one that's golden like the sun, one that's silver like the moon, one that's as bright as the stars) and then usually a cloak made of precious animal furs. She runs away in this disguise to the next kingdom over, and that's where it dovetails with the usual "Cinderella" type: she works as a servant, wears her magical dresses to the ball, gets the prince to fall in love with her, there's some kind of recognition token, and they get married and live happily ever after.

I find this story bizarre and endlessly fascinating, and it's one of my favorite fairy tales, which always makes me hesitate when someone asks what my favorite fairy tale is because it's like, errr, do I want to summarize this one or not? Anyway, utilizing Rooth's work, Goldberg uncovered two variants of 510B that haven't received as much attention. See, in addition to fleeing an incestuous marriage and menial labor while unrecognized, two essential components of the classic European versions of 510B are the "splendid dresses and the parties" (Goldberg 36), which obviously go hand in hand as the heroine gets to wear the splendid dresses *to* the parties and meet her lover there.

But in other 510B subtypes, the heroine wears a flayed old woman's skin to escape from an unwanted marriage: in versions from Sudan, she doesn't want to marry her brother, and in versions from Japan, she is merely outcast, but is gifted a magic skin that turns her into an old woman (Goldberg 34-36). In the other subtype, dubbed "The Hiding Box," we see tales from Scotland to Mexico and throughout the Middle East where the persecuted heroine hides in a wooden box to escape to a better life.

Goldberg argues that these tales are so distinctive that they ought to have their own numbers in the Tale Type Index rather than being subsumed under 510B (42). And further, she suggests that the flayed old woman's skin may well be the origin point of the animal skin tales, the modern 510B: "Because together they make a perfect contrast, the ugliness of the skin disguise attracted the motif of the splendid dresses. This in turn attracted or strengthened the introduction of the Unnatural Father" (41).

Can we ever definitively prove this assertion? Maybe...and maybe not. And I know that I, as a 510B scholar, am much more interested in digging into the potential meanings of the tale, like what happens when we pit feminist interpretations against psychoanalytic interpretations, and why this tale has been so persistent and popular for centuries (though granted, it hasn't received the Disney treatment, probably because incest is not considered an appropriate topic for kids in the U.S. these days).

But historic-geographic work, while time-consuming, provides an amazingly useful starting point for other scholarly works, as I hope I've shown here. So even though we mostly teach it in "history of the study of folklore" classes rather than as currently accepted and practiced methodology, it's worth knowing about and knowing when to draw on it.

REFERENCES:

Apo, Satu. "Historic-Geographic Method." In *The Greenwood Encyclopedia of Folktales & Fairy Tales*, edited by Donald Haase. Greenwood Press, 2008. 452-454.

Dundes, Alan. *The Meaning of Folklore: The Analytical Essays of Alan Dundes*, edited and introduced by Simon J. Bronner. Utah State University Press, 2007.

Goldberg, Christine. "The Donkey Skin Folktale Cycle (AT 510B)." *The Journal of American Folklore*, vol. 110, no. 435, 1997, pp. 28–46.

Rooth, Anna Birgitta. *The Cinderella Cycle*. Gleerup, 1951.

STRUCTURE AND STRUCTURALISM

ONE OF THE traits unique to fairy tales is their narrative structure, or the way in which the building blocks of their plots get assembled, time after time, no matter which motifs get swapped in or out. I love to nerd out about this stuff—who doesn't?!—so in this chapter I'll explain some of the major approaches to fairy-tale story structure (these approaches are known as structuralism) and which tools tend to be used by scholars today.

What is story structure? It's when you peel back the superficial layer of fairy tales—usually their motifs—and see what's under the hood. Let's take "Cinderella" as a handy example. If you look at Perrault's 1697 version, a fairy godmother is the one who gets her to the ball in high fashion. If you look at the Grimms' version (er, the one from 1857) it's a white bird from the hazel tree that grows over her mother's grave. If you look at Basile's 1630s version, the main character, Zezolla, who is nicknamed the Cinderella Cat, a fairy who comes out of a golden date tree is the one who decks her out and sends her to fancy events.

Taking a structuralist approach here, we don't get distracted by whether the magical figure who sends Cinderella off in couture is a fairy godmother, a bird from a tree, or a fairy from a tree. What matters is the action that furthers the plot: dressing up Cinderella and sending her out of her stepmother's clutches so she can meet her prince (or king, depending on the version). The individual motifs are interesting, and we can assume that they're culturally relevant, so we shouldn't totally leave them out of our analysis...but when looking at structure, we at least set the motifs aside for now to focus on the underlying event that furthers the plot.

There were a couple of early stabs at this approach in scholarship, but what I want to focus on here is the distinction between syntagmatic and paradigmatic structuralism, as expressed in the works on Vladimir Propp and Claude Lévi-Strauss, with later contributions by Bengt Holbek.

Let's start with this syntagmatic vs. paradigmatic thing. The easiest way to distinguish between the terms is associating syntagmatic with sequential and paradigmatic with underlying paradigms. As Alan Dundes explains in his introduction to the most current translation of Propp's work, calling "linear sequential structural analysis" syntagmatic borrows "from the notion of syntax in the study of language" (xi). So in English, the order that you put the words in a sentence in matters, since that's how our syntax is set up. It wouldn't make a ton of sense for me to say "tale fairy book this I like" when I really mean "I like this fairy-tale book" (unless I'm imitating Yoda, I guess). Similarly, when we study fairy tales from a syntagmatic structural perspective, we care about the order in which the events happen: Cinderella has to acquire magical clothes *before* she goes to the ball, ya know?

In contrast, paradigmatic structural analysis is based more on the "notion of paradigms in the study of language" and focuses on "latent content," as in, underlying binary oppositions in a narrative like life/death or day/night (Dundes xii). The champion of paradigmatic structural analysis was French anthropologist Claude Lévi-Strauss. A paradigmatic analysis might take into account sequential structure, but it's not really emphasized to the degree that it is in syntagmatic structural analysis.

Which one is better? Eh, depends who you ask. Dundes of course had an opinion about this, one I largely share: "Generally speaking, the syntagmatic approach tends to be both empirical and inductive, and its resultant analyses can be replicated. In contrast, paradigmatic analyses are speculative and deductive, and they are not as easily replicated" (xii). One of the major benefits of paradigmatic analysis is that it's inherently tied to the values of the culture from which the narrative comes, because how else do you know which binary oppositional paradigms you need to be looking at? Whereas in syntagmatic analysis, you can pluck the stories out of their cultural context and still perform a reasonably thorough analysis. Which is...not ideal, after a certain point, because folklore is always inherently tied to the culture that performs/transmits it.

Fun fact: Lévi-Strauss and Propp actually debated the merits of their individual approaches in a scholarly exchange in the early 1960s. I think they each kinda missed each other's points, something which I made sure to include in a presentation I did on the topic in a graduate seminar. I also used sock puppets to have Propp and Lévi-Strauss deliver their points to one another in front of my classmates, which probably branded me as an eternal weirdo, but that's no surprise.

Moving on to the specifics of structuralist approaches. Vladimir Propp (1895-1970) was a Russian scholar who worked on folklore, specifically folk narrative. In 1928 he published a book titled (in English) *The Morphology of the Folktale*, but it was in Russian, and wasn't translated into English until 1958. Propp used formalist techniques—basically, looking at structures in literature—to analyze patterns in fairy-tale structure, and his book was one of the first major contributions in this area (especially once it reached the English-speaking world).

First off, the title of the book can be confusing. Propp was specifically working with fairy tales, those magic-, quest-, and transformation-focused folktales, despite what it says on the cover. And I guess "morphology" isn't an everyday word for most people unless you're in linguistics or botany. But it basically just means the study of forms, or the basic shapes of things and how they relate to each other. I am not a great gardener (we joke about having a "brown thumb" rather than a "green thumb" in my family), but my understanding of plants is that even with very strange-looking ones, they often have the same structures: roots, bulbs, stems or stalks, and errr, whatever else plants have. The roots may look drastically different from one species to the next, but they all perform the same function of sucking up nutrients from the soil. That's the association we're going for with "morphology" here: looking at the component parts/structures of fairy tales to understand *how* they work in the story, even if they look quite different from one another superficially.

Back to Propp. He basically sat down with a classic collection of Russian fairy tales by Aleksander Afanasyev, read one hundred of them, and tried to puzzle out the structural commonalities. The classic description of what he noticed (which is frequently reprinted) is as follows:

1. A tsar gives an eagle to a hero. The eagle carries the hero away to another kingdom.
2. An old man gives Súčenko a horse. The horse carries Súčenko away to another kingdom.
3. A sorcerer gives Iván a little boat. The boat takes Iván to another kingdom.
4. A princess gives Iván a ring. Young men appearing from out of the ring carry Iván away into another kingdom, and so forth. (19-20)

In these examples, we see a variety of magical means for getting from Point A t o Point B. But as Propp notes, it literally doesn't matter who's getting the hero from Point A to Point B, what matters is that the hero is transported. That's the action needed to further the plot. Or, in Propp's words:

> The names of the dramatis personae change (as well as the attributes of each), but neither their actions nor functions change. From this we can draw the inference that a tale often attributes identical actions to various personages. This makes possible the study of the tale *according to the functions of its dramatis personae.* (20, italics in original)

So, we study the tale according to which functions make

things happen in the story's plot, not according to who performs those functions. I do need to note one thing here before we move on, though, since it's potentially confusing: the term "function" has more than one meaning in folklore and fairy-tale studies. Here in structuralism land it means the action needed to progress the plot, but in more general folklore studies, we often talk about the function of an item or genre of folklore in society, to capture the sense of why it exists and the role it plays in people's lives. Sorry, wish I could make these words not overlap, but we seem to be stuck with them.

Anyway, Propp goes on to ascertain that there are 31 functions underlying the plots of most fairy tales, which can be carried out by 7 major figures or dramatis personae. I'll go ahead and list them all, but the list is a bit of a beast, so don't feel like you have to memorize it. I'll make sure to focus in on some of the most important ones, too.

The 31 functions are:

1. One of the family members absents themselves from home
2. An interdiction ("don't do this") is given, often to the hero
3. The interdiction is violated
4. The villain makes an attempt at reconnaissance / getting intel
5. The villain receives info about their intended victim
6. The villain attempts trickery / deception
7. The victim unwittingly agrees / submits
8. The villain therefore causes harm; this can take a lot of forms, but we usually call it villainy OR lack, since sometimes the real danger comes from lacking

something essential like a wondrous item or healing object

9. Mediation: the hero is approached about the villainy / lack to fix it
10. The hero agrees to go on the quest or whatever
11. The hero leaves home
12. The hero is tested by the donor figure
13. The hero reacts to the test (showing mercy / kindness, performing a service)
14. The hero thus acquires the use of a magical helper or agent
15. The hero is taken / delivered / led to the object of their search
16. The hero and villain fight in combat
17. The hero is branded (with some kind of identifying mark)
18. The villain is defeated
19. The initial misfortune is fixed or the lack is liquidated
20. The hero returns
21. The hero is pursued / chased
22. The hero is rescued from pursuit
23. The hero arrives (home? elsewhere?) unrecognized
24. A false hero rolls in and tries to take the hero's place with unfounded claims
25. A difficult task is proposed to distinguish them or reward the real hero
26. The task is resolved in the hero's favor
27. The hero is recognized
28. The false hero or villain is exposed / revealed
29. The hero is given a new appearance
30. The villain is punished

31. The hero is married and ascends to the throne

It's important to note that you don't need to have every single function showing up in a fairy tale; some tales cluster around just a handful of them. The model Propp went with is ATU 300, "The Dragonslayer," where we have a princess kidnapped from home (fulfilling the early functions) and the hero tested and given magical help so he can fight the dragon. The "branding" is often the princess leaving a mark on his body or clipping his hair, so that when a false hero claims to have really killed the dragon, there's proof that it's a lie (that, or the hero cuts out the tongues of the dragon to show as evidence). The false hero is killed, the actual hero marries the princess, and they live happily ever after.

Incidentally, this is something Disney got right: the breakup of the natal family is often key to kicking off the fairy tale's plot. So now you know why there are so many dead mothers in Disney stories.

All these functions can be carried out by very few or very many characters, but again, our goal is to not get distracted by the superficial details. Instead, Propp encouraged scholars to view seven main character roles within most tales:

1. The villain
2. The donor (the one who tests the hero in order to give them magic help)
3. The magic helper (this may or may not overlap with the donor figure)
4. The sought-after person, usually glossed as the princess in Dragonslayer tales; sometimes her father the king is lumped in with this category too

5. The person who dispatches the hero or calls him to action (this is obviously a minor category that's not present in all tales)
6. The hero
7. The false hero

Again, not every tale will have each of these seven tale roles. Or they might be conflated; sometimes you get a villainous donor figure, like in my fave weirdo tale type ATU 510B, where the incestuous father—who is obviously the villain—gives the heroine the magical dresses that help her secure her future. Or the tale roles might be duplicated, such that you have the hero needing to rescue three different sought-after people (but their underlying role in the narrative is the same).

There are some notable exceptions to Propp's morphology, but again, fairy tales can be a pretty fluid genre so this isn't a surprise. Some classics like "Little Red Riding Hood" and "Hansel and Gretel" don't end in marriage, but they're right up there with other canonical tales. Some tales like "Bluebeard" and other serial-killer-husband tales focus tightly on the interdiction/violation sequence (don't go in the forbidden chamber...guess what happens next) and actually seem to want to prevent marriage rather than enabling it. And so on.

Propp's work has gone on to inspire many scholars, myself included. Being able to get at the bones of a narrative text is quite useful. There are valid questions raised about whether Propp's model is too reductive, or whether we can reasonably expect it to work in texts from every single culture, but my sense is generally that it can be adapted as needed. And it is really useful to have something concrete to point to when defining fairy-tale structure; generally it starts with a family's dissolution, tests the protagonist and/or sends them on a journey, and ends with the creation of a new family and/or the elevation of the existing family in terms of social status. That model exists in stark contrast to, say, contemporary legends, which may also contain an interdiction and violation, but usually end abruptly in some gory or mysterious manner. Again, narrative structure is a useful analytical tool to understand and utilize.

That's how syntagmatic structural analysis got started in fairy-tale studies. I won't summarize paradigmatic analysis in as much detail, in part because my understanding is that Lévi-Strauss was working more with myths than fairy tales so it's not super relevant to us right now, and in part because I never found it all that useful. However, the idea of oppositional binaries that came from Lévi-Strauss turned out to be integral to another model of structural analysis that came about later.

I'm primarily going to refer to Danish folklorist Bengt Holbek here as the next evolution of structuralist fairy-tale analysis, but he in turn builds on pioneering work by Algirdas Greimas and Elli Köngäs-Maranda (their work is very sophisticated and quite good, but if I go into it in depth, I risk getting out of the 101-level scope I'd set for this book...feel free to look up semiotic squares if you want to go hard!).

Holbek basically looked at the previous syntagmatic and paradigmatic structuralist work and extracted some of the most useful insights from both. I imagine him sitting in his office and being like, "31 functions? Bit much there, bro, let's simplify those down to 5 moves, which also correspond to the main three binary oppositions we see expressed in fairy-tale structure."

Building on the work of others, Holbek asserted that fairy tales have not one but two protagonists (mind blown!), that fairy tales deal with three thematic oppositions (low vs. high status, youthful vs. mature status, and male vs. female identity), and that fairy tales depict these two protagonists navigating these oppositions over the course of five moves. As Holbek writes, the wedding that caps off most fairy tales "is the crowning achievement of efforts at three levels: that of gaining independence from parents and other authorities of the preceding generation; that of winning the love of a person of the opposite sex; and that of securing the future of a new family" (410).

Holbek also classifies tale types as either masculine or feminine based less on the gender of the protagonist than on the gender of the low-born or low-ranking protagonist who essentially moves up in the world through the course of the tale. The gender of the protagonist may not matter in tales like "Jack and the Beanstalk" (ATU 328) where you might have a girl instead of a boy as the hero (look up "Molly Whuppie" for examples of this). But in tale types that are a bit more rigid, Holbek notes that a "masculine" tale will have a low-born young guy as the main character, who ends up with a high-born young woman, and in feminine tales it's generally the opposite.

Here is how the grouping of Propp's 31 functions into Holbek's 5 moves looks:

1. Move I = functions 1-8, the absenting of a family member up through the lack or villainy that really kicks off the plot
2. Move II = functions 9-14, which when we see functions 12-14 highlighted we call the donor sequence: the donor figure tests the protagonist and gifts them with magical help

3. Move III = functions 15-22, usually the combat sequence, but this is also usually where the male and female protagonists meet, interact, and become romantically interested in one another

4. Move IV = sometimes functions 25-26 (difficult task), but it depends since this isn't present in all tales; it's commonly found in feminine tales where the hero's mother does not accept the new bride (example below)

5. Move V = functions 23-31, some difficult task/recognition up through the punishment of the villain and the wedding and ascension to the throne

To take an example, in the Grimms' version of "Cinderella" move I is where her mother dies (family member absent) and the stepmother and stepsisters move in (they commit villainy against her). Move II is when she's pious and prays at the tree over her mother's grave (tested and found to be mature/good/etc. by a donor figure, in this case, her mother's spirit/God/whatever). Move III is when she goes to the ball and meets the prince. Brief move IV when the "task" of recognition is solved. Move V is when she marries the prince (ascension to the throne) and the stepsisters get their eyes pecked out by birds at the wedding (punishment of the villain).

Move IV is tough to pin down, so I'd recommend reading Perrault's and/or Basile's versions of "Sleeping Beauty" (content note for the Basile one re: sexual assault). Those don't end like the Disney one, but rather show Sleeping Beauty shacking up with the king...but facing persecution in his household, from his mother or his existing wife, depending on which version you read. That is classic move IV territory, since the threat is coming from inside the house, and the protagonist is kept from their happily-ever-after by one more obstacle, one that requires their spouse to subdue the threat (sometimes quite violently).

Holbek isn't the only scholar to point this out, but it's pretty relevant to his structural analysis: the major villain that the main protagonist of the tale faces is usually their same gender. Boys tend to face off against giants and dragons, while girls tend to combat witches and stepmothers. And in that elusive Move IV, when the protagonist is helpless in their new home, having actively struggled throughout the entire tale to get there, it's usually their partner who needs to step up and take down the threat. In the "Sleeping Beauty" texts mentioned above, once the prince (or in some cases king) realizes that his mom or wife is cannibalistic and evil, he has her killed. From a structural perspective, then, we can view the dual protagonists of a fairy tale as having alternating periods of being passive and active; when one character is passive (in an enchanted slumber, transformed into an animal, etc.) then the other character is more active, and vice versa.

Just like how Propp's functions can be told out of order— like, in "Beauty and the Beast," we may not know exactly why the Beast was enchanted until the tale's end—so can Holbek's. But the underlying structural logic is usually still present.

In Holbek's massive book *Interpretation of Fairy Tales* he goes on to articulate an interpretive method that overlays with his structural analysis, which he then applies to a corpus of Danish tales collected by the famous (in some circles) folklore collector E. Tang Kristensen in the late 1800s. I'll talk about that in the next chapter, but for now our take-home is that structural analysis, no matter how you slice it, is a tool meant to facilitate better overall understanding of the phenomenon under study.

Also? The cool thing about studying structure in folklore texts is that it's applicable to more than just folktales and fairy tales. Most verbal genres have some kind of underlying structure; for example, proverbs have the structure of Topic, Comment. It can be as simple as two words, one the topic and the other the comment on it, like "Time flies" or "Money talks." But even nonverbal genres have unifying structures too, like superstitions which are generally "If A, then B, unless C," so for example: "If you spill salt then you'll have bad luck, unless you throw it over your left shoulder." And sorry all, no citations for these, they come from my lecture notes from classes with Alan Dundes in the way-back-when of my undergrad, but you can find publications by Dundes on these topics if you search.

Let's recall, though: structural analysis is cool, but it's not usually our end goal. As Dundes reminds us: "Clearly, structural analysis is not an end in itself! Rather it is a beginning... It is a powerful technique of descriptive ethnography inasmuch as it lays bare the essential form of the folkloristic text" (xiii). But it's on us to seek out and make explicit the relationships between the structure of the text and its meaning, context, and function.

REFERENCES:

Dundes, Alan. Introduction to the Second Edition. *Morphology of the Folktale*. Vladimir Propp. Translated by Laurence Scott. University of Texas Press, 1968. xi-xvii.

Holbek, Bengt. *Interpretation of Fairy Tales*. Folklore Fellows Communications No. 239. Academia Scientiarum Fennica, 1998 [1987].

Propp, Vladimir. *Morphology of the Folktale*. Translated by Laurence Scott. University of Texas Press, 1968.

INTERPRETIVE AND ANALYTICAL
APPROACHES TO FAIRY TALES

THIS CHAPTER COMES RIGHT after the structure and structuralism one on purpose, so I'd recommend going back and reading that one if you haven't already!

Ah, the quest for meaning in fairy tales. This topic has occupied folklorists, psychoanalysts, literary scholars, feminists, and Marxists for centuries. Here, I'll give a general overview of these interpretative and analytical approaches, along with some examples of when they do and don't play nicely together.

Some people parse these terms a bit differently, so here's how I use them: interpretation refers to the quest for meaning, while analysis refers to breaking things down into their component parts in order to understand them better. An interpretive approach to fairy tales is looking for meaning, asking how we make sense of these things, while an analytical approach is asking which parts make up the whole, how they relate to each other, and how that informs our overall understanding of them. As you can see, these terms are very close in meaning, so it's probably fine to use them interchangeably in this context.

At their most basic, interpretive and analytical approaches to fairy tales are about understanding what makes them compelling, and parsing their various meanings. Both scholars and laypeople tend to latch onto an interpretive or analytical framework that appeals to them most, and then go about applying that framework to fairy tales. A framework is like a lens: it influences how you view the world. So to feminist scholars, fairy tales have a lot to say about gender, whereas to a therapist, fairy tales might speak more on the workings of the subconscious mind.

I tend to view interpretive and analytical approaches as sorting into roughly two categories: literal and symbolic approaches. I discuss this extensively in my master's thesis, published as "Sorting Out Donkeyskin" with the citation shared below, but in brief, scholars have long debated whether to pay more attention to the surface, superficial layer of fairy tales or the deeper, latent layer of fairy tales. Do we interpret the motifs that are explicitly there in the text, or do we try to get under the surface, under the hood as it were, to try to get at the tale's inner workings? How do you even *do* that?

With the more literal-oriented approaches, like feminist and sociohistorical approaches, we look to the social context in which tales are told to inform our analysis: "As products of sociohistorical circumstances, folktales reflect the conditions, values, religious beliefs, social concerns, politics, and ideologies informing the lives of a certain people at a specific time" (Trinquet 887). Lots of scholars have taken these approaches, from the historian Robert Darnton suggesting that themes of hunger in fairy tales reflect actual times of famine in history to Jack Zipes with his many (often Marxist) takes on how the ruling classes have used fairy tales to inspire obedience and subservience in the general population (as in, if all these protagonists are good, humble, and kind and get richly rewarded for it, maybe we can enculturate the masses to believe the same thing! Which is kinda like a secular riff on the whole "religion is the opiate of the masses" thing).

Similarly, anthropological approaches have used the content of the tales as a key to understand the cultures in which they're embedded and transmitted. Leaving aside some earlier anthropology-oriented folks who saw "primitive" universals in fairy tales (like Andrew Lang), modern-day anthropological approaches tend to assert that tale motifs directly correspond to cultural customs and beliefs. This builds on the classic work of early anthropologists like Franz Boas and Bronislaw Malinowski, who saw "the purpose of the story [as] not merely to entertain but to legitimize the values of an entire society" (Bierhorst 49). James Taggart's work on tales in Spain and Kirin Narayan's work on tales in India are both great examples of modern-day scholarship in this vein, making concrete connections between gender roles and marriage practices/rituals in the society and in the tales circulating within that society.

Feminist approaches are also considered among the literal approaches to fairy tales, because when we do feminist scholarship, we say "hey, look at the gender roles in those tales, they correspond to the gender roles in that society" except for when they don't, which also makes for an interesting conversation. There are whole books devoted to this topic; *Fairy Tales and Feminism* (edited by Donald Haase) is one of the better ones in my opinion. As Haase notes: "scholarly research explicitly devoted to feminist issues in fairy-tale studies began in earnest in 1970 and was propelled by the feminist movement's second wave" (vii). Of course, there were earlier hints of it, and one of the more interesting ways to look at gender in fairy tales is to be like, what if people who aren't/weren't familiar with feminist theory used fairy tales to have similarly sophisticated conversations about gender in their own lives?

To drill a bit deeper into feminist approaches to fairy tales (since it's my specialty), the major conundrum comes down to: are fairy tales filled with positive or negative representations of gender roles? And what impact do these representations have on real human beings? We are woefully bad at answering that second question (with the exception of some pioneering work by Kay Stone, she's awesome, look her up), but in regards to the first one, we've had lots of vigorous debate. Are there disgustingly heteronormative stereotypes about good girls and bad witches in fairy tales? Yes. Are there subversive representations of women doing unexpected things in fairy tales? Also yes.

Queer approaches to fairy tales are also a thing, albeit a newer thing, and they sorta skirt the line between literal and symbolic approaches, so I'll use them as my bridge to connect the two. On the one hand, we definitely see some less-heterosexual stuff in certain fairy tales. For example, my colleague Psyche Ready has analyzed tale type 514, about a magical sex change that makes everyone involved happy (search for her name and you'll find both a comprehensive blog post and an open-access article on the topic). On the other hand, queer theory is being fruitfully applied to fairy tales, as in the 2012 edited collective *Transgressive Tales: Queering the Grimms*, and queer theory is...how shall I put it gently...not very transparent, accessible, or literal-minded. So queer approaches to fairy tales, while I love them all, are a bit of a mixed bag: sometimes going with the literal side of things, sometimes the symbolic side of things.

In contrast to literal approaches, symbolic approaches insist that there is some deeper meaning to fairy tales. Usually, to get there, you need a framework that tells you what symbols are and how to interpret them. In brief, a symbol is something that stands in for something other than itself...but thanks to some linguistics nerdery, there's an additional dimension to symbols to consider: they are signs just like language is, as well as literal signs like a stop sign or traffic signature (in the sense that they point towards something, in this case a meaning). However, symbols are a specific subset of signs that are arbitrarily assigned and culturally determined. There is no reason you'd assume that a stop sign meant "stop" if you hadn't been socialized to view it as such, you know? So in this view, symbols are *not* universal, they are learned and transmitted by culture. This is an important point, so hold onto it for now, and go read some Saussure if you want more on this front.

Psychoanalysis and analytical psychology both have different takes on how we should interpret symbols. Freud, the father of psychoanalysis, paved the way for future scholars to view symbols as a way to discuss taboo desires: the desire of a boy for his mother (the Oedipal complex), the desire of a girl for her father (the Electra complex), all that forbidden id stuff, and sex stuff in general. Jung, his disenchanted disciple who founded analytical psychology, saw symbols as a means to connect with the collective unconscious and the archetypes that parcel human experience into concrete categories: the Mother, the Crone, and so on.

Technically, scholars in both traditions discuss symbols as universals (which, again, they are not!), but Freudian symbolism is more apt to be culturally relativized than Jungian symbolism. This is because one of the main tenets of Freudian psychology is that infantile conditioning shapes adult projections and fantasies. In other words, Freudians tend to believe that the way a culture treats babies and children (in terms of affection, potty training, and so on) shapes how adults engage with creative storytelling later in life. That's a tenet you can test out in different cultures, which Alan Dundes did in a variety of his studies. In contrast, Jungian scholars tend to say "a universal is a universal is a universal" and not leave much room for cultural variation. Jungian symbols are absolutes; Freudian ones less so.

In both schools of thought, motifs are best viewed as symbols for the latent (or under-the-surface) content of fairy tales. I summarize more of the nuances of these approaches in my article cited below, but in brief, you'll find Freudian interpretations of fairy tales searching for symbols of family trauma in tales, whereas you'll find Jungian interpretations of fairy tales searching for evidence of archetypes in tales, talking about the anima vs. animus (or the feminine vs. masculine aspects of the psyche) and individuation, and stuff like that.

Personally, I'm not convinced by either. One of the better-known Freudian approaches to fairy tales appeared in Bruno Bettelheim's 1976 book *The Uses of Enchantment*, which remains popular to this day. Basically, Bettelheim posits that fairy tales assist children with their unconscious development into adulthood, by giving them fantastical scenarios wherein internal processes play out to a happy ending. Jack Zipes has done a great takedown of Bettelheim's work (among other ills, he's suspected of plagiarism), but for me, Bettelheim is so Freudian as to be truly off-putting and useless.

I'll share a quote about Cinderella so you can see what I

mean: "She selects him [the prince] because he appreciates her in her 'dirty' sexual aspects, lovingly accepts her vagina in the form of the slipper, and approves of her desire for a penis, symbolized by her tiny foot fitting within the slipper-vagina" (271).

This is a great quote to horrify students with, but otherwise, it's off-putting because it's so darn vague. If Cinderella's foot is a penis, is everyone else's foot a penis? When is a foot a penis or not? Is a slipper always a vagina? WTF?

Freudian approaches almost always come back to sex, which I'm not particularly bothered by because I try to cultivate a sex-positive attitude. But the biological essentialism and heterosexism of this portrayal of sex kinda gross me out. Plus Freud's ideas are irrevocably tainted by patriarchy; penis envy is just one concept among many that gets it totally wrong.

Similarly, I'm not a fan of Jung. He had some weird ideas about "primitive" peoples that come across as pretty racist today, and I also have a problem with his idea of archetypes since they're supposedly universal. In my mind, anything that's universal becomes so general as to be useless for analysis. Like, yes, every culture tells stories and has folklore. Woohoo! Okay, how does that help us??? Further, Jung has written that archetypes are essentially unknowable in which case, err, miss me with trying to bring them into evidence-based academic discourse. Finally, Jung has said that every culture has a Christ child archetype which is inaccurate and Eurocentric.

As much as I find some symbolic and psychological approaches to fairy tales distasteful, I will grant this: they're necessary because fairy tales have fantastical elements in them. Literal approaches will only get you so far because if we're trying to map every element in the fairy tale to something in the real world, er, bad news, we don't have talking horses or dragons or magic rings.

Bengt Holbek got around this by hypothesizing that the fantastical elements in fairy tales are the means by which communities can discuss their real-world anxieties, hopes, fears, and dreams. Even so, scholars still have to decide how to parse the fantastical elements, through which lens to interpret them. Like, you can't decide a magical flower represents a hymen one day and a mother figure the next, you know? You need some kind of consistency. Holbek went with a fairly standard Freudian approach to symbols, which isn't my favorite thing, but at least he was consistent (my Portuguese colleague Francisco Vaz da Silva has a lot to say on the matter).

These days, neither Freudian nor Jungian symbolism are particularly well-regarded in academic spaces. Fairy-tale scholars agree that there's some kind of meaning under the hood, some need to unite literal interpretations with symbolic ones. We get bonus points for making sure our interpretations are able to pass the test of cultural relativism: ensuring that the imagery and themes make sense within a given cultural context, according to that culture's own standards, rather than being imposed from outside. My inclination is to examine the uses of gendered symbols in fairy tales in their own cultural context as a way for people to have difficult conversations about fraught topics. It's not exactly easy to criticize nastily strict gender roles when you're living inside them, you know?

I do need to quickly detour to mention another two parallel tracks of scholarship that aren't so much about the literary/symbolic divide, but still have a lot to contribute to the interpretation of fairy tales. These are the literary and performance angles.

In literary approaches to fairy tales, scholars focus on the artistic uses of language, style, and imagery. The classic example here is work by Swiss scholar Max Lüthi, who laid out a series of fairy-tale traits—their characters are depthless and isolated, their color palettes metallic and simple—in order to better analyze them. On the flip side, a whole host of scholars ask questions about the uses of fairy tales in literature and other creative media, asserting that the connections are many and fruitful. The method outlined by Dundes is to first identify, then interpret. So if you see a "Little Red Riding Hood" motif in a poem or film, first you need to recognize it as such (rather than assuming the author just whole-cloth made up the idea of a girl in a red hood), and then you need to analyze it and ask what changes the author made and why.

In performance approaches to fairy tales, scholars try to gather data on the people who perform folk and fairy tales, plus their cultural context that makes it a good life choice in the first place. Linda Dégh was a Hungarian folklorist who did pioneering work here, arguing that the lives of the storytellers and the stories they told were intertwined and had to be studied in tandem. Ironically, the performance approach arose in part as a response to the literary approach; just taking tales as standalone works of creative genius means taking the risk of missing out on the ways in which culture shapes them. Performance studies in folklore and related academic fields had a larger backstory than I have the space to get into here, but for our purposes it's pretty much what it says on the label: wanting to study folklore as it's performed in social life, rather than fixating on recorded texts like butterflies pinned to a board.

Additionally, there are a few academic subfields where really interesting conversations about fairy tales are taking place. One is disability studies. Another is ecocriticism (environmental studies, essentially). Running with the disability studies example for a moment, we see the literal vs. symbolic distinction play out with real-world consequences. Scholars have long viewed disabling factors in the fairy tales as symbolic, meant to convey additional meaning: voiceless maidens are mute as a reflection of their powerlessness, disfigured villains (like Cinderella's stepsisters in the Grimms' version who are blinded by birds) are that way as a punishment for their evil deeds, and so on.

But this interpretation leaves actual, real-life disabled people being like, "Sooo if all these depictions of disability are metaphors or symbols, do disabled people ever get representation in fairy tales?!" It's a valid question. The two books that cover it best in my opinion are by Ann Schmiesing (author of *Disability, Deformity, and Disease in the Grimms' Fairy Tales*) and Amanda Leduc (author of *Disfigured: On Fairy Tales, Disability, and Making Space*). I'll review them in more depth in the recommendations section, but they grapple with the question of how to interpret disability in fairy tales and the consequences of how we answer this question.

I'll leave you with one more interpretive approach to consider before wrapping up this chapter. It came from my mentor, Alan Dundes, and it incorporates structure in very cool ways.

In yet another nod to linguistics, Dundes coined the terms allomotif and motifeme, which are modeled on concepts like allophone and phoneme in the study of languages. If you need a brief refresher on that, basically, in language the phoneme is the ideal or mental version of a sound that becomes part of a word, whether it's a consonant or a vowel. In contrast, the allophone is what people actually pronounce when they're talking. There are multiple potential allophones you could speak aloud in place of the one phoneme, and still be understood. For example, since I'm from California and grew up with a Valley Girl accent, the "u" in dude is a phoneme that I might pronounce as a long, drawn-out vowel with my lips rounded, whereas someone else might pronounce it as a short, simple, unrounded vowel. Both expressions of the vowel are allophones, or acceptable interpretations of the phoneme a.k.a. the idealized version of the vowel. Or to take another example, sometimes people in the midland portions of the U.S. say "warsh" instead of "wash." How did that allophone inserting the "r" into the middle of the word creep in? I have no idea, but it's a thing that happens. Again, allophones are all the variants that people actually say out loud, while phonemes are the way the sound "should" be (but of course this might be contested according to who makes the rules, how far the dialect has stretched, and so on).

Just as the phoneme is the mental version of a sound and the allophone is the sounded-out-loud version of a sound, the motifeme is the structural slot of a motif in a tale, while the allomotif is the range of motifs that get used in that slot by taletellers. In a Proppian structural sense, we would specify that we're talking about one of his thirty-one functions as a potential motifemic slot. Here's how Dundes puts it:

Thus for any motifemic slot in a folk-tale, there would presumably be two or more alternative motifs, that is, allomotifs, which might occur. If we have a full-fledged comparative study of a tale available, we probably have a good idea of what the range of allomotifs are for any one motifeme. (321)

The classic example would be that in different versions of "Cinderella," you have different donor figures standing in for whomever/whatever gives her magical dresses and gets her to the ball. The role of getting that particular thing done is the motifeme, and the specific characters who fill it in are the allomotifs. So in the Grimms' version, the allomotif is the birds living in the tree growing over her mother's grave, whereas in the Perrault version, the allomotif is the fairy godmother. According to a motifemic analysis, we could therefore say that the birds in the tree over the grave are symbolically equivalent to the fairy godmother: not only do they fulfill the same structural slot in the story, they also have parallel meanings. Both birds and godmother are stand-ins for the absent mother, who should have been the one arming Cinderella with beautiful dresses so she could secure her happily-ever-after.

A really tight motifemic analysis would utilize tales from the same culture, or even the same taleteller. For instance, Dundes observed that in variants of ATU 570, "The Rabbit Herd," the hero was threatened with getting his head cut off (allomotif #1), getting his phallus cut off (allomotif #2), or being thrown in a snake pit (allomotif #3) in versions collected in the Ozarks by Vance Randolph. One taleteller even knew multiple allomotifs and would swap in the one deemed most suitable for the audience (Dundes 321).

I've used motifemic analysis when comparing multiple versions of ATU 451, "The Maiden Who Seeks Her Brothers," since the conditions of the brothers' transformation into birds and the tactics of disenchantment (silence and suffering from the heroine) can vary. As I concluded in my book chapter on the tale type in *Transgressive Tales*, the symbolic equivalences uncovered by motifemic analysis reveal that the heroine is in danger both from her natal family and her marital family.

There is no safe place for women in these stories, which is a cogent (if coded) critique of patriarchal gender and kinship roles. Pretty cool, right?

The best part? Gathering all this data means you're working with concepts that come directly from the folk, not some scholar's or psychoanalyst's head. This is one of the best arguments in favor of utilizing some kind of motifemic analysis in your own work, assuming you're dealing with multiple versions of a tale type. Comparative work remains the gold standard in fairy-tale studies and folklore studies, but doing a deep dive into one or two texts is also acceptable, if you have more of a focus on the literary and/or artistic aspects of the text.

Obviously, fairy tales mean *something* or they would not have persisted this long or taken this many forms. There's a reason the magic mirror metaphor dominates our scholarly conversations, too: we are constantly in dialogue about to what extent fairy tales mirror culture, and how realistic we can expect that mirroring to be.

REFERENCES:

Bettelheim, Bruno. *The Uses of Enchantment: The Meaning and Importance of Fairy Tales*. Random House, 1989 [1976].

Bierhorst, John. "Anthropological Approaches." In *The Greenwood Encyclopedia of Folktales & Fairy Tales*, edited by Donald Haase. Greenwood Press, 2008. 48-50.

Dundes, Alan. *The Meaning of Folklore: The Analytical Essays of*

Alan Dundes, edited and introduced by Simon J. Bronner. Utah State University Press, 2007.

Haase, Donald. Preface. *Fairy Tales and Feminism: New Approaches.* Wayne State University Press, 2004. vii-xiv.

Jorgensen, Jeana. "Sorting Out Donkeyskin: Toward an Integrative Literal-Symbolic Analysis of Fairy Tales." *Cultural Analysis* vol. 11, 2012, pp. 91-120.

Trinquet, Charlotte. "Sociohistorical Approaches." In *The Greenwood Encyclopedia of Folktales & Fairy Tales*, edited by Donald Haase. Greenwood Press, 2008. 887-890.

Vaz da Silva, Francisco. "Fairy-Tale Symbolism: An Overview." *Oxford Research Encyclopedia of Literature.* Oxford University Press, 2017. Accessed 30 June 2022. https://doi.org/10.1093/acrefore/9780190201098.013.79

HOW TO LEGIT START STUDYING
FAIRY TALES

OKAY, so you're super inspired to interact with fairy tales, not just as a fan or consumer, but taking things to the next level. Now what?

Reading this book is already a great first step, if I do say so myself. I'll outline some further steps in this chapter.

Not everyone has the time, money, or inclination to pursue graduate work in folklore or a related field, I get it. Sometimes you get lucky and can take classes from a fairy-tale-leaning professor in English, in an ethnic studies or children's literature department, and so on, or catch our public-facing lectures or online courses. But after having spent my entire adult life in higher education—yes, I was that nerd who went straight from high school to undergrad to grad school—I can state that while academia is one very thorough way of learning one's way around a topic, it's not the only way. And it's certainly not great if you think you're landing a job in your field after getting your degree, only to find that there are very few jobs anymore. *stares in disillusioned contingent academic*

So while I will always encourage people to support folklore programs by enrolling where possible, I also know it's not feasible or desirable for everyone. And there are lots of great options for educating yourself in the meantime.

The first and most important step in my view is to familiarize yourself with the 200+ years of fairy-tale scholarship. One of the most annoying assumptions non-specialists make about fairy tales (and folklore in general) is that since they have some understanding of the topic, that means they know *everything* about it. That, friends, is not true.

It's important to know not just who the Grimms were, that they were scholars as well as tale collectors, but also to know that they were in correspondence with some of the most important intellectual figures of their day. You should know about Johannes Bolte and Georg Polivka's work, and the collections of Giuseppe Pitre, E. Tang Kristensen, and Laura Gonzenbach. Most nations have had a handful of star tale collectors, and it's useful to have some rough idea of who they were (Kristensen was a star in Denmark, Afanasyev was in Russia, etc.).

You might want to specialize in a national or linguistic tradition, which is cool...and which probably means you should learn that language if you don't know it already. English is a pretty acceptable language for international scholarship these days, but knowing French and German will give you access to a lot of important historical scholarship on fairy tales (Russian and Italian wouldn't hurt, too).

Obviously, you need to know what tale types and motifs are, and you should be referring to ATU numbers instead of AT numbers (since the ATU index is the updated version). And if you can't acquire your own copy of the ATU index, find a university library near you that will either order a copy or borrow it on inter-library loan.

If you've read the book thus far, you'll know that most folklorists and fairy-tale scholars are not super interested in questions of way-back-when origins, since those are generally impossible to prove. It's also essential to keep in mind the transnational nature of most tales; they are constantly cross-pollinating and crossing borders, so it's usually a mistake to assume that a tale was an original creation if you haven't checked to see if there are other versions of it floating around.

Not to get all "when I was your age..." ranty, but back when I studied with Alan Dundes at UC Berkeley during my undergraduate degree, Google searches didn't exist yet. Nor did many of the more sophisticated online search catalogs in libraries. So I will run through a couple old-school search techniques in case they're useful to you, like if you time travel to the 1990s or something.

If you have access to a university library, you too can have the pre-Google experience. Every few years, scholars would publish summaries of recent scholarship that would essentially aggregate knowledge for future people to look up. You would find these books in your library's card catalog (which us old folk remember using!), look up these reference books, and then they'd point you towards scholarship on your topic that you maybe hadn't heard of. Some stellar examples include the *Internationale volkskundliche Bibliographie* (the *International folklore and folklife bibliography* in German, which at least has abstracts in German, English, and French), the 1976 *Folklore Theses and Dissertations in the United States* edited by Alan Dundes, and *The Centennial Index: One Hundred Years of the Journal of American Folklore* by Bruce Jackson (there's a more recent supplement to that one, too).

So you'd pick your research topic, find the location of these physical books, look up your topic in them, and get the titles of research articles or books on your topic to then look up. If you're really on top of things, you could then pillage their bibliographies or works cited lists for yet more ideas on what's been written on your topic. Honestly, this is a good practice in general; if I'm reading an article or book I really like, I usually scan the bibliography at the end to see if I've missed any scholarship on the topic.

Nowadays, many of these aggregators are available online. Again, it helps to have a library log-in; some public libraries have access to all this stuff, and many university libraries will grant you the ability to do short-term research if you ask nicely. You can also, if you just want to get an idea of what's out there, search online for the Indiana University Library Research Guide on the Folklore Reference Collection at Indiana University and see the various bibliographies, encyclopedias, and so on that are available online or in print.

If you've hooked up with a library log-in, you can also use search aggregators like WorldCat to search through multiple databases such as JSTOR and Project Muse, which is where many folklore and fairy-tale studies journals live online. You can also specify if you want the search results to include books, book chapters, articles, monographs, and so on.

(Brief aside: if you're wondering what a monograph is, it's essentially a highly distilled study of one very specific topic that might have been someone's master's thesis or PhD dissertation, which has now been published as a free-standing pamphlet or book; it's usually not of interest to the general public since it's so specialized, but we do still talk about monographs in academia.)

The gold standard, of course, is the peer-reviewed article.

Academic journals accept article submissions, and the editor then scrubs the author's name and reaches out to scholars with expertise in that field to review the article and weigh in on whether it's worth publishing. This system of anonymity— often called double-blind review—is ideal because it means no one's biases will get in the way of evaluating the present work. The reviewers (usually 2, sometimes 3 per article) will then recommend publishing the article as is or with minor or major revisions, or sometimes rejecting it outright. Sometimes books go through peer review as well, but usually only if they're associated with a university press rather than a mainstream literary press.

Peer-reviewed journals where you are *guaranteed* to get the best fairy-tale scholarship include *Marvels & Tales* and *Fabula*. Both are devoted to folktales and fairy tales. If you go a bit broader, you'll find great folklore scholarship and sometimes specifically fairy-tale scholarship in journals like the *Journal of American Folklore*, *Western Folklore*, the *Journal of Folklore Research*, and other adjacent journals.

Additionally, lots of scholars have published regional and national motif and tale type indexes, so if there's an area of the world that's caught your attention, give it a look and maybe you'll find that someone's done all the collecting and sorting for you. There's a ton of material out there!

Now that you know some basics of fairy-tale scholarship, so you don't make a newbie mistake like fixating on origins, here are some tips about framing your scholarship in a useful and interesting way.

The way I think about it, scholarship is a conversation. It's ideally an evidence-based conversation, not just a flurry of hot takes, but it's people in dialogue with one another about a topic. Our conversation about fairy tales spans centuries and multiple countries and languages, which is pretty cool. And just like it'd be rude to interrupt a conversation without knowing what's already been said, it's a tad impolite to bust into the fairy-tale scholarship conversation without knowing what's already been published on your specific topic.

When we publish scholarship, we generally call this the "lit review," short for literature review. Basically, you don't want to reinvent the wheel; if a scholar's already asserted or proven something, you should make a note of that rather than trying to DIY the same thing. The lit review is important for a couple of reasons: first, you don't want to risk looking uninformed by neglecting an important development in your area of inquiry, and second, it can actually guide your research. Sometimes you notice something that prior scholars missed, or you realize that an earlier hypothesis needs a bit of nuance that you can help give it.

Once you've figured out what interests you in fairy-tale-land and what's already been written about it, it helps to know which methods and theories are best suited for your kind of inquiry. If you want to work on the psychological aspects of fairy tales, get thee to some Freud. If you want to work on the artistic and literary aspects of fairy tales, brush up your close reading skills. If you're interested in a particular nation's tradition, try to find out if you can visit one of their archives. It's also useful to get a sense of whether you can even prove what you're setting out to do: is your inquiry grounded in textual or historical evidence, or based more on subjective interpretation of a story? Subjective stuff is fine, just be up front about it and don't try to generalize or universalize your findings if it's not appropriate to do so.

Since scholarship is a conversation, at some point you'll need to get feedback from others! You can do this by presenting your findings at a conference if you're feeling super academic-y. Good ones for fairy tales include the annual meeting of the American Folklore Society and the International Conference on the Fantastic in the Arts, regional American folklore conferences like the Western States Folklore Society annual meeting, and global ones like the International Society for Folk Narrative Research. They all have websites on which you can learn more, but be aware: 1) proposals often go through peer review so you'll need to brush up on academic writing and citation conventions, and 2) sometimes they make you buy an academic association membership in order to present, and then there's usually a fee to register for the conference too, so you could be looking at spending a lot of money to participate.

Otherwise, you can always just post your thoughts in a blog post or Facebook group devoted to the topic. On Twitter, for example, hashtags like #FairyTaleTuesday and #Folklore-Thursday are great places to share your thoughts, with links to blog posts that people can click on and read.

In my experience, the best scholarship combines something you're passionate about with something you've done a ton of research on and are thus qualified to have an informed opinion on. So get out there and figure out where the intersections of joy, curiosity, and research skills take you!

SHORT ESSAYS & BLOG POSTS

WHY WE SHOULD STOP OBSESSING OVER "DARK" FAIRY TALES

THOSE OF US on the scholarly side of fairy-tale fandom have noticed a trend in the last few years that perplexes us: a draw towards supposedly "dark" fairy tales, those apparently older, more gruesome and violent and sexual texts. I'm going to unpack some of those meanings here and argue that this trend reveals more about us than about the tales themselves.

Scholars do use the term so we're not guilt-free here; I noticed it in a journal article by Susan Wood about Hans Christian Andersen's tales and how their "darkness" is there to use pain and sorrow in a transcendental way. Jack Zipes has written that French filmmaker Jacques Cocteau brings out the dark side of the fairy tale. If you want these citations plus my full argument, check out my piece in *Humanities*, cited in full below (it's open access, so you can read it for free on the internet!).

But I see the term used waaay more by fairy-tale fans: people who are reading and rewriting fairy tales for fun and perhaps profit. Some books have "dark" in the title referring to the fairy tales therein, while lists on Goodreads and a variety of entertainment-oriented websites classify certain tales as darker (hence more attention-worthy) than others. There's an assumption that the "earlier" or "original" tales are "darker" hence cooler/better/more interesting.

And on the one hand, yeah, I get where this comes from: if you've only been exposed to the sanitized and saccharine versions of fairy tales common in Disney films and picture-books, it can be a revelatory experience to learn about the earlier texts and see that they didn't pull any punches. A lot of earlier versions aren't shy about violence and vengeance.

To fixate on this one facet of tales, though, kinda misses the point: the earlier tales were still a reflection of their society (the good, the bad, the ugly) and they were also sometimes still censored.

One of the not-so-happy reasons that a lot of the Grimms' tales include violence is that violence was seen as an accept-able tool for teaching kids morals in the 19th century. So while the Grimms themselves, and their subsequent translators, often removed sexual themes from their stories, the violence was seen as fine to stay in many renditions. And that sends a message about them and their values, not some supposed coolness factor.

Authenticity is always a moving target, too. So while we may be drawn to the idea that the "darker" tales are more authentic, the question is: authentic to whom, and where, and when? Getting our hands on unexpurgated tale texts is under-standably delightful, and I don't mean for my critique to take away from that experience. But the tales of our time are authentic to *us*, so it does strike me as a bit weird to focus on another culture's or time period's authenticity as *the* authenticity worth starting fights over.

Additionally, the term "dark" has some problems that make it not ideal, in my opinion. We do live in a global society where various forms of racism have been around for a long time and are still present. As a result, there are plenty of instances where the connotations of something being "dark" aren't just limited to mystery or the unknown, though there are plenty of proverbs, sayings, and famous quotes to that effect. Darkness is often equated with evil, which is especially problematic in a society that makes a big deal out of some people having darker skin while others have lighter skin, and wherein skin color was used as a justification for colonialism and oppression.

The unfortunate thing is that fairy tales have actually participated in this manner of racism, associating darkness with bad and lightness with good. Ann Schmiesing has written about the racial and racist undertones of dark skin color in the Grimms' collection, and Nancy Canepa among others has noted that in Basile's groundbreaking collection, the *Tale of Tales*, it's always black slave girls who are the most treacherous and evil characters. That is…not a good look.

Further, calling a tale dark is a bit vague. Do we mean it's more sex-filled? More violent? Which kind of violence, like how graphic is it? How many people need to die for it to count? Those are all questions about the content, but are we talking more about motifs (individual "dark" acts, items, characters) or themes (death, grief, etc.)? Or is it more of a structural question, like we're looking at sad endings instead of happy endings? Or are we talking about questions of genre-crossing, where "dark" fairy tales actually cross into horror? More like gore or more like psychological horror?

At the end of the day, I just don't think calling a fairy tale "dark" is that useful of a description. I've seen alternatives proposed, like grim (too close to the name of the Grimm brothers in my opinion, so that could lead to confusion), bitter, and Gothic. In my article cited below, I explored a new-ish trend in fairy-tale literature I'm seeing, which I decided to call fairy-tale torture porn. And yes, that level of specificity is warranted.

I like reading about sex and violence as much as the next person. So I get the sheer glee when we encounter fairy tales that, counter to so much of our lived experience where they're "just" for kids, participate in a much more complex and full human spectrum sort of storytelling. I am here for it; goodness knows I read and write more than my fair share of what can be considered "dark" fairy tales.

But, returning to my earlier assertion, this sort of pleasure in playing with assumptions says more about us than about the tale traditions. Many of us have grown up with Disney's dominance in fairy-tale retellings, and so just discovering that there's more to the story than their version of it can feel freeing and exhilarating. And I do think that fairy tales can and should address the full spectrum of human experience, so the less-cheery side of tales can be really compelling too.

I will make some recommendations for these kinds of texts in the last section of this book, but let's recall: "dark" fairy tales are really just fairy tales. Sometimes they're early versions that escaped censorship, and sometimes they're retellings toggled to highlight topics that are taboo or run counter to the Disneyfied trend. They're fun...but they're better when we understand them (and ourselves).

REFERENCES:

Jorgensen, Jeana. "The Thorns of Trauma: Torture, Aftermath, and Healing in Contemporary Fairy-Tale Literature." *Humanities* vol. 10, no. 47, 2021.

FOLKLORE, FAIRY TALE, AND THE "ORIGINAL" VERSION

As a FOLKLORIST, I've grown to loathe the concept of the "original" when it comes up in my college classes or out in the broader world. This is due to two conflated meanings that I'll unpack here, and once we understand these meanings, I think we'll all be better positioned to have awesome conversations about fairy tales and folklore more generally.

The first – and incorrect – way that references to the "original" crop up in my classes is as an assertion of origin. As in, a student saying that the "original" Cinderella was dark and gory.

Um, no. First, that's usually a reference to the Grimms' version of Cinderella, in which the stepsisters cut off toes and/or heels to try to fit into the shoe, and get their eyes pecked out by birds at Cinderella's wedding to the prince. But even then, are we talking about the 1812 version of Cinderella, from when the Grimms first published their collection of tales, *Kinder- und Hausmärchen (Children's and Household Tales)*, or from the 7th and final revision which appeared in 1857, or any of the intervening revisions? And then what about translations? We know from various folklore studies that Victorian-era English translators changed bunches based on social norms and ideas about acceptability for child audiences.

Between publication and translation issues, it's difficult to talk about the "original" version of a fairy tale, even when someone has a specific version in mind. Then you throw in the fact that it's incredibly difficult to determine when the first existing version of something from oral tradition came into being, and yeah… it's hardly worth talking about unless you happen to have access to a time machine and can clear up the debate for once and for all. (For what it's worth, though, the oldest written version of something resembling Cinderella comes from 9th century China, which means it was likely circulating in oral tradition well before that!)

See, I'm not drawn to the pursuit of the origins of older folklore. It might be an intriguing research question, for some people, some of the time… but it's not why I'm here. I'm in folklore studies because we have our scholarly fingers on the pulse of what people (consciously or not) find relevant enough to transmit, perform, and enact.

Anyway, in folklore studies the question of the "original" is essentially a meaningless one, unless you're working with a phenomenon that is so recent or so thoroughly documented that you can, in fact, point at the first instance of something. But usually it comes together from a swirl of existing cultural material that gets remixed in just the right way to cohere and resonate with people.

The second meaning that the "original" can have in folk-lore studies (and one that bugs me far less, though I wish we had better language for it) is meaning the first version that stuck with *you*. So it's a more subjective meaning, and therefore can't really be debated in the same way as the first meaning. Which is fine – but people need to realize that the first version they were exposed to isn't necessarily going to be the same for everyone. The language of intertextuality is useful here (it's basically the idea that all texts are forever in conversation with other texts), but unless I'm making my college students memorize those terms, I don't expect everyone to start chatting someone up by asking what their personal pretext or hypotext is.

In *Fairy Tales and Feminism: New Approaches*, Donald Haase covers reception and reader response approaches to fairy tales in his introductory essay. One of the scholars he mentions, Kay Stone, has done pioneering work with women's and children's memories of and responses to gender roles in fairy tales. Among Stone's findings is the impressive insight that women selectively remembered the heroines of fairy tales, sometimes making them more active and heroic than passive, even when their roles in the text seem largely passive. Otherwise, there hasn't been a ton of work in this area that I know of (at one point I was going to do a study, but the Institutional Review Board permissions were complicated, given that I wanted to work with children).

For fairy tales specifically, yes, we can blame Disney and their aggressive copyright laws for a lot of the hype around the "original" version of something, down to the color and cut of a princess's dress. But we should also take into account the intellectual fascination with morphologies and genealogies dating back to the Romantic era and the philological foundations of modern literary, historical, linguistic, and anthropological studies. I've always got a rant about authenticity up my sleeve, and how every cultural tradition was at one point invented, and it ties in nicely here. Like, maybe there was an "original" back in the day at some point, when two texts collided, or people accidentally rearranged some old things to make a new thing…but if it's as good as lost to the sands of time, why should we fixate on it? Usually, the fixation around authenticity is someone trying to stake a claim, whether to defend their heritage against threats or try to sell you something, just sayin'.

If we each have our own personal first-exposure version of a text – whether a tale type, or a custom, or a proper way of preparing a holiday food – then that can be a potentially interesting avenue of study. When was someone first exposed to the text? By whom? Which facets of it stuck with them (motifs and themes; structure; context) and which are more malleable? How does this color their interactions with other versions of the same plot, text, or tale type?

The personal-first-exposure meaning (we need to find a better term than "your original version") is intriguing and grants that our unique life experiences shape our interactions with cultural materials. This is more empowering – and more accurate – than trying to determine which version of something came first, since that's often a question that leads back to historically privileged individuals and groups (e.g. those with literacy, the power to record their lives, and so on).

So please remove the word "original" from your vocabulary when in a folklore context. And if you can be mindful of my other folklore pet peeves that'd be awesome too, such as when people assume we write children's books, or that all folklorists are obsessed with origins or with Joseph Campbell.

REFERENCES:

Haase, Donald. *Fairy Tales and Feminism: New Approaches.*
Wayne State University Press, 2004.

EXPLORING A TALE TYPE: SAMPLE PAPER ON ATU 510B

So, in the fall of 2017 I taught an elective on gender and sexuality in fairy tales. I gave my students an assignment: to select a tale type, then research its historical and geographical distribution, using at least three versions to document the forms the tale type tends to take. After assembling at least three texts, they were supposed to describe the content of the stories (as in, motifs and themes), the contexts in which they were told and collected, and the structures they exhibit. In another paper this semester, we dove more into interpretation and function...but in my mind, this first assignment paves the way for the second. Before you can begin interpreting a tale type, you need to know its basic context, because context always informs meaning...it's not like meaning is some free-floating attribute out in space, it always comes bundled along with culture and people and their values.

At some point in the semester, it occurred to me that not everyone's been doing folkloristic research for over a decade so maybe I should write up a sample document. I decided to write about my favorite tale type, ATU 510B, which I also wrote my master's thesis on. My hope was to model what basic, entry-level type of folkloristic looks like for my students...here's hoping I succeeded!

Aarne-Thompson-Uther tale 510B, "Peau d'Asne"/"Donkeyskin"/"The Dress of Gold, of Silver, and of Stars [Cap O Rushes]," is found in many regions and time periods throughout European, Semitic, and adjacent cultures. The best-known versions come from Charles Perrault and the Grimm brothers, and in this paper, I will focus on three lesser-known versions to survey how tradition and variation play out in this tale type. I will survey the content, contexts, and form/structure of these three versions, and in a future paper will discuss the tale's potential functions and interpretations.

As Hans-Jörg Uther demonstrates in his 2004 revision of the tale type index, ATU 510B is found in the British Isles, Scandinavian countries, Romance-language-speaking countries, Germanic countries, East European states, Slavic states, and throughout the Middle East and Mediterranean (as well as European-colonized locations in North and South America). Thus while this tale type is not universally known, it is certainly widespread, which makes it all the more intriguing due to its disturbing content.

The three versions I work with here come from 20th century Palestinian-Arab tellers, 19th century Sicilian tellers, and 20th century French tellers. In terms of situational context, they vary greatly in terms of the amount of information we have about collector and informant, though in terms of cultural context, they all come from patriarchal cultures. The Palestinian-Arab version, "Sackcloth," was collected by

Ibrahim Muhawi and Sharif Kanaana from a 58-year-old woman, Almaza, between 1978 and 1980. The collectors were also responsible for translating it into English. The Sicilian version, "Betta Pilusa," was collected by Laura Gonzenbach in the 1860s in Sicilian (of which she was a native speaker), which she then published in German. Jack Zipes then translated her tales into English, noting the difficulties of translation but stating: "Despite the different languages, Sicilian and high German, Gonzenbach managed to convey the spirit of insurrection and provocation with which the tellers imbued their tales" (*Beautiful Angiola* xxxii). The French version, "The She Donkey's Skin," was collected in 1960 from a peasant woman in her 70s from the region of Limousin. It is unclear whether the tale was collected by Geneviève Massignon, editor of the volume in which it appears (Folktales of France), or by one of her field team. It was translated by Jacqueline Hyland and appears in the English-language series Folktales of the World edited by renowned folklorist Richard Dorson. Though we lack detailed informant information for these texts, it is clear that they all have been circulating in oral tradition (quite recently, in the case of two of them), rather than being derived directly from a literary tale collection such as those of Perrault, the Grimms, or Straparola.

The content of these tales revolves around the same motif: father-daughter incest. As Uther outlines the plot in the tale type index, a king promises his dying wife that he will marry someone who fulfills a particular condition. This turns out to be their daughter. She flees after obtaining magical dresses and/or a disguise from him, often under advice of a sympathetic helper figure, and then works as a servant in another king's castle. After wearing the magical dresses to three subsequent balls, she either reveals herself to the prince or is found out by him to have been the servant working in the castle all along (frequently, he has taunted or abused her). They marry. How closely each tale's structure and content conforms to this plot outline varies.

The French version, "The She Donkey's Skin," has the father deciding to marry his daughter after the mother's death, based on a condition she set on her deathbed: "Do not marry again unless you find a woman as beautiful as I am" (Massignon, 149). The girl requests beautiful dresses from her father (the number is not specified), and then flees in a magic chest and donkey skin that her godmother gave her. She settles at a farm belonging to a king, and there the prince teases her three times: he pokes her with a fire poker, gives her a puff from bellows, and then prods her with a stick. After each of these encounters, she cleans herself up, puts on a beautiful dress, and teases the prince at the ball when she dances with him, telling him her name is something like "Poker Poke" or "Bellows' Puff." Finally, the prince falls ill and refuses to eat soup made by anyone but her, but then he spies on her as she puts on her beautiful garb to come meet him. They are married, and no mention is made of the incestuous father.

In the Palestinian-Arab version, "Sackcloth," there is no condition that the dying wife imposes; the father simply realizes: "No one seemed more beautiful in his eyes, so the story goes, than his own daughter, and he had no wish to marry another" (Muhawi and Kanaana, 125). Nor are there three magical dresses, though the girl takes the fine clothes her father gives her in preparation for their wedding when she flees. She has a "tight-fitting sackcloth" commissioned that will cover her whole body (ibid 126), and in it, she looks like a man, and a freakish one at that, so she is able to escape the dreaded marriage and go to work in another household. There, she attends a wedding in her beautiful dress, and inspires the prince's mother to bring him along (cross-dressed) so that he can see the beautiful girl for himself. Once the prince sees her, he wonders where she comes from, and hides the next day, only to observe her coming and going from his own household. He orders Sackcloth to bring him his meal the following day, and though she drops a number of platters while on the way up, eventually the two are alone together, and he tells her to remove the sackcloth and reveal herself. They are married.

In the Sicilian version, "Betta Pilusa," the dying wife tells her husband not to remarry unless a particular ring fits the prospective wife. The daughter tries it on since it's among the mother's jewels, and the father declares that he must marry her. The girl's father confessor tells her to ask for a dress the color of the sky, a dress the color of the sea, and a dress the color of the earth. The devil provides the father with all these dresses, and also with the girl's final request: a dress made from the fur of a gray cat. The girl flees in the cat fur dress. The king mistakes her for an animal and almost shoots her, but then takes her to live in his chicken coop. Living under the name Betta Pilusa (which Zipes translates as "Hairy Bertha"), she attends three balls and charms the king each time. He gives her gifts, which she as Betta Pilusa cooks into buns to give the king. He threatens the cook until the cook reveals who baked the bread, and then the king threatens Betta Pilusa until she removes her cat skin dress and agrees to marry her.

All three versions have the following motifs in common: the dead mother and incestuous father, the three trips to a festive event, the hairy or ugly disguise, the relegation of the protagonist to the kitchen, and the lack of punishment for (or mention of) the father at the tale's end. As with many fairy tales, the number three is a prominent motif (the three requested dresses appear in two of the versions considered here). Intriguingly, it is only in "Sackcloth" that the protagonist is daughter of a king; in the other two versions, it's specified that she is the daughter of a gentleman or a rich man. In all three versions, however, she marries either a king or a prince (the king's son). Thus, her lowly status relative her husband-to-be depends more on her being displaced from her own household than on what precise rank she held at birth.

Larger themes addressed include family, obligation, food, and marriage. These themes seem very much in tune with the life contexts of the tale's tellers. Jack Zipes observes of the French women writing fairy tales during the height of the literary fairy-tale trend in France in the 1690s: "the sad state of the dark side of the classical fairy tales is that women writers often felt compelled to give more expression to male needs and hegemony than to their own" ("Setting Standards" 53). Though these three versions come from different cultural contexts, I would argue that their themes seem in line with the daily concerns of their tellers. The tellers were likely of lower or middle class, and thus the amount of attention to kinship obligations and food preparation seems appropriate.

Structurally, each of the three tales casts the incestuous king as a hostile donor figure – combining the Proppian roles of villain and donor – to varying degrees. In "Sackcloth," the father provides beautiful dresses, but the heroine provides her own disguise in which to escape, and at no one's prompting. In fact, her father consults a cadi (a local Islamic authority) to establish his claim over his daughter, and the cadi backs up the father's right to act on his desires. The father in the French version has the devil's backing in obtaining the magical dresses. In terms of advisors, the French protagonist benefits from the advice of her godmother (who is also a fairy), and the Sicilian protagonist gets advice from her priest. The sought-after love object, the prince or king's son, takes initiative in each tale to seek out the mysterious maiden who turns out to have been living in his household all along, showing that this tale role is not completely passive.

ATU 510B is a tale type with controversial content but remarkable conformity across time and space. Despite varying cultural contexts, versions from Sicilian, Palestinian-Arab, and French narrators align to present a tale showing a young woman escaping her father's incestuous advances and establishing herself in a new household. This may happen with more or less magical intervention, and more or less guidance from a helper figure, showing that at the tale type's core is a resilient and independent woman.

REFERENCES:

Massignon, Geneviève. *Folktales of France.* The University of Chicago Press, 1968.

Muhawi, Ibrahim, and Sharif Kanaana. *Speak, Bird, Speak Again: Palestinian Arab Folktales.* University of California Press, 1989.

Uther, Hans-Jörg. *The Types of International Folktales: A Classification and Bibliography.* Academia Scientiarum Fennica, 2004.

Zipes, Jack. *Beautiful Angiola: The Great Treasury of Sicilian Folk and Fairy Tales Collected by Laura Gonzenbach.* Routledge, 2004.

---. "Setting Standards for Civilization through Fairy Tales: Charles Perrault and the Subversive Role of Women Writers." In *Fairy Tales and the Art of Subversion.* 2nd edition. Routledge, 2006. 29-57.

WHY THE TRANSLATION YOU READ OF A FAIRY-TALE COLLECTION MATTERS

PART of the fun of being a fairy-tale scholar is revealing particularly gory versions of beloved tales to people. Here, I take a different tack.

As folkloric texts, fairy tales are already subject to astounding variation: Cinderella's benefactor has been a fairy godmother, a tree growing over her dead mother's grave, or a magic talking fish in different versions. Adding translation to the list of things that can vary – and might be intentionally altered – complicates matters.

When people tell me they've read the Grimms' tales, I always ask: which edition, and which translation? Because the Grimms released seven major editions of their tales between 1812 and 1857, and once we establish which edition it was, the translation makes a huge difference as well. Martin Sutton chronicled the changes made by Victorian-era English translators in his book *The Sin-Complex*, noting that the British translators were particularly keen on removing sexual and scatalogical motifs from the tales. The Grimms, too, toned down the sex in their stories, but left in plenty of violence and bodily fluids, due to cultural differences about what was deemed appropriate for young readers.

Another fascinating case study emerges in the tales authored by Charles Perrault, a French courtier whose *Mother Goose Tales*, published in 1697, also became part of the canon of classical fairy tales.

Scholar Christine Jones strikingly demonstrates how the rearranging of the order of Perrault's tales in the collection alters their reception and impact. In his original publication, Perrault started with "Sleeping Beauty," though his story has the heroine coming back to live with her husband and having to fight for her life against his Ogress mother who wants to eat her and her children. It's a long and violent tale.

In contrast, early 18th century English translations of Perrault's tales start the collection with "Little Red Riding Hood" and "The Fairies." Perrault's LRRH dies in bed with the wolf, while "The Fairies" has a happy ending (good girl rewarded by fairy; bad girl punished by fairy; this tale type, ATU 480, is appropriately called "The Kind and the Unkind Girls").

As Jones points out, this has implications for the reception not just of Perrault's tales, but the entire genre of fairy tales:

What happens when the text leads off with the shortest stories in the corpus? Readers are set up to read fairy tales a certain way. The short plots encourage us to look for a simple point—the nugget of action or "moral of the story" that teaches a lesson. Readers who approach the collection this way will logically seek out a similarly small nugget buried in the much longer stories to follow instead of relishing their narrative complexity. We can see in that perception of the genre something very close to popular ideas today about what a fairy tale should look like and do for children.

There's a whole body of scholarship on translations of folklore, literature, and culture, and this is why: translation is not a passive act, a silent rendering, a reflection. It actively creates something new, synthesizing the original text with a host of embedded assumptions about culture, norms, and more.

In order to best understand and appreciate fairy tales, we have to know by whom – and how – they were translated.

REFERENCES:

Jones, Christine. "Mother Goose's French Birth (1697) and British Afterlife (1729)." *The Public Domain Review*, 2013, https://publicdomainreview.org/essay/mother-gooses-french-birth-1697-and-british-afterlife-1729. Accessed 19 February 2022.

THE GRIMMS ON CENSORSHIP

IF YOU'RE A FAIRY-TALE SCHOLAR/NERD like me, you're probably making your way through (or at least aware of) Jack Zipes's new translation of the first edition of the Grimms' fairy tales. While reading the introduction, which details how the brothers collected and edited their tales, I came across a fascinating quote about how they view censorship, which I wanted to share here.

To briefly give some context, Jacob and Wilhelm Grimm were scholars whose interest in German folklore began as a combination of art and science: they were gathering tales to help some friends in the literary scene achieve enough material to publish, and they were also interested in the historical evolution of language and genre. Documenting the oral traditions (*Naturpoesie*) of the German people was also a political means to an end, as Germany was not yet united and was suffering under Napoleon's wartime rule.

So in 1812 and 1815, the Grimms published volumes 1 and 2 of their fairy tales... which also contained a bunch of scholarly annotations. This first edition wasn't that well received by the public; many readers thought the stories were too crude, violent, and sexually explicit. The annotations didn't really resonate with the general public, either, and the topic seemed trivial to some. For the next 40 years, the Grimms continually revised their tales, putting out new editions, until the final (and for many, definitive) edition of 1857 was published. The stories from that edition are probably the ones you've read, unless you also read German.

Are the tales meant for kids? Yes and no. As scholars have extrapolated from their writings, the Grimms were writing for fellow scholars, but also believing that young and old readers alike could derive both wisdom and entertainment from these tales. They vehemently rejected the idea that the tales should be withheld from children on the basis of their being unsuitable for them, and here's where things get interesting.

The Grimms weigh in on the subject:

In publishing our collection we wanted to do more than just perform a service for the history of *Poesie*. We intended at the same time to enable *Poesie* itself, which is alive in the collection, to have an effect: it was to give pleasure to anyone who could take pleasure in it, and therefore, our collection was also to become an intrinsic educational primer. Some people have complained about this latter intention, and asserted that there are things here and there [in our collection] that cause embarrassment and are unsuitable for children or offensive (such as the reference to certain incidents and conditions, and they also think children should not hear about the devil or anything evil). Accordingly, parents should not offer the collection to children. In individual cases this concern may be correct, and thus one can easily choose which tales are to be read. On the whole it is certainly not necessary. Nothing can better defend us than nature itself, which has let certain flowers and leaves grow in a particular color and shape. People who do not find them beneficial, suitable for their special needs, which cannot be known, can easily walk right by them. But they cannot demand that the flowers and leaves be colored and cut in another way. (Zipes xxix-xxx)

Although the Grimms did increasingly edit their tales for certain kinds of content (changing wicked mothers into wicked stepmothers; removing mentions of pregnancy; removing overt incest), this assertion is still a fascinating one. Why, indeed, should artists and content creators/curators be beholden to the complaints of a few? If people can be expected to overlook things that don't serve them in nature, why can't they do so with art?

I very much think that the Grimms are correct, and that people can and should be responsible for their own content intake much of the time. Concerned parents can try to monitor what their children are reading, or better yet, raise the kids with values congruent with their own, so that if kids encounter "objectionable" material then hopefully they won't be too vulnerable to it.

It also amazes me that almost the exact same argument for censorship we hear so often today – "but think of the children!" – was being made TWO centuries ago. It's clearly a powerful rhetoric that resonates with a lot of people, though I think it's overused and misused in many cases.

The "art is like nature; take it or leave it" argument might be flawed, though. Goodness knows that some folks take what is natural – say, sex and sexuality – and try to obscure it, making it seem like it doesn't exist. But it seems to me that the Grimms have, two centuries ago, articulated a very important anti-censorship argument: that we inhabit a world that is not always to our liking, and we must make our peace with this fact.

REFERENCES:

Zipes, Jack. Introduction. *The Original Folk and Fairy Tales of the Brothers Grimm: The Complete First Edition.* Princeton University Press, 2015. ix-xliii.

HANS CHRISTIAN ANDERSEN
ON ART

I'VE BEEN DOING some reading on Hans Christian Andersen lately, and it's really spurred me to think about my own inter- actions with art. In addition to reading Andersen's tales, I've been reading Jack Zipes's book *Hans Christian Andersen: The Misunderstood Storyteller*, which (in my opinion) does a great job of using contextual information from Andersen's life to illuminate his fairy tales and stories.

Fun fact: Andersen never married, and is believed to have never had sex (despite apparently visiting brothels a couple of times in his life). Contemporary scholars debate whether he was gay, bisexual, or "spiritually androgynous" yet asexual in practice (Bom and Aarenstrup). Based on the fact that he proposed to two women, and yet in numerous letters and diary entries described his passionate feelings for men, it seems likely that he wasn't 100% heterosexual (as much as that category existed in 19th century Denmark or anywhere else for that matter). Either way you slice it, he felt like he didn't fit in and was thus lonely and misunderstood.

Perhaps related to his loneliness was his drive to create. He was amazingly prolific, penning not just the tales we know and love him for, but also poetry, essays, novels, plays, travel books, and memoirs. Zipes gives us a quote from one of his diaries:

> What could become of me, and what will become of me? My powerful fantasy will drive me into the insane asylum, my violent temper will make a suicide of me! Before, the two of these together would have made a great writer. (7)

Other quotes reveal that Andersen believed he was guided by God to become a great artist, that he had a gift to share with the world. In Andersen's tales, too, we see notions of inner nobility (such as in "The Ugly Duckling") and ruminations on the nature of art ("The Nightingale")… and those are just from some of his better-known works! There are tons more.

All this has me thinking, as an artist, about what makes me similar to and different from Andersen. I also feel driven, perhaps to the point of narcissism and solitude. I don't, however, believe that I have a God-given destiny to become an artist… though I do feel like I have talents and skills that I ought to use, if only because I have them and don't want them to get rusty. When it comes down to it, what's the difference between the two? If I believe I have a gift and ought to use it to create art, does it really matter whether I believe it came from God or is just a part of my personality and makeup?

One of Andersen's tales, "The Pen and the Inkwell," shows the two titular objects arguing over which of them has agency and is thus responsible for creating the masterpieces they write. The poet who wields them ends up writing a parable about how the bow and violin that create marvelous music are not, however, the creators of their art:

How absurd it would seem if the bow and the violin should be proud and haughty about their accomplishments. Yet we, human beings, often are: the poets, the artists, the scientists, and even the generals often boast in vain pride. Yet they are all but instruments that God plays upon. To Him alone belongs all honor. We have nothing to pride ourselves upon! (Haugaard, 640)

I believe that artistic inspiration comes from somewhere, but that "somewhere" doesn't need to have a religious explanation tacked on to it in order to be meaningful. The important thing about art is that it moves us, not where it comes from. To be sure, many artists use art therapeutically, to resolve feelings and address struggles – so in that sense, yes, it matters where art comes from. But I don't think that the only rational or valid origin for art lies in religion.

To me, a more powerful account of art can be seen in "The Nightingale." A nightingale that sings miraculously beautiful songs agrees to come and sing for the emperor, but it's banished after a mechanical bird arrives and sings flawless, perfect (but ultimately boring and unchanging) music. After all this, the nightingale returns and sings for Death before Death can claim the emperor's life. Art is so moving that it can persuade Death to leave – and it almost teaches the emperor a valuable lesson about de-commodifying art. Almost. The emperor still wants art on his terms, but relents and agrees to let the nightingale come and go as it pleases.

Perhaps there are people who will never understand how artists and art work, but as long as they're able to enjoy its beauty from time to time, this tale suggests, then our worlds will intersect and enlighten one another. Perhaps art doesn't always provoke lasting social change, but moments of reflection are still worthwhile.

One of the enduring gifts that Andersen gave the world was his meta-art, or his art that reflects on art. I appreciate this as both an artist and a scholar, and I continue to seek it out in my engagements with others. If nothing else, connecting with others (such as collaborating) prevents me from going to the extreme of hermiting myself up all the time or becoming too proud. Encounters with others always have the potential to be humbling, and if we read into and across Andersen's tales, we find the encouragement to engage, encounter, and transform.

REFERENCES:

Bom, Anne Klara and Anya Aarenstrup. "Homosexuality." *The Hans Christian Andersen Centre*, https://andersen.sdu.dk/rund tom/faq/index_e.html?emne=homo. Accessed 19 February 2022.

Andersen, Hans Christian, et al. *The Complete Fairy Tales and Stories*. Translated by Erik Christian Haugaard, First Anchor books ed., Anchor Press, 1983.

Zipes, Jack. *Hans Christian Andersen: The Misunderstood Story-teller*. Routledge, 2005.

WHY I HATE THE NATURALIZATION OF FEMININITY, AND YOU SHOULD TOO

LET'S make it seem like women's bodies are self-contained vessels of naturally-occurring perfection! That's a great idea... said no woman ever. And we see it in fairy tales as well as in fashion and body art trends.

Anecdote time: I'm putting on a racer-back bra under a new shirt. I turn to check out the back in the mirror, to make sure the bra straps aren't showing. They aren't, but I can see little bumps under the shirt where the bra can be adjusted.

No big deal, right? It's not as bad as visible bra straps, right?

But what makes visible bra straps bad? What makes the mere suggestion of undergarments inappropriate? Obviously there's a chunk of sex negativity mixed in, with the idea that the garments that come into contact with sexy body parts should be hidden forever because sex is filthy, dirty, icky, immoral, bad, only good when in the context of heterosexual monogamous procreation, etc.

When it comes to the manifestations of misogyny, there's a

lot to talk about. We could talk about purity policing. We could talk about slut shaming. We could talk about rape culture.

And those are all good conversations to have, but right now I want to talk about the naturalization of femininity. By this, I mean all the ways in which women's bodies and selves are molded into an ideal in ways that should be invisible. No one should see all the work going into your diet, wardrobe selection, or beauty regime...because it's natural. It needs to happen routinely and perfectly, as though you rolled out of bed this way. I'm calling it "naturalized" because it's not only presented as natural, but also as part of a process that obscures its origins.

This cultural concept goes a long way back. We see it in fairy tales, for example, where the natural beauties like Snow White and Cinderella outshine their rivals effortlessly. Women in fairy tales do go to great lengths to enhance their beauty, but always in ways that conceal the origin of the effect once it's put into place.

My fairy-tale scholar colleague Laurence Talairach-Vielmas sums up this phenomenon nicely:

As Snow White's wicked stepmother's irresistible offer illustrates, what we generally learn as children is that all princesses are beautiful and may even try to improve their beauty. In fact, their beauty is their wealth—quite literally, since being beautiful enables them to win a prince and a fortune. Hence, what fairy tales foreground is the idea that femininity is closely linked to aestheticization, and that beauty is a feminine virtue which needs to be cultivated. Whether it be

Psyche enticed by Prosperine's beauty cream or Snow White lured by the Wicked Queen's gaudy stay-laces, these female characters exemplify how much their own fate depends on their physical appearance, on their power to construct a self which matches male exceptions. (5)

And then we get to pop culture and fashion, where the same message prevails, and invades our lives in ever more pervasive and personal ways: the need to shave or groom body hair, the need to be slender or skinny, the need to have one's breasts look just right. The moral connotations of being fat are one example of this. The freak-out over women wearing "revealing" clothes is another. And again, it's not just that these ideals are harmful in and of themselves, but that women are being held to such high standards that upon arriving at said ideals, the work to get there must be invisible. Not to mention the intersectionality at play, too, in that these ideals are largely based on ideas that are white supremacist, classist, and ableist in nature; women who deviate from those norms, by birth or social construct or choice, are less likely to be considered candidates at attaining beauty.

Little of what I'm writing here is new; Naomi Wolf made many of the same criticisms in *The Beauty Myth* (which, btw, I am not a huge fan of Wolf's recent work or opinions, but this book is a feminist classic). One of my favorite passages in the book is:

Just as the beauty myth did not really care what women looked like as long as women felt ugly, we must see that it does not matter in the least what women look like as long as we feel beautiful.

The real issue has nothing to do with whether women wear makeup or don't, gain weight or lose it, have surgery or shun it, dress up or down, make our clothing and faces and bodies into works of art or ignore adornment altogether. *The real problem is our lack of choice.* (272, italics in original)

What I am pointing out, however, is that multiple aspects of Western culture not only push a restrictive and unattainable ideal of femininity, but they also do so through the mechanism of naturalizing femininity into an invisible (but necessary) effect. This is, of course, another form of emotional labor that women are expected to take on (look pretty! but don't talk about or reveal all the work that goes into it!).

And don't get me wrong: I love body art, adornment, and beauty in general. My feminism encompasses the notion that self-adornment can be creative, playful, fulfilling, and radical when we make it so (but of course it can also be a tool of the patriarchy).

To borrow a line from Black lesbian feminist Audre Lorde, can we use the master's tools to dismantle the master's house? The answer, of course, is "it's complicated." I suggest that we start with de-naturalizing feminine beauty, deconstructing it, and having a bit of raucous fun from there. And, of course, keep the conversation going!

REFERENCES:

Talairach-Vielmas, Laurence. *Moulding the female body in Victorian fairy tales and sensation novels*. Ashgate Publishing, Ltd., 2007.

Wolf, Naomi. *The Beauty Myth: How Images of Beauty Are Used Against Women*. Harper Perennial, 2002 [1991].

WHY THE FAIRY-TALE METAPHOR FOR TRUMP'S WORLD... ACTUALLY WORKS

HELLO. Fairy-tale scholar here.

I'm here to tell you that fairy tales have been in and out of vogue for the last few centuries, but when they're in, they're usually politically relevant. Sometimes writers use fairy tales to critique current regimes, other times to uphold them. Scholars like Jack Zipes have compellingly made the case that when viewed from a Marxist perspective, fairy tales are not actually all that revolutionary or subversive; more often than not, they uphold the status quo.

Sadly, this is especially true in contemporary America.

Perhaps – and please note that I wrote this piece originally in mid-2017 – you saw some of the coverage of the Trump family's nepotism that compared the whole phenomenon to royalty. And for many Americans, anything "royal" pings our fairy tale senses. For instance, Jude Ellison Sady Doyle wrote a piece for *Elle* titled "Ivanka Trump Will Not Fix 'Women's Issues'–She Will Distract From Them." Doyle opens the piece:

For those of us who overdosed on Disney princess memorabilia growing up, good news: Thanks to Donald Trump and his legion of terrifying yet well-coiffed children, Americans are now closer to living in a monarchy than we have been since 1776. And Ivanka Trump—blond, pretty, well-mannered, given massive amounts of power over the citizenry thanks to nothing but her genetic makeup—is the closest thing we'll get to a princess. Which is how we'll all get to find out: Princesses are terrifying.

If you've not seen the animated video for the "Historically Accurate Princess Song" by Rachel Bloom, it's a must watch (you can find it easily on YouTube). It's a humorous and visceral reminder that stories about monarchies do not serve everyone equally, and I love to gross out my college students with it (content note for assault, incest, and anti-Semitism among other things).

Whither the association of fairy tales with royalty? It's partly a feature of the genre's structure, or the way in which fairy-tale plots tend to proceed with consistency towards a highly specific happily ever after.

The way fairy tales are structured, we follow the adventures of a protagonist who either starts in a low station in life, or has fallen from status. They meet a donor figure, perform tasks to demonstrate their kindness or maturity, and are gifted a magical agent to help them succeed in achieving a quest, fighting adversaries, and/or disenchanting/winning a spouse. At the tale's end, our protagonist has either risen to royal status through marriage, or been restored to their former position (usually with the addition of a marital partner).

When princesses appear as protagonists in fairy tales, they're often enchanted and need to be rescued (by their partner-to-be, the tale's other main character) or they're cast out from home and need to go on a quest for redemption. As supporting characters, princesses run the gamut from vapid to sullen, prizes to be won, generous helpers, window dressing, sexual competition. In terms of the Grimms' tales alone, sometimes they even get to be murderous, scheming against their husbands as in "The King of the Golden Mountain," while the princess in "King Thrushbeard" is vain and must be taught humility through humiliation.

Tales that feature princesses do not show revolution or social change. The monarchy is intact at the tale's beginning, and remains that way at the tale's end. In this sense, fairy tales preserve political power structures, though they might be subversive on other levels, allowing for exploration of gender roles or notions of humanity.

Scholars have long argued that fairy tales function to, among other things, provide communities with a means of collective day-dreaming. The supernatural elements of fairy tales thus operate as a metaphorical code for the real-life dilemmas that people face. Danish folklorist Bengt Holbek, for example, saw in 19th century tales told by Danish peasants a symbolic system that posited villains as the prospective spouse's parents that the protagonist would have to overcome to be successfully married.

But if fairy tales offer wish fulfillment – and I think they do, at least some of the time – they usually do it on an individual level. The low-ranking protagonist who rises to a higher social station does so alone. They don't change the social system for everyone. Hell, they don't change it at all in most cases.

This is why I find it eerie that fairy tale metaphors are employed to the extent that they are, in describing Ivanka Trump and Trump's world more generally. As Doyle states:

The goal of Trumpism is not to benefit women. The goal is to benefit one woman, Ivanka, or the one type of woman she represents. [...] We're not meant to benefit from her; we're meant to look at her, and think about how we can be more like her. We're meant to blame ourselves for falling short, as we have with every other Exceptional Woman to date. Ivanka is the Disney princess; we're the peasant chorus members who watch, and serve, and sigh at her pretty hair. Hell, maybe we'll even pitch in some background vocals on a few of the big musical numbers. Peasants always do, in those movies, even though they're probably all starving.

The failure to question whether exceptional figures, literal or real princesses, have our best interests at heart is understandable on some level; after all, the stories we're raised on valorize royalty and nobility. Throw in the American dream, telling us we can achieve high social status that's not technically based on birth but just as good, and you've got a potent mix of ideologies.

Throw in the lack of intersectional feminism among white women in particular, and my reading of the appropriateness of the fairy-tale metaphor gets even more dire.

I've seen arguments that white women voting for Trump is more a general Democratic failing. In general, it seems that white women have little reason not to continue to uphold the status quo, as many of feminism's gains have benefited them (I guess I should say us, though I'm trying to suck less at feminism by being more intersectional). And that's for women supposedly sympathetic to the plight of other women! What about the rest?

Here, I turn to Sarah Jones's piece, *"The Handmaid's Tale* Is a Warning to Conservative Women." Jones focuses on the character of Serena Joy, a former televangelist and now high-ranking wife in Gilead who nonetheless seems to suffer for it. Offred notes: "She stays in her home, but it doesn't seem to agree with her. How furious she must be, now that she's been taken at her word."

Jones writes:

The dilemma of Serena Joy feels deceptively easy to resolve. She's in this for power, and understands that it's hers if she says the right things to the right audiences. Schlafly achieved international fame, and Conway has the ear of the president. With Gilead, however, Atwood reminds such women that they might not like the results of their labor; that by the time they come to regret it, the culture they helped create will have developed far beyond their control. Serena Joy is a warning, not only to her feminist antagonists, but to conservatives, too.

When narratives like *The Handmaid's Tale* and fairy tales depict women in power, they show us potential paths, routes, and outcomes. Fairy tales don't have a lot to say about what happens after the happily-ever-after, after the princess has preserved her grip on her royal heritage. But we can imagine, once the enchantment is over, once the compact and crystallized story ends, that it's a return to the messy human world with all its conflicts.

Fairy tales are not ideologically neutral. They show us the naturalization of femininity and women's beauty; they normalize certain patterns of sexuality. They provide templates for belief and behavior.

If we have reason to compare the people with political power to the people in fairy tales, we should be wary. We should ask who can access this power, and what their incentive is to do so, and strive to be intersectional in our analysis.

The fact that it's so easy to liken Ivanka Trump to a princess should bring to mind not just classic fairy tales about princesses, but also cautionary tales, of wolves in the woods, predators dressed in grandma's clothing. With any luck, some narrative savvy will help us undress the metaphors and make it out of the woods alive.

REFERENCES:

Doyle, Jude Ellison Sady. titled "Ivanka Trump Will Not Fix 'Women's Issues'–She Will Distract From Them." *Elle*, 15 December 2016, https://www.elle.com/culture/career-poli tics/a41444/ivanka-trump-distraction/. Accessed 19 February 2022.

Jones, Sarah. *"The Handmaid's Tale* Is a Warning to Conserva-

tive Women." *The New Republic,* 20 April 2017, https://newre
public.com/article/141674/handmaids-tale-hulu-warning-
conservative-women. Accessed 19 February 2022.

LIVING IN THE HOUSE OF
CANNIBALS

W<small>HEN</small> I <small>WAS</small> <small>LIVING</small> in Estonia in early 2012 to finish my dissertation, some folklore colleagues and I watched an Estonian film titled *Nukitsamees*, which translates to "Little Bumpy" (the title character is a little witch child with horns). The plot begins rather like the Western fairy tale "Hansel and Gretel" with a brother and sister lost in the woods, taken to the home of a witch where they live with the constant threat of being eaten. When they escape, they take the witch's child with them, and though he is unruly, he eventually chooses to live a human life. There is much rejoicing, singing, dancing, and valorizing of the heteronormative family.

What really struck me about the film, however, was the grim terror that the children experienced while living in the witch's house. While it was quite graphically depicted in the film, this is a feature of many related stories as well: the despondence and despair of the children upon discovering what they've stumbled into. The tale plot about children living in the house of cannibals – be they giants or witches – is quite widespread throughout Europe and Asia (we're not just talking "Hansel and Gretel" but many tale types with this motif, from lesser-known versions of "Jack and the Beanstalk" and "Molly Whuppie" to plenty of other tales).

These tales address very real fears of abandonment and child abuse, but more than that, I believe they deal with the experience of living in an environment that is experienced as harsh, hostile, and dangerous. The children are forced to work all day and night; they know that they could be punished or killed for any arbitrary reason; they know that their bodies will sustain the bodies of their captors, giving the captors life built on death.

What is this really about? I think these stories are about patriarchy, or, more broadly, a hierarchically stratified society that thrives upon the labor of the disenfranchised, literally building the lives of the empowered upon the bodies of the disempowered. In the case of women's experiences of patriarchy, everything I wrote in the above paragraph applies: women's labor in the domestic sphere is endless, filling each day and night; women (and men too) are policed and punished for any number of arbitrary transgressions when they step outside their gender roles; and women's reproductive labor is the foundation of society's continuation. Sexual assault remains astoundingly prevalent and functions as a powerful threat to keep women in their places, while cultural rhetoric places the blame on women who are raped as though they somehow asked for it.

Much of the same could be said for the working class in a capitalist society; for people of color in a racist society; for the urban poor in a classist society; for the untouchables in a caste society; and so on. These are the people whose bodies bear the brunt of mainstream society's desires and needs. Those who live more comfortable lives are unaware that they are simply being fattened by the witch before being shoved into the oven.

Stories like "Hansel and Gretel" and *Nukitsamees* give us an emotional vocabulary with which to articulate experiences of fear, complicity, and hostility. Those of us who study culture know that most people can't articulate the basic principles of the culture they live in, just like they can't articulate all of the principles of the language they speak. We're like fish who can't tell that we're swimming in water. Our culture is so infused with power relations that we can't even begin to say where they begin and end.

The setting – a terrifying house that is not a home – intensifies the cultural conflicts we all experience. The hostility is coming from inside the house (sorry, couldn't resist the temptation to make a *BSG* reference) when that is the very last place that should be experienced as hostile. Fairy tales as a genre make these artistic distortions, playing with significant themes like home and family, in order to critique these very institutions.

While I wrote this essay as a blog post in 2012, it still resonates with me in 2022: we are still watching horrors unfold, and many of us are still helpless to do much about it. Even those of us who are cozily weathering political turmoil and a global pandemic are struggling, as being a bystander can entail its own form of trauma. And there is no value in taking a comparative approach to terror and trauma; there's no ranking system that applies. All we can do is tell story after story, looking for the jagged edges of where experience ends and story begins, looking for language to convey experiences so strange as to seem inexpressible.

The imagery of terror in stories holds up a mirror so that we can see what our lives are like. Some of us are living comfortably in cages or cradles; some of us are breaking our backs stoking the fire; too many of us have already been eaten, rent limb from limb, or know people who have suffered terribly.

We are all living in the house of cannibals.

A RANT ON HELEN OYEYEMI'S FAIRY-TALE NOVEL BOY, SNOW, BIRD

I'LL START with a spoiler-free summary, in case anyone's thinking of reading the book and wants to know if it's for you. I like the summary at the review site *Raging Biblioholism*:

Boy Novak escapes her brutal father in post-WWII New York and heads north, to the Massachusetts countryside. There, in a small town some way out of Boston, she begins a new life and falls in a kind of love with widower Arturo Whitman and his daughter Snow. But a surprise revelation upon the birth of Arturo & Boy's daughter changes everything she thought she knew about the town, about her husband, and about herself...

As a folklorist I'll add that it's a loose "Snow White" retelling with other fairy-tale references woven into the text at stylistic and structural levels. I caught a whiff of "Bluebeard" (a husband with secrets around his former dead wife), a lot of "Cinderella" references in the wicked stepmother stuff, many frame tales in the letter exchanges, and so on. The characters were often sparse in terms of description and motivation, which is very in keeping with fairy tale style. Folklorists like Kimberly J. Lau have gone into a few more of the fairy-tale intertexts, especially focusing on the role of race and tricksters in the book (Lau). And I've written a piece on this book too, comparing it to a text that I think does the thing I rant about here so much better (Jorgensen, and btw my article is open access so anyone can read it).

So, I enjoyed the writing for the most part. And I enjoyed ruminations on women's independence, how abortion was subtly woven in as an issue, and so on. I loved lines like this one: "If you wish to be truly free, you must love no one. But of course if you take that path you may also find that in the end you're unloved."

But...

(and here's where explicit spoilers come in)

...

...

...

Having Boy's abusive father Frank turn out to be Boy's biological egg donor, a brilliant woman named Frances who was raped and then suffered a psychotic break that led to her gender transition, is FUCKING TERRIBLE.

Oh my gods, where do I even begin???

First, trauma does not cause people to be transgender. Surprise! Yes, trauma can do a lot of things to people. I've written about being trauma-informed and try to bring trauma knowledge to my teaching whenever possible, but basically, it helps to know a bit about how trauma works, and that trauma is not always sexual in nature, when we encounter it in literature and want to critique it. Not all trauma causes PTSD, either. I'm not surprised to hear that the violent rape Frances endured in the novel was traumatizing... but to link the trauma to this character transitioning is totally inaccurate and perpetuates damaging stereotypes about trans people being damaged, traumatized, mentally ill, etc.

Second, trauma does not cause people to become abusive. It can be the case that traumatized people stay in relationships where they are being abused for a variety of reasons, some of them physiological in nature (especially in cases of developmental trauma, where the brain is still growing and hence things that are unsafe get coded as "normal"). And obviously, sometimes people who have experienced trauma become abusers; I think there's research out there on this topic but I'm drawing a blank right now on where to find it (I'm jetlagged, don't judge me). But to so clearly link the two, as Oyeyemi does, is super problematic, especially in a culture where trauma continues to be misunderstood and not taken seriously.

Third, people with mental illnesses and trans people are more likely to experience abuse than to commit abuse. This comes up every time there's a gun control debate and people start blaming those with mental illnesses – because, nope, people with mental health issues are ten times more likely than the general population to experience violence (I've seen this number in quite a few places, so I'm beginning to think it's common enough knowledge to not need a citation). As noted above, linking a trauma history with becoming abusive is super problematic, and it's even more so when we throw a different gender identity into the mix. Right now, mainstream representations of trans people are so limited and stereotyped that any representation risks being seen as The Representation, which is a problem for many marginalized groups wherein an individual becomes symbolic of the entire (often quite diverse) group. So if your only representation of a trans character is one who's mentally ill, traumatized, and abusive, then screw you, you are NOT helping.

In the *Raging Biblioholism* post, the author attempts to sidestep the serious damage done by this depiction: "Because I don't think, at least based on my understanding of the book, that Frank/Frances is meant to be considered a trans character in the strictest sense – but, rather, a person placed under a spell."

I'm sorry, but no. We don't get the luxury of turning a marginalized character's identity into a magic spell or a metaphor, not when we're clearly supposed to read other characters as representing themselves in a more literal, realistic sense. I make the same point about disability in The Shape of Water in a forthcoming book chapter; to read disability as a metaphor for powerlessness is bullshit, in a culture where representation of disabled folks as themselves, as real people, is still lagging terribly.

I like a lot of the points that Melinda Guerra makes in her review of the book, some of which I quote here:

Even in the most charitable reading, one which would suggest Oyeyemi wants to extend her exploration of passing to make gender too a thing in which a character has "passed," the disregard for the character's declared, preferred gender is astonishing, not to mention such an explanation would still reinforce the harmful myths the trans community faces.

Adding to all of this, Boy suddenly has compassion for her abuser, a matter about which no one seems concerned, and in these pages Frank's identity as a person who repeatedly abused Boy is suddenly gone, eclipsed by his new narrative role as a problem for Boy to travel back to and solve. Adult survivors of childhood abuse can face a variety of feelings about their abuse and toward their abusers, and to feel a pull toward reconciliation and salvation could fit within the realm of possibilities. But for Oyeyemi to send the survivor on a trip back toward her abuser, armed with a belief she can "free" her mother from Frank (which, again, is completely belittling of trans experiences) is unsafe for Boy: she is walking into a situation which is not only very possibly physically unsafe, but emotionally unsafe as well– Boy has done little to no dealing with the abuse she suffered, and is exposed and vulnerable as she returns.

Ultimately, Oyeyemi handled the revelation at the heart of Boy's family dysfunction so poorly, I'm surprised that no editor or publisher was like "ummm...?!" It was hastily tacked on at the very end of the book, too, making it narratively unsatisfying for me. And this is a secondary complaint, but I disliked the framing of trans-ness as a magic spell in the same way that I disliked the references to mirrors being potentially kinda magical in the book; this was yet another instance of a mostly-mainstream author coming to play in the speculative fiction sandbox by borrowing some of our tropes, but then not playing nice with our toys. One could argue for a more ambiguous, slipstream, magical realism reading of the novel's use of fantasy motifs, but I feel like the author let readers down by giving us some intriguing clues about the role of fantasy in the novel, and then utterly ignoring them for the rest of the book.

So while the book was in some ways nicely written and in some ways a pleasant travel read, the author handled gender and trauma in a way that left me utterly unable to recommend the book. I will certainly never teach it, because I wouldn't want to perpetuate these horrible stereotypes and assumptions, nor would I want to potentially make my classroom unsafe for trans, non-binary, or gender non-conforming students (I've taught materials with sexual violence, rape, and trauma before, so those elements aren't the problem here – it's the utterly untroubled manner in which the author makes the links discussed above).

If you decide to read this book (even after all the spoilers here), do what I did and get a copy from your library, so as not to financially support the folks who think all this stuff is okay. Ugh. For a palate cleanser, I'm reading N.K. Jemisin, by the way, who handles issues of trauma, gender, and speculative fiction a billion times better.

REFERENCES:

"Boy, Snow, Bird." *Raging Biblioholism*, https://ragingbiblio holism.wordpress.com/2016/05/09/boy-snow-bird/. Accessed 19 February 2022.

Guerra, Melinda. "(Book Review) Boy, Snow, Bird by Helen Oyeyemi." *Fourth & Sycamore*, 7 June 2016 https:// fourthandsycamore.wordpress.com/2016/06/07/book-review-boy-snow-bird-by-helen-oyeyemi/. Accessed 19 February 2022.

Jorgensen, Jeana. "A Tale of Two Trans Men: Transmasculine Identity and Trauma in Two Fairy-Tale Retellings." *Open Cultural Studies*, vol. 5, no. 1, 2021, pp. 181-193. https://doi. org/10.1515/culture-2020-0128

Lau, Kimberly J. "Snow White and the Trickster: Race and Genre in Helen Oyeyemi's 'Boy, Snow, Bird.'" *Western Folklore*, vol. 75, no. 3/4, 2016, pp. 371-96.

ACADEMIC ARTICLES

INNOCENT INITIATIONS: FEMALE AGENCY IN EROTICIZED FAIRY TALES

ORIGINALLY PUBLISHED IN *MARVELS & Tales: Journal of Fairy-Tale Studies* vol. 22, no. 1, 2008, 27-37.

OBSCENE AND BAWDY FOLKLORE HAS SUFFERED A LONG HISTORY OF neglect and censorship. In 1965, Gershon Legman lamented the "prudery-ridden" reception of Aleksander Afanasy'ev's *Russian Secret Tales*—a collection of bawdy Russian folktales with a troubled publication and translation history (xi). In 1998, Alan Dundes, in his Foreword to Afanasy'ev's tales, echoed Legman's frustration with "narrow-minded censorship" (n.p.). He states: "bawdy folklore is badly under-represented in the totality of folklore publication. It is the exception rather than the rule when a sampling of bawdy folktales finds its way into print" (n.p.). Bawdy folktales, like fabliaux and toasts, are difficult to study due to their under-representation in collections and the lack of scholarly attention given them. This difficulty extends, with certain differences, to the study of eroticized fairy tales: there exists a wealth of scholarship on fairy tales, but only some of it deals with explicit sex. In this article, I define and explore eroticized fairy tales in relation to classic and literary fairy tales, focusing on the contemporary erotic tales' depictions of women, sexuality, and agency.

There is some precedent for eroticism in literary fairy tales, such as sexual scenes in Basile's *Pentamerone* and the *Arabian Nights*. Lewis Seifert remarks that although love is depicted psychologically and not physically in most French tales— explicit depictions of sexuality so rare as to seem prohibited— a few tales contain "sexually suggestive (as opposed to erotic) descriptions or allusions" (118). My focus here is not on literary tales that are erotic or sexually suggestive, but rather on contemporary tales that eroticize formerly nonerotic or latently erotic classic fairy tales. Eroticized tales privilege the erotic encounter as a focal point of the plot, though the degree to which sex forms the plot is variable. Whether sex is the pretense for the plot or merely a happy side effect, graphic descriptions are the standard result in eroticized fairy tales. Content is one of the main ways that eroticized fairy tales differ from most other fairy tales: there is little explicit sex to be found in most literary fairy tales, especially the classic tales of the Grimms, Perrault, and the French *conteuses*. The overt sexuality of eroticized fairy tales, however, could be viewed as a carnivalesque inversion, making the implicit explicit. Since so many fairy tales end in marriage—to the extent that Vladimir Propp has marriage as the fairy tale's ultimate function—sex is an underlying concern of fairy tales, though it rarely comes to the forefront as it does in erotic literature. By exposing sex, authors of eroticized fairy tales open new areas of discussion that intersect with current concerns about fairy tales.

The eroticized fairy tales that comprise this study are at the same time a literary phenomenon, subject to the whims of editors, consumers, and other market forces, and a post-modern phenomenon. They fit within a larger matrix of ideologically charged literature that conveys numerous messages, and part of this genre's ideological significance derives from its fairy tale connections. Cristina Bacchilega, in *Postmodern Fairy Tales*, calls fairy tales "ideologically variable desire machines" (7). Fairy tales deal with desire on several planes, including but not limited to desire for material goods, power, and sexual union. It is sexual desire, often intertwined with the desire for power over another human being, which comes to the forefront of eroticized fairy tales. Since fairy tales have been incorporated into children's literature over the past two centuries, there is also an element of gleeful perversion in eroticized fairy tales. As Karen Rowe phrases it, the mass popularity of erotic (as well as gothic) fairy-tale fictions "testifies to a pervasive fascination with fairy tale romance in literature not merely for children but for twentieth-century adults" (210). At risk of disregarding the nuances developed by feminist fairy-tale scholars over the past thirty years (see Haase, "Feminist Fairy-Tale Scholarship"), I ask: what is the power and appeal of eroticized fairy tales? And how do they portray and affect women?

Related genres, such as romance novels and postmodern fairy tales, can offer some clues. Romances, like fairy tales, typically deal with a series of fantastical transformations that end in heterosexual marriage. Though romances often feature spunky or rebellious heroines, they ultimately choose to be in a monogamous, heterosexual marriage, conforming to patriarchal norms. Janice Radway, in *Reading the Romance*, suggests: "despite the utopian force of the romance's projection, that projection actually leaves unchallenged the very system of social relations whose faults and imperfections gave rise to the romance and which the romance is trying to correct" (215). While romances and postmodern fairy tales may or may not be erotic or explicitly sexual depending on their authors and audiences, I would argue that unlike romances, postmodern fairy tales tend to problematize the desires they represent. I would further argue that the category of postmodern fairy tales can encompass eroticized fairy tales, but the uncritical portrayal of desires separates eroticized fairy tales from other, more radical postmodern fairy tales such as those of Angela Carter. According to Bacchilega, "some postmodern revisions may question and remake the classic fairy tale's production of gender only to re-inscribe it within some unquestioned model of subjectivity or narrativity" (23). The subtype of eroticized fairy tales I shall discuss in this paper conform to Radway's and Bacchilega's notions of stories that appear to dispute certain, often sexual, standards, but on a deeper level leave them uncontested.

The eroticized fairy tales I chose to study are marketed as such in short story collections. The four collections that inform this paper are: *Once Upon a Time: Erotic Fairy Tales for Women*, edited by Michael Ford; *Erotic Fairy Tales: A Romp through the Classics*, by Mitzi Szereto; *The Empress's New Lingerie and Other Erotic Fairy Tales*, by Hillary Rollins; and *Naughty Fairy Tales from A to Z*, edited by Alison Tyler. These are selected from a handful of English-language erotica that contain fairy tales in their titles. Many of the tales conform closely to fairy-tale plots, whereas others utilize fairy-tale motifs in a pastiche plot. Among the tales included in the four collections, I was able to identify a dozen tales that follow a similar theme, which I have termed the "innocent initiation." The innocent initiation tales feature a sexually naïve heroine who, as a part of the plot, is thrust into a sexually charged situation. She is initiated into sexual pleasure without knowing precisely what is going on, and she unconditionally enjoys the event. The focus of these stories is on the experience of the female protagonist, yet the structure of these stories—because of their similarity to fairy tales—calls into question the heroine's agency.

A few examples of this type of tale will suffice. The first is titled "The Twelve Months," and it appears in Szereto's *Erotic Fairy Tales*. The plot is that of ATU type 480, "The Kind and Unkind Girls," specifically the subtype Strawberries in the Snow. In this story, the heroine, Maruska, is repeatedly sent out from her stepmother's trailer to seek things impossible to find in winter: first violets, then strawberries, and finally red apples. Each time Maruska wanders into a circle of a dozen rocks, where men personifying the twelve months of the year reside. The twelve months help Maruska attain each objective, but first she must pleasure them individually. The author describes how the heroine straddles each month's lap, feeling "something rigid burrow[ing] into her tender place, making it wet and sticky and even a little sore" (304). After the sex sequence, the author concludes: "Never had Maruska imagined that sitting upon a lap could be so enjoyable" (304). The heroine's sexual initiation is presented as pleasurable though not as a result of her conscious decision. Additionally, the heroine's sexuality, specifically her lack of sexual experience, is what motivates the donor figures to aid her. This can be seen as an instance of women's sexuality serving as a token of exchange in a cultural context where men have power and agency and women do not (see Rubin's "The Traffic in Women" for a theory of sexual exchange).

A second example of an innocent initiation tale is a version of "Cinderella," ATU type 510A. Titled "Down in the Cinders," this story is by Marcy Sheiner and it appears in *Once Upon a Time: Erotic Fairy Tales for Women*. In this version, Cinderella enjoys her downtrodden state since she derives pleasure from taking on a submissive role. The stepsisters in this story enjoy taking a dominant role in a bondage context. Cinderella's sexual initiation, however, is noteworthy not only for the overtones of sexual dominance and submission, but also because she does not understand her own feelings of sexual arousal. The author details the immense pleasure Cinderella feels when doing menial work for her family, which leads her to "lie down among the cinders where she slept, and touch herself until she reached satisfaction. She had no idea what this was or why it happened, but she knew for sure it was wicked" (278-79). The plot progresses with this submissive, agoraphobic Cinderella pushed by a kindly neighbor woman to attend the ball, where the prince falls in love with her and promises to wed her. Yet on the wedding night, Cinderella's stepsisters intrude to teach the prince, who is himself also a submissive type, how to properly appreciate Cinderella's unique charms. Again, the heroine does not make sexual choices for herself. The stepsisters provide an interesting contrast to Cinderella as they are active characters, and moreover not villainized as in many other versions of ATU 510A; their meanness is accounted for by their particular sexual leanings, and in the end they help Cinderella. This collapses the helper and antagonist roles, a conflation common in contemporary revisions of fairy tales. This tale illustrates the complexity of women's roles in eroticized fairy tales, although an overly optimistic reading of the tale is problematic because the stepsisters and Cinderella are necessarily (for the plot to work) presented as oppositional and essentialized.

Stories fitting the innocent initiation subtype include revisions of Rapunzel, Rumplestiltskin, Sleeping Beauty, and Snow White, plus a pastiche tale called "Earthly Delights" that references fairy-tale motifs without adhering to any particular plot. These tales have some characteristics in common that distinguish them from other eroticized fairy tales and from non-erotic fairy tales: passivity on the heroine's part and actions by other characters that awaken and appreciate the heroine's inner lusty nature.

Other eroticized fairy tales, when they feature a female protagonist, sometimes place her in the role of seductress or villainess, rather than naïve initiate. Red Jordan Arobateau's "The Shoes That Were Danced to Pieces" in *Once Upon a Time* features twelve princesses who indulge their deviant lesbian fantasies every night upon their escape from their parents' palace. Carol Queen's "Puss in Boots: Or, Clever Mistress Cat" in the same volume is about how a servant, Kitty, asks her destitute mistress for a pair of boots by which to make their fortune; after becoming a successful courtesan, Kitty teaches her mistress how to also ply that trade. Both of these heroines are sexually empowered when they choose to become lovers and continue in their trade, despite the stigma associated with prostitution.

The revision of "Little Red Riding Hood" in Hillary Rollins's *The Empress's New Lingerie* reveals tensions between sexual undercurrents in classic and updated fairy tales, particularly ATU type 333. Feminist criticism, notably Jack Zipes's *The Trials and Tribulations of Little Red Riding Hood*, has demonstrated that many canonical versions of ATU 333 make Red responsible for her fate, paralleling the popular victim-blaming defense of rape. Rollins's "Red," which opens her collection, follows this pattern. Described as extremely attractive, Red is told by her mother not to "spill [her] treasures into the lap of some stranger along the way" (17). As though the double entendre were not clear enough, the mother admonishes Red: "Uh uh uh, don't you deny it, young lady. I've seen the way your hips sway when you walk to the market. I've seen the way you yield to the caress of the wind on your thigh or the sting of icy water on your hard little nipples when you bathe in the stream" and so on (17). Following her mother's lecture, Red reflects on her changing body and secret desires, feeling shamed by these impulses she is unable to satisfy by herself. When Red meets a threateningly wolf-like man on the path, she succumbs to his seduction. She does not seem to know what is happening: "But for reasons she could not comprehend, her entire body trembled" (20). She is compared to a rag doll and to a caught and trussed-up rabbit. Defenseless, she feels that "no one had ever worshipped her fiery ringlets like this before, and even as she feared it, she thrilled to his violent touch" (21). The man eventually pleasures Red (in her grandmother's bed, even), yet contradictorily the parallels to rape are visible in the text.

This eroticization of violence parallels the eroticization of the folktale. The belated appearance of a woodcutter indicates the influence of the Grimm version of the tale over the Perrault version. The woodcutter, however, does not save Red from the wolf's ravaging. He watches, gaining voyeuristic pleasure from the experience, only deciding to use his axe at the time when Red cries out. She is, however, enjoying herself sufficiently to tell the woodcutter "No." This tale's statement that Red does not need rescuing by the woodcutter, and moreover can articulate such, is a subversive comment on patriarchal intertexts and prior versions of ATU 333.

Like many well-known fairy tales, eroticized fairy tales

feature highly stylized descriptions, focusing on bright colors, well-defined shapes, and intense emotions. Max Lüthi's work is an example of the dialogue that can exist between non-erotic and erotic fairy tales. In *The European Folktale*, Lüthi claims that folktales are practically asexual, yet in emphasizing their idealized and stylized aspects, he perfectly describes eroticized fairy tales. These stylistic features, in addition to the sensual writing style, obscure the question of why the female protagonist's first sexual encounter should be so unrealistic. In my sample of eroticized fairy tales, there are almost no *male* protagonists who experience a sexual initiation, and indeed, the assumption underlying the heroine's experiences is that their male initiators *must* have had more experience than them. The sexual asymmetry is ideologically charged. Moreover, the heroines in these tales do not in general initiate sexual contact; instead, the secondary male (and occasionally female) characters do. This aspect of innocent initiation tales brings up the question of agency, or the condition of exerting power or acting. If a female character does not act with agency, she is not a subject; she is an object. And if the main character of a story is objectified, not acting but being acted upon, then readers are forced to identify either with the protagonist only as a sexual object, or with the performer of the sexual acts.

The objectification of innocent heroines is a problem that extends beyond eroticized fairy tales. Agency is a relevant topic in discussing nonerotic fairy tales as well, but fairy-tale scholarship has in general been slow to adapt this term. However, Angela Carter's fairy-tale fiction has invited enough feminist analysis that it can provide a model for this discussion. Her work treads the erotic border, and has attracted a great deal of scholarship that repetitively claims that Carter rewrites fairy tales with a feminist agenda. According to

Stephen Benson, emphasizing the "feminist" endings of Carter's tales disregards "the many folktales that offer instances of just such female agency" (48). Which folktales display female agency, and just how much agency, remains a tricky question. In Jack Zipes's collection of feminist fairy tales, *Don't Bet on the Prince*, he simultaneously celebrates folktale heroines who are active and aggressive while acknowledging that due to historical and market factors, oppressive patterns have both developed and lingered in fairy tales (7). I think it is safe to say that some folktales contain self-sufficient heroines, while other, often literary renditions of the tales depict more passive heroines. Even more recent revisions of fairy tales frequently complete the circle by returning to independent heroines—except, I would argue, in the case of eroticized innocent initiation tales. One interesting point about eroticized fairy tales is that while the heroines only sometimes require rescue due to plot complications, they always require sexual attention. Since sex, or at least erotic sensation, is usually the expectation in erotica, it makes sense to have present a sexual partner (or seven, in "Snow White"). From a feminist perspective the difficulty arises when the heroine does not imitate either folktale or revision models and discover her pleasure for herself, but instead conforms to the fairy-tale passivity that has rightfully come under attack.

It is significant that most of the innocent initiation eroticized tales in my sample are based on well-known fairy tales from the Grimm collection or from Disney films. Thus, authors of innocent initiation tales start from texts that already show patriarchal bias. Since these authors deliberately evoke certain associations, intertextuality becomes a key notion in my analysis. Even the act of choosing to rewrite one fairy tale instead of another, or choosing one version's title over another, is meaningful. As Alessandra Levorato points out in her book *Language and Gender in the Fairy Tale Tradition*: "rewritings are built on prior texts, and they often rely on the reader's knowledge of earlier versions in order for their full meaning to be carried across" (193). The prior texts informing the stories in my sample four collections of eroticized fairy tales have varied origins beyond folktales and fairy tales, from nursery rhymes to legends. Yet as I mentioned earlier, all of the tales that fit the innocent initiation type with one exception build on familiar fairy tales. Interestingly, they also primarily feature heterosexual couplings. Not all of the eroticized fairy tales in the four collections of stories are heterosexually oriented, so the innocent initiation stories actually stand apart from some of the other stories on the basis of their sexual encounters being predominantly heterosexual.

I would argue that tale characters' heterosexuality is one among other conservative elements drawn straight from fairy tales. While not all of the sex occurs in a marital situation, often, such as in the eroticized rewrites of "Sleeping Beauty" and "Cinderella," marriage is the implied or stated next step in the narrative. Some of the sex in these stories involves multiple partners, as in "Snow White and the Seven Dwarves." There is bestiality in the retelling of "Little Red Riding Hood" and sexual power play in "Cinderella," noted earlier, as well as in "Rapunzel" and "Rumplestiltskin." I mention these sexual elements not to be gratuitous, but rather to draw a comparison between them and similar elements in Angela Carter's collection *The Bloody Chamber*, which is hailed as a feminist work. Yet Carter problematizes sexual desire by the way she evokes it in her tales, whereas the authors of innocent initiation tales leave certain questions about desire unasked. Thus, the incorporation of unconventional sex into a rewritten fairy tale is no guarantee of the story being progressive.

The fact that eroticized fairy tales are meant as entertainment does not lessen their ideological impact or importance. As Bacchilega points out, fairy tales employ narrative strategies that, among other things, naturalize certain types of desire while negating others. These strategies can be visual as well; Zipes states in "Breaking the Disney Spell" that Disney "animated the fairy tale only to transfix audiences and divert their potential utopian dreams and hopes through the false promise of the images he cast upon the screen" (74). Eroticized fairy tales make sexual desire seem natural and inherent to practically everyone and everything, but innocent initiation tales in particular portray female characters as though their sexual desires have lain dormant until just the right moment. In the two versions of "Sleeping Beauty" within my sample, the protagonist is literally dormant until the prince awakens her— and her desire—with a kiss located such that Freudian displacement comes to mind. This initiation is extremely metonymic, equating subjectivity with the ability to desire, because the heroine and her sexuality are simultaneously awakened. In other tales in my sample, the heroines experience sexual urges without understanding what they are, and only their initiatory sexual experiences truly fulfill these urges. Often the initiations occur without the girls understanding what exactly is happening, but they enjoy the sensations nonetheless. Nor do the female protagonists initiate sexual contact —in the rewrite of "Rumplestiltskin," for example, the heroine is abducted to be the king's pleasure slave, where she shamefully finds herself aroused despite her impending rape. The message behind these tales is that not only does the heroine lack the agency to make choices about when and where and with what or whom she has sex, but also that she cannot make decisions about whether or not to be a sexual being.

Clearly, the characters in erotic fiction will have sexual dimensions to their personalities, but the heroines in innocent initiation tales are portrayed dualistically in regards to desire. On the one hand, these heroines are inherently sexual creatures. On the other hand, these heroines are innocent about sex, even after the fact. This duality is a manifestation of the virgin/whore complex, a double bind constraining women to be sexy, but not too sexy; sexual, but not overtly sexual. The emphasis that authors of innocent initiation tales place on their protagonists' inexperience commodifies innocence. The heroines are sexy—to other characters with whom the readers might also identify—precisely because they are naïve. Innocence thus becomes a trope meant to evoke desire in the reader because within the story, innocence signifies sexual eagerness that is ready to be exploited. Female characters in traditional folktales at least have the option to refuse to be sexual beings; for example, the protagonist of ATY 510B, Donkeyskin, makes herself sexually unappealing and unavailable by wearing an animal fur disguise after her father tries to marry her, and only later casts off this disguise to tease a prince into marriage.

The final point I would like to make about eroticized fairy tales in general is that by making use of certain rhetorical devices, they reinscribe fairy tales within the realm of the feminine. As Marina Warner has discussed in *From the Beast to the Blonde*, women's contributions to the body of fairy-tale literature have been immense, from the labels of Mother Goose tales and old wives' tales to the association of fairy tales with children's entertainment, hence the domestic sphere. Eroticized fairy tales are often written by women, and collections of them are aimed at female consumers, often explicitly. Why women choose to write disempowering tales can be attributed to many factors, ranging from unconsciously following genre constraints and embedded ideologies to actively choosing to write what will be deemed sexy and hence successful, yet it is difficult to make hypotheses without interviewing these authors. If the titillation a reader experiences at depictions of women's innocent initiations provide an experience that the reader values and wishes to consume more of, then the piece of writing can be deemed successful from an economic perspective, providing the rational to pay writers for more works. Still, it is difficult to generalize about readers' experiences given that the same text can be read in many different ways. Finally, in the case of the innocent initiation tale, women's sexual experiences are commodified even as the main female characters are objectified and deprived of agency. All of these traits reinforce the notions that fairy tales belong to women, fairy tales are about women, and yet fairy tales disempower women by granting them superficial pleasure while denying them any real agency.

In conclusion, eroticized fairy tales are complex revisions of fairy tales wherein the treatment of female agency and desire conveys certain ideological messages. Though these tales are sexually explicit, much of their content simply makes manifest the power relations that are already expressed in nonerotic fairy tales. The coherence of eroticized fairy tales relies upon the underlying assumptions of both writers and readers. Levorato describes this phenomenon: "the reader in accepting to construct the coherence of the text in this way is constituted as a subject who accepts this interpretation of gender roles" (118). The innocent initiation type of eroticized fairy tale offers a polarized view of gender roles, which draws on roles already prevalent in fairy tales.

These representations of sexuality, including the ideologies fueling them, implicate many people and groups in their productions and reproductions of cultural expressions, including scholars. Folklorists occupy multiple places on the chain of transmission, sometimes unintentionally: for instance, Mitzi Szereto, author of the stories in *Erotic Fairy Tales: A Romp through the Classics*, refers to folklore scholarship—from tale collections to cognates—in her introductions to each tale. Further work using reader response models as well as questionnaire- and interview-styled fieldwork is the next step in understanding not only why writers eroticize fairy tales, but why consumers purchase and read them, and what kinds of effects these tales might have on their understandings of fairy tales and sexuality. How many of us leave fairy tales in the realm of childhood or, for those of us who study fairy tales, in the workplace? How often and in which forms do fairy tales, as opposed to other cultural materials, fuel people's fantasies? Eroticized fairy tales, distinct from nonerotic and erotic folk and fairy tales as well as from postmodern fairy tales and romantic fiction, offer intriguing opportunities for scholars of sexuality and intertextuality to explore and perhaps play.

REFERENCES:

Bacchilega, Cristina. *Postmodern Fairy Tales: Gender and Narrative Strategies*. Philadelphia: U of Pennsylvania press, 1997.

Benson, Stephen. "Angela Carter and the Literary Märchen: A Review Essay." *Marvels & Tales* 12.1 (1998): 23-51.

Carter, Angela. *The Bloody Chamber and Other Stories*. New York: Penguin Books, 1979, 1993.

Dundes, Alan. "New Foreword." *Russian Secret Tales: Bawdy Folktales of Old Russia*. Baltimore: Clearfield, 1998. n.p.
Ford, Michael, ed. *Once Upon a Time: Erotic Fairy Tales for Women*. New York: Masquerade Books, Inc., 1996.

Haase, Donald, ed. *Feminism and Fairy Tales: New Approaches*. Detroit: Wayne State UP, 2004.

---. "Feminist Fairy-Tale Scholarship." Haase, *Feminism and Fairy Tales* 1–36.

Hoard, Florence. "Earthly Delights." Tyler 33–44.

Hoffman, Frank. *An Analytical Survey of Traditional Anglo-American Erotica*. Bowling Green, OH: Bowling Green UP, 1973.

Legman, Gershon. Introduction. *Russian Secret Tales: Bawdy Folktales of Old Russia*. Baltimore: Clearfield, 1965. v-xxxix.

Levorato, Alessandra. *Language and Gender in the Fairy Tale Tradition: A Linguistic Analysis of Old and New Story Telling*. New York: Palgrave Macmillan, 2003.

Lüthi, Max. *The European Folktale: Form and Nature*. Trans. John D. Niles. 1982. Bloomington: Indiana UP, 1986.

Propp, Vladimir. *Morphology of the Folktale*. Trans. Laurence Scott. Rev. and ed. Louis A. Wagner. 2nd ed. 1968. Austin: U of Texas P, 1996.

Radway, Janice A. *Reading the Romance: Women, Patriarchy, and Popular Culture.* 1984. Chapel Hill: U of North Carolina P, 1991.

Roemer, Danielle K., and Cristina Bacchilega, eds. *Angela Carter and the Fairy Tale.* Detroit: Wayne State UP, 2001.

Röhrich, Lutz. "Erotik, Sexualität." *Enzyklopädie des Märchens.* Ed. Kurt Ranke et al. Berlin: Walter de Gruyter, 1984. 4: 234–78.

---. "Erotik und Sexualität im Volksmärchen." *Liebe und Eros im Märchen.* Ed. Jürgen Janning and Luc Gobyn. Kassel: Erich Röth Verlag, 1988. 20–48.

Rollins, Hillary. *The Empress's New Lingerie and Other Erotic Fairy Tales: Bedtime Stories for Grown-Ups.* New York: Harmony Books, 2001.

Rowe, Karen E. "Feminism and Fairy Tales." Zipes, *Don't Bet on the Prince* 209–26.

Rubin, Gayle. "The Traffic in Women: Notes on the 'Political Economy' of Sex." *The Second Wave.* Ed. Linda Nicholson. New York: Routledge, 1997. 27–62.

Seifert, Lewis. *Fairy Tales, Sexuality, and Gender in France, 1690–1715: Nostalgic Utopias.* Cambridge: Cambridge UP, 1996.

Sheiner, Marcy. "Down in the Cinders." Ford 277–92.

Szereto, Mitzi. *Erotic Fairy Tales: A Romp through the Classics.* San Francisco: Cleis Press, 2000.

Thomas, Hayley S. "Undermining a Grimm Tale: A Feminist Reading of 'The Worn-out Dancing Shoes' (KHM 133)." *Marvels & Tales* 13 (1999): 170–83.

Tyler, Alison, ed. *Naughty Fairy Tales from A to Z: 26 Racy Retold Fairy Tales, Fables, and Nursery Rhymes.* New York: Plume, 2003.

Warner, Marina. *From the Beast to the Blonde: On Fairy Tales and Their Tellers.* New York: Farrar, Straus, and Giroux, 1994.

Zipes, Jack. "Breaking the Disney Spell." *Fairy Tales as Myth/Myth as Fairy Tale.* Lexington: UP of Kentucky, 1994. 72–95.

---, ed. *Don't Bet on the Prince: Contemporary Feminist Fairy Tales in North America and England.* 1986. New York: Routledge, 1997.

---, ed. Introduction. Zipes, *Don't Bet on the Prince* 1–36.

---, ed. *The Trials and Tribulations of Little Red Riding Hood.* 2nd ed. New York: Routledge, 1993.

THE MOST BEAUTIFUL OF ALL: A QUANTITATIVE APPROACH TO FAIRY-TALE FEMININITY

PUBLISHED as "The Most Beautiful of All: A Quantitative Approach to Fairy-Tale Femininity." *Journal of American Folklore* vol. 132, no. 523, 2019, 36-60. © 2019 by the Board of Trustees of the University of Illinois.

INTRODUCTION

The time is ripe for a consideration of bodies in fairy tales. The body offers a lens to understand the construction of gender in expressive culture, as Christine A. Jones and Jennifer Schacker acknowledge in their introduction to *Marvelous Transformations*. They posit that studying "Little Red Riding Hood" (ATU 333) offers "an exceptionally clear illustration of how we have been trained by many critical theories not to see the trees for the forest of tale history" (2013:26). In attending to the prominence of the protagonist's body in the Grimms' version of the tale, Jones and Schacker become attuned to how "the conversation between the title character and the wolf shifts from Little Red Cap's reason for being in the forest to a focus on her body" (32). In this version, as she is carrying the cake and wine under her apron, Little Red Cap's body becomes metonymous with the treats held against it. The importance of worldly knowledge and discursive skills to attaining bodily safety—especially for women—is a theme that Jones and Schacker draw out masterfully (32-5).

The fairy tale genre eludes easy definition. Jones and Schacker assert that "The fairy tale genre for centuries has been malleable and dynamic" (2013:487, emphasis in original), encompassing both print and oral transmission, characterized by alternatively compact or complex plots, but unified by a (content-based) defiance of "the constraints of realist fiction" (488). In his chapter on the fairy tale *in Folktales and Fairy Tales: Traditions and Texts from around the World*, Donald Haase lists three definitive elements: "(1) the structure is episodic and constructed primarily on motifs; (2) the genre is unabashedly fictional, the setting indefinite ...; and (3) protagonists over-come obstacles to advance to rewards and a new level of exis-tence (achieving wealth, power, marriage, and/or social status)" (2016:321). Transmission is an additional defining factor, since as a genre of folk narrative most fairy tales circu-late with identifiable variation. Hence, crucial folkloristic tools such as the motif and tale type indexes are essential for their study. Kay Turner and Pauline Greenhill propose that fairy tales, "oral or literary in derivation, feature human and non-human principal characters in developed fictional narratives, along with elements of wonder and the supernatural" (2012:3). It is the role of wonder, and its relationship back to the real world (and gendered bodies therein), that concerns me here.

The significance of gender as a structuring concept in lived (and narrated) experience is one of the central tenets of feminist theory. My contribution to this conversation is to use computational methods to analyze how femininity and women's bodies are constructed in Western fairy tales. I begin by discussing feminist critiques of women's depictions and roles in fairy tales and then outline recent developments in computational folkloristics. This discussion sets the scene for my analysis of the descriptions of women's bodies that appear in a data set of body descriptors found in 233 fairy tales from both oral and written traditions. I use straightforward statistical measures based on the frequency counts of these body descriptors to enter into a dialogue with assertions made by feminist scholars, assessing claims about five categories: beauty; hair, eyes, and skin; bodily fluids; suffering; and morality. This statistical analysis of body descriptors derived from fairy tale texts reveals patterns in the gendered depictions of women's bodies that both confirm and complicate earlier feminist critiques of fairy tales. Women's bodies are bounded by expectations of beauty, but often in non-specific ways, contributing to the double bind that constrains femininity and gender norms.

Feminist Critiques of Women's Bodies in Fairy Tales

In recent decades, feminist folklorists have moved from a simple criticism of the representations of women in fairy tales to a more complex discussion of how gender and ideology interact in the production, transmission, and reception of fairy tales.

Feminist scholars often consider women in fairy tales to be too passive, pretty, and domestic (if protagonists), or too wicked, ugly, and vicious (if antagonists) (Lieberman 1972; Stone 1985). This assertion is directly related to the body: the unrealistically high standards of beauty that female protagonists must achieve to be judged worthy of a mate, or, alternately, the correlation of ugliness with evil and unworthiness in antagonists and false brides. Laurence Talairach-Vielmas writes, "what we generally learn as children is that all princesses are beautiful and may even try to improve their beauty" (2007:5). Beauty is linked with not only success in fairy tales, but also with character. Much earlier, Marcia Lieberman noted: "Good-temper and meekness are so regularly associated with beauty, and ill-temper with ugliness, that this in itself must influence children's expectations" (1972:385). Thus, feminist scholars view beauty as a problem in and of itself in fairy tales, but they also draw attention to its associations with other supposedly feminine traits.

Helplessness and patience, along with contentedly accepting one's fate (being a "nice" girl) are key characteristics of the critique of feminine passivity in the fairy tale (Yolen 1988; Waelti-Walters 1982). As Jack Zipes observes, the versions of "Cinderella" by both Charles Perrault and the Grimms "set models for girls of the upper class who need to show off their beauty and docility to win the appropriate mate" (2016:360). Passivity is also projected onto women sexually; Ruth Bottigheimer notes that unlike related genres such as fabliaux, in fairy tales "Men act on women's bodies," intruding "their bodies into the private space of terrified girls or women" (2004:48-9).

The concatenation of various feminine traits makes it important to study them in connection with one another. Lori Baker-Sperry and Liz Grauerholz conclude "that messages in the Grimms' fairy tales, especially those that have been reproduced often, are consistent with other messages women and girls receive about the importance of feminine beauty" (2003:724). As Kay Stone notes, "The emphasis on ideal female beauty, passivity, and dependence on outside forces suggested

in the fairy tales is supported by Western culture in general"
(1985:141). Thus, fairy tales are but one outlet of Western
society insisting on the imbrication of traits that are supposedly inherently feminine: beauty, goodness, passivity, dependence, and an affinity for the domestic sphere (see also Tatar
1992, 2003).

In addition to general traits of idealized femininity, feminists have criticized physical appearances that recur in fairy
tales. Marina Warner comments on the "teeming population of
blonde fairytale heroines" (1994:362) and demonstrates how
"fairness was a guarantee of quality" in the social system of
meanings that penetrates the fairy-tale tradition (364). Blonde-
ness connotes both Christian virtue (366) and class privilege,
as "blonde hair implies pale skin, which in turn entails lack of
exposure... either to the rays of the sun in outdoor work, or to
the gaze of others" (368). Though attending to symbolic
meaning rather than social meaning, Francisco Vaz da Silva
characterizes ideal fairy-tale heroines as white (which symbolizes purity) splashed with red (2007:245-8). Dorothy Hurley
(2005) and Baker-Sperry and Grauerholz (2003) find that
beauty and whiteness (as a racial category) are often correlated
in fairy tales. This position argues, in contrast to Max Lüthi's
observations about colorlessness in fairy tales (that few people
in fairy tales are distinguished by color [1986]), that the fairy
tale's image of beauty does carry social meaning.

To summarize the claims made by feminists and other
scholars of fairy tales, one would expect female protagonists'
bodies in fairy tales to display the following traits: they must
be beautiful; their beauty includes Western stereotypical attributes like white skin and blonde hair; their bodies are passive,
pliant, and patient; and their beauty correlates positively with
other features such as kindness. Constrained by stereotypes

and cultural norms, this view of women's bodies in fairy tales is limiting and dismal.

In order to test these proposals quantitatively, I examine the appearance of five main groupings of traits: general mentions of beauty; descriptions of hair, eyes, and skin; bodily fluids like blood and tears; suffering; and morality.

Quantitative Methods for Fairy-Tale Studies and Project Scope

The application of quantitative methods to folklore studies has been labeled "computational folkloristics" (Tangherlini 2016a). One of the movement's biggest proponents, Timothy Tangherlini, says these developments "offer folklorists new opportunities for the analysis of traditional expression" (2016b:5). These new opportunities have been practiced in relation to both narrative and non-narrative genres; as an example of the former, see Peter Broadwell and Tangherlini's work on legends (2016) and Folgert Karsdorp's work on fairy tales (2016), and as an example of the latter, see Davor Nikolić and Nikola Bakarić's work on tongue twisters (2016).

In fairy-tale studies, early quantitative studies relied on simple metrics such as counting and comparing character attributes. Ruth Bottigheimer hints at a quantitative approach in her essay "Silenced Women in the Grimms' Tales," listing tales in which female characters lose their voices and counting the distribution of the word "speak," noting that it "appears more often in conjunction with authority figures" (1986:126). Kathleen Ragan studies the correlations between gender of character, tale collector, and collection editor using quantitative methods (2009), and Mark Alan Finlayson demonstrates how to automate computer learning about Vladimir Propp's functions from a corpus of Russian folktale texts (2016).

Sources

Because fairy tales exist on a spectrum from oral to written, it is important to strike a balance between folkloric and literary sources in analysis. This strategy also ensures that my expertise as a folklorist will benefit others in fairy-tale studies and those on the fringes of computational folkloristics, as it has been lamented that scholars unfamiliar with folkloristics ignore non-literary versions of tales (Dundes 1989:119). Cautionary tales already exist; Tangherlini relates the disciplinary creep that occurs among scholars intrigued by the materials:

Jamie Tehrani, in his attempt to revive the search for fairy-tale origins through the application of computational methods developed for the study of evolutionary biology, could have avoided the various pitfalls related to his source materials, which undermined his conclusions, had he worked with domain experts. (2016b:7-8)

Similarly, Jonathan Gottschall et al. utilized folktales as grist for their mill of Darwinian quantitative studies of sex roles in society. Among other things, they found that "when information on attractiveness was present, this information was, overall, more than twice as likely to be conveyed about females than males" (2003:372). Gottschall et al. reached this conclusion by ignoring cultural context and translation. As Donald Haase points out, Gottschall et al.'s "problematic assumptions...not only undercut his methodology but also perpetuate colonialist perspectives still entrenched in our field" (2010:29). A quantitative approach to fairy tales, therefore, is at its strongest when it takes into account all of the nuanced context that folklorists have spent centuries compiling tools to understand.

I follow Zipes in establishing an interest in "classic" fairy tales, which he defines as works by those major writers and collectors from the seventeenth through twentieth centuries who "are significant because they helped evolve, expand, and reform the discourse and have thus been rewarded with 'classical' status in our cultural heritage. The reasons for their 'classicity' vary, for their symbolic acts were made either to legitimize or criticize the course of the western civilizing process" (2006:10-1). Taking Zipes' "our cultural heritage" to refer to Western society provides an excellent leaping-off point. Of course, the classic tale is a moving target. Defining a genre in part by how it retrospectively appears is problematic; it risks privileging the etic over the emic, the scholarly category over the native category.

Viewing classic fairy tales in terms of their longevity means, from a folkloristic perspective, that their relationship to cultural values has been a productive one, even if the genre seems largely defined by outsiders in retrospect. As Jones points out, this type of work is a timely project, as demonstrated in her new translation of Perrault's tales, a choice which "stems from how much press the Mother Goose characters attract in our own culture and how badly they are in need of rethinking and reinterpretation" (2016:85). As scholarship is a type of reinterpretation or intervention (Joosen 2011), I propose that attention to gender and bodies in classic fairy tales will add to our understanding of the interaction of genre and social value.

Classic fairy tales, because they have persisted for so long and can be shown to have a significant effect upon both children and adults, are worth studying in-depth. Baker-Sperry and Grauerholz examined gendered descriptions of beauty in fairy tales both from the Grimms' collection and from reproductions of the Grimms' tales up through current times. Their hypothesis is that "women's beauty appears to play a more important role in fairy tales during certain time periods, possibly serving as a means of normative social control" (2003:714). They acknowledge that "[o]ne limitation of our study is that we cannot determine the extent to which messages concerning feminine beauty found in fairy tales have in fact been internalized or by whom" (723), though they cite feminist research indicating that even young girls show an awareness of the beauty ideal and knowledge of when they fail to live up to it. While it would take another study to ascertain what people actually think about the bodies in fairy tales —classic or contemporary or both—it is important to establish, from the outset, how bodies in classic fairy tales are textually constructed and represented. Consequently, the target corpus for this study consists of classic European fairy tales as well as tales from modern ethnographically collected sources that display a large overlap of tale types, demonstrating that many of the same tales have retained their popularity with modern narrators, attesting to their classic status.

Practical concerns placed constraints on the number of collections I was able to work with. Jennifer Schacker analyzed four tale collections in *National Dreams* and provided a nuanced account of the cultural context in which the tales were translated and received by the Victorian English public (2003). Bengt Holbek (1998) and Propp (1968) each studied tales from a single collector, while Lüthi (1986), James Taggart (1990, 1997), and Vaz da Silva (2002) analyzed tales from multiple tellers and various collections. The collections used here are *Beauties, Beasts, and Enchantment: Classic French Fairy*

Tales, translated by Jack Zipes ([1989] 2009; covering the classical French tradition from the 1690s onward); *The Collected Fairy Tales of the Brothers Grimm*, translated by Jack Zipes (Grimm and Grimm 2003; based on the 1857 edition of the Grimms' tales with additions from their notes); *Italian Popular Tales*, compiled and translated by Thomas Crane and edited by Jack Zipes ([1885] 2001; spanning Italian literary and folk tales mostly from the 1800s); *Folktales of France*, edited and translated by Geneviève Massignon (1968; tales she and others collected in the 1950s); *Folktales of Germany*, edited and translated by Kurt Ranke (1966; compiled from fieldwork collections from approximately 1850-1950); and *Folklore by the Fireside* by Alessandro Falassi (1980; tales he collected in Tuscany in the 1970s and translated). It is worth noting that two of these collections come from Richard Dorson's important Folktales of the World series, which has been influential in folkloristics as a set of rigorously collected, categorized, and translated folktales. My analysis includes only the proper fairy tales (those numbering 300-749 in the ATU tale type system, with a few exceptions for tales that fall outside that category but are still clearly tales of magic or appear in combination with magic tales) from each collection. This selection balances between tales collected by single collectors and tales written by single authors, folk and literary versions of tales, and classic and contemporary versions of tales.

Working in translation offers both constraints and unique opportunities. As tales are always being translated and transmitted to new cultures, it is possible to treat translations like any other version of a tale: a variant. Bottigheimer notes that: "new translations are often new tellings of an old tale" (2013:559). Additionally, all translations are mediated texts; as Jones points out, any "translation can achieve the status of 'original' for its culture" (2016:15); this is partly what I am after. As Jones notes, "ideas about [Perrault's] fairy tales—and particularly their female characters—spread quickly in translation, with long-lived and wide-reaching impact in the English-speaking world" (2-3). The study of fairy tales in the Anglophone world is a worthy pursuit on its own merit. I make no claims as to the ability of this study to illuminate meanings of the body or gendered bodies in the original cultural contexts of these tales; rather, I view this corpus of tales as a usefully representative sampling of classic tales disseminated in (and thus disseminating) an Anglophone lens.

A brief note on the translators themselves: each collection used here was translated by folklorists with a scholarly or educated public audience in mind, which promises a higher degree of linguistic accuracy. Zipes notes of Thomas Crane's translation, for instance, that it is "remarkably accurate" due to how "he mastered different Italian dialects and slang" (2001:viii). And while Zipes has now translated the Grimms' tales again (based on the 1812 edition of the tales), his anthologizing of the French tales used here must be treated with caution, as his translation began with J.R. Planché's nineteenth-century English translation of the French tales and made corrections from there (discussed in Malarte-Feldman 1999; Zipes [1989] 2009). We must thus keep in mind that these are mediated texts (see also Sutton 1996).

Methods

The tales were coded for both metadata and body descriptors. Each tale was coded according to 14 metadata points (Tale, Collection, Author, Teller, Collector, Year of Writing/Collecting, Year of Publication, Tale Type, Region, Original Language, Gender of Teller/Writer, Gender of Collector, Gender of Editor, and Gender of Protagonist). Then each tale was coded for 14 features related to mentions or descriptions of a body. The 14 feature categories were divided into text-based categories (Noun, Adjective, Surrounding Text, Page Number, Gender, Young/Old, High/Low, Quoted Speech, Skin Tone) and interpretive categories (Positive/Negative Value, Grotesque, Violence, Nudity, Move). "High" and "Low" refer to social status, while "Young" and "Old" refer to the character's age: youthful characters are of child-bearing age or younger, while old characters are beyond child-bearing years or are the parents of children who are already mature, derived from Holbek's modification of Elli Kongäs-Maranda's opposi-tional categories (Holbek 1998:347-8). The "Move" category is drawn from Holbek's modification of Propp's 31 tale functions.

The resulting data set is the first hand-coded database of body descriptors in fairy tales, combining objective and subjective elements. To code each of the 233 tales, I made an entry into a spreadsheet every time a body or body part was mentioned or described. Rather than relying on full-text extraction or trusting an algorithm to correctly identify every mention of a body and to also extract metadata such as the gender of the character involved (additionally, not all texts were available digitally at the time due to copyright restric-tions), I entered sentence fragments surrounding each body-part noun or adjective. Age and social class are more subjec-tive categories and sometimes had to be inferred from contex-tual information in the tale. Whether a body was ascribed positive or negative value, whether it counted as grotesque, and whether violence was being done to that body were also subjective judgments.

Much of the information presented here is based on simple word counts. This is not a new method (see Bottigheimer

1986), though it is made easier with recent technology. Co-occurrences can also yield information about how women's bodies are modified and described; here, I arrive at co-occurrences by finding instances where an adjective (such as describing the color of the hair of a character) co-occurs with a noun (the aforementioned hair), and I align that co-occurrence with the extracted features for that given sentence (e.g., metadata indicating the gender of that character). These co-occurrences were left unweighted for each tale. The resulting matrix consists of 11,144 rows, with each row constituting an extracted feature, and 27 columns, with each column related to either a data or metadata feature. Of these, 5,454 describe women's bodies and 4,877 describe men's bodies (the remaining 814 are either gender-neutral or implicate both genders).

Results

The adjectival descriptors connected with women in my database are particularly revealing as to the construction of femininity in fairy tales. Of all the bodies referenced in my database, 48.9% are female and 43.7% are male. Of the nouns that refer to gendered bodies, 51.18% refer to women's bodies (2,923) and 48.82% refer to men's bodies (2,788). This disparity between men's and women's bodies increases when we consider adjectives. Of all the adjectives that refer to a gendered body, 54.75% refer to women's bodies (2,530), while 45.25% refer to men's bodies (2,091). The increasing percentages in the order listed also show that descriptive attention to women's bodies takes up more tale space than that of men's bodies: 48.9% of the bodies in the corpus are female, 51.18% of the nouns are attributed to female bodies, and 54.75% of the adjectives refer to female bodies.

Certain words immediately leap out as clustering more

around women than around men. These include nouns, adjectives, and themes. I used themes to classify actions that happened to bodies in a given text, such as when a character died or was transformed, but the specific words "death" or "transformation" did not appear in the text. Calculating the frequency of word use with the genders, however, is more complicated than it appears on the surface. I first had to take into account that more of the body words coded in the database appear with women than with men, which might skew results if I simply tried to use basic percentages. Some words are used so consistently with one gender but not with the other that basic percentages are still useful, such as how "beauty" is used with women 360 times and with men only 8. In other cases, however, additional useful information is obtained when the word usage is analyzed in context of the frequency of male and female references overall.

By listing some of the body-part nouns used more commonly with women than with men, I hope to give a sense of how women's bodies are represented in fairy tales. Some nouns are used entirely with women and never with men. These are listed, in descending order, with each word followed by its frequency of use: tresses (14), bosom (10), cripple (9), sex (4), locks (4), being (4), complexions (3), lip (3), liver (3), lungs (3), wrist (2), wrinkles (2), elbows (2), braids (2), spirit (2), stature (2), and strand (2).

None of these words are sex-specific; the word "breast" is used with both men and women, though more with women, and bosom can appear in conjunction with any gender. It should be noted that some of these word associations come only from one tale. For instance, "liver" and "lungs" each appear three times, but every appearance is from the Grimms' "Snow White," when the wicked queen demands that the

202

protagonist's liver and lungs be brought to her as proof of Snow White's death. "Sex" appears in only one collection —*Beauties, Beasts, and Enchantment: Classic French Fairy Tales*— and only in tales by female writers. "Sex" appears once in "Beauty and the Beast" by Gabrielle-Suzanne de Villeneuve; once in "The Blue Bird" by Marie-Catherine d'Aulnoy; and twice in "Belle-Belle, or The Chevalier Fortuné," also by d'Aulnoy. In each of these cases, feminine gender (often that of the protagonist, and "sex" as a gloss for what we would now understand as gender) is commented on, ostensibly in contrast to the unmarked masculine norm. This is notable when viewed in light of the cultural context, as the female salon writers in early modern France were revising prevailing gender roles and assumptions about biology and genetics in their fairy tales.

Other nouns in my data set appear with both women and men, but predominantly with women. For the purposes of this investigation, I am considering words that appear with women at least 60% of the time to be predominantly woman-associated words. These are as follows (in the format of word/number of appearances/percentage of time used with women): hair/144/71%, hands/101/63%, tears/75/69%, mind/62/70%, blood/62/70%, birth/61/74%, finger/49/65%, nose/20/61%, lap/18/86%, lips/16/62%, cheeks/16/70%, fingers/14/64%, features/14/74%, teeth/13/62%, forehead/13/77%, ugliness/11/73%, side/11/79%, and complexion/10/90%.

Many of these words are related to appearance and can be used to rate attractiveness (or lack thereof) by describing facial features. Only one is specifically feminine: "birth" (though "lap" is commonly used to refer to a woman's seated position when holding or nursing a child). The association of women with extremities—"hands," "finger," and "fingers," which appear in this list, and "thumb," "heel," "toe," and "toes"—is interesting. These associations could be a reflection of women's work, which in Western Europe has included house-work and handiwork such as sewing and cooking and thus would require the attention to detail that dexterous hands and fingers grant.

The link between extremities and women's bodies can be read in at least two ways: metonymically or in terms of symbolic and real dismemberment. The extremities could metonymically symbolize the marginalization of women in Western culture: the small and marginalized body parts associated with women depict the smallness and marginalization of women in a society where men held the majority of the power.

Another reading of these nouns that are predominantly used with women is that they emphasize surfaces and interiors, portraying women as images or as collections of dismembered pieces. This tendency to dismember women has been noted by visual culture theorists. Ann Schmiesing, in her discussion of disability and dismemberment in the Grimms' tales, discusses how "Females are typically given disabilities that make them more passive, whereas males often—but not always—have disabilities that mark them as Other without significantly reducing their agency" (2014:83). Thus women are often bodily Othered in multiple ways in fairy tales.

There are 93 adjectives associated solely with women (versus 88 adjectives shared between women and men, and 93 adjectives associated solely with men). Because there are so many, I will list those that recur here (as with the nouns, counting those with two or more mentions). These are as follows, with each word followed by its frequency of use: fairest (9), prettiest (9), homely (7), thick (7), pregnant (6), loveliest (4), poorest (4), prettier (4), fairer (3), flat (3), lazy (3), slender (3), tender (3), attractive (2), blonde (2), blue (2), broad (2), chubby (2), deceased (2), haggard (2), homelier (2), honest (2), hooked (2), immense (2), miserable (2), naked (2), proud (2), scrawny (2), smaller (2), sweet (2), and ugliest (2).

Again, the number of appearance-related adjectives is striking, and again, some caveats must be made. The two mentions of "broad" and the three mentions of "flat" can be traced to a single tale, "The Three Spinners" from the Grimms' collection, in which the helper figures are three old, ugly women, including one with a broad, flat foot from treading while spinning. The words "broad" and "flat" are used solely to describe the old woman's foot in this single tale, proving that not all of these adjectives can be taken generally to represent femininity in all of the six collections (and fairy tales in general). However, the fact that so many of the adjectives are related to appearance and physical attractiveness is useful information and indeed accounts for the variations across texts: the adjectives used to describe women may vary by place and language, but still these types of adjectives persist, even in translation.

The adjectives that appear predominantly—at least 60% of the time—with women are also worth discussing, because they establish gendered patterns of representation. Here I list those that have at least ten mentions or more, again in the format of word/number of appearances/percentage of time used with women: beautiful/418/98%, old/411/61%, dear/68/62%, golden/55/75%, fair/53/87%, ugly/52/80%, lovely/46/94%, wicked/43/80%, pretty/36/90%, wise/21/91%, long/17/65%, evil/15/75%, younger/15/65%, red/12/67%, and pale/11/73%.

The fact that most of the words have an evaluative or

descriptive function related to appearance is striking. The evaluative words—"beautiful," "fair," "lovely," "ugly," and "pretty"—appear with women at least 80% of the time, indicating that physical appearance is of great importance for female fairy-tale characters. Words that describe rather than evaluate appearances are used more frequently with women than with men, too, as words like "golden," "long," "red," and "pale" appear in connection to physical descriptions of skin and hair. Additionally, "beautiful" was used so frequently that of all the adjectives used with women, "beautiful" accounted for 16.52% of them. Approximately one in six times, if a woman is described as anything, she is described as "beautiful." This supports feminist analysis of other fairy-tale texts found in the scholarly literature and will be expanded upon in my analysis below.

As seen in this last list, "old" is the next most-commonly used adjective with women after "beauty." Age and wisdom frequently relate in the figure of the fairy godmother, popularized in French fairy tales such as Perrault's "Cinderella" and its subsequent mass-market versions (like Disney's Cinderella film). Despite the fact that fairy godmothers occur less frequently in oral tradition, there still exist plenty of symbolic links between aged female figures, kinship obligations, and narrative traditions in early modern Europe. My prior work on fairy godmothers led to this observation: "The implied age and judgment of fairy godmothers, more than other donors/helpers, positions them to impart traditional wisdom, and to instill not just heroes and heroines but also tale audiences with aspects of worldview" (Jorgensen 2007:224). The data in this project implies that, even if fairy godmothers are not explicitly named as such, the correlations between traits support the existence of elderly female helper figures. The same is true of female villainesses: not every single one need be named a wicked stepmother or evil witch, but the frequency of descriptions of women as evil and wicked suggests that these types of women are very common in my data set. This also resonates with Schmiesing's findings that "female villains are often depicted with a disability or other physical anomaly that is meant to further mark their wicked deeds without in any way compromising their ability to perform them, but this has the effect of casting female agency as wicked" (2014:84). Conflating agential female embodiment with disability or age is thus a problematic feature of fairy tales.

By examining adjectives that are applied frequently or exclusively to women as a whole, it becomes apparent that both descriptions and evaluations of physical appearance are highly patterned. My data set reveals that evaluative appearance words are used with men, but not with the same frequency, intensity, or breadth of descriptions. The adjectives used with women range from stand-alone adjectives to those used in connection with body parts. For example, in "The Ram" by d'Aulnoy, the enchanted ram who is the heroine's counterpart tells her, "It was there that I saw you, beautiful princess" (Zipes [1989] 2009:395). In this case, "beautiful" is applied to the princess' whole person, not to any particular body part. Later, when the exiled princess returns home unrecognized, the king is so taken with her beauty that he offers her "a golden basin and vase filled with water so that she might wash her beautiful hands" (398). Thus, "beautiful" is one of the adjectives that can be used alone or to modify a noun. This is the case with many of the adjectives, regardless of whether they serve evaluative or descriptive functions. However, a pattern has yet to emerge with word co-occurrences and types of adjectives. This is in part because while the terms "descriptive" and "evaluative" adjectives are useful shorthand ways of describing the apparent functions of the adjectives, it is difficult to come up with a precise-enough definition to concretely separate instances of the two enough to get a count for statistical purposes. Additionally, since I am working with tales in translation, I do not wish to delve too deeply into the linguistic differences between descriptive and evaluative adjectives, as they may differ between languages.

Discussion

The results presented above can be considered in the context of the five topics related to women's bodies and constructions of femininity in fairy tales I have previously identified: beauty as a feminine trait; hair, eyes, and skin; bodily fluids; suffering; and morality.

Beauty

For purposes of classification in my database, I counted as nouns items I called "themes," since technically "beauty," "death," and "cannibalism" are nouns even though they do not refer to body parts. Beauty is the most frequently used theme with female fairy-tale characters, at 360 mentions in my database outranking all other themes and most other words, both nouns and adjectives. Men were connected with "beauty" only eight times in my database, meaning that "beauty" was used with women 97.83% of the times it occurred. Moreover, "beauty" was used so frequently with women that of all the nouns used with women, both explicit body-part nouns and themes, "beauty" accounted for 6.31% of them. "Beauty" is by far the most common theme used with women; the next most frequently used theme is "birth," with 19 mentions with women and 4 with men. The remainder of the themes are either used with men more than with women or in relatively equal numbers between men and women, or they are used in such small numbers that they provide supporting evidence at best. Some of the frequency of "beauty" can be attributed to the fact that it sometimes appears as a character name. These instances include the titular character in the tale "Beauty with the Golden Hair" by d'Aulnoy (ATU 531), the character "Beauty" in the tale "Beauty and the Beast" by Jeanne-Marie Leprince de Beaumont (ATU 425C), and the character "Beauty" in "Beauty and the Beast" by de Villeneuve (ATU 425C). If I were working with a smaller sample of tales, I would be concerned that the presence of these titular characters would skew the results, but as the naming conventions in fairy tales include these sorts of names based on personal details and appearances, I believe that the inclusion of these tales contributes to an understanding of the overall patterning of bodies and identities in fairy tales.

But does "beauty" actually mean "beauty" in the sense of physical attractiveness, or are there other social and symbolic meanings being referenced in fairy tales? Isabel Cardigos believes "the 'beauty' of fairytale heroines is a transparent code for their fertility potential" (1996:48). In other words, fairy-tale heroines are described as the most beautiful when they are romantically available. Cardigos elaborates on this symbolic equation, stating "the ugliness of the 'black bride' is a male perception of the 'wrong' times of woman" (209). Vaz da Silva concurs with the equation of beauty with symbolic availability, stating that the famed fairy-tale tricolor complexion (red as blood, white as snow, black as ebony) as an expression of feminine perfection hints at far-reaching links between "trivalent goddesses and ideal womanhood" (2007:242). The association of beauty with the supernatural is another aspect of the symbolism behind feminine beauty in fairy tales. Vaz da Silva posits that "unearthly beauty discloses a 'fairy nature'" and "specifically, the extraordinary beauty of Cinderella's mother betrays her otherworldly origin" (2002:203). Beauty is a sign of not only otherworldliness, but also the cyclical transformations that occur in fairy tales: "the heroine relegated to temporary death by the stepmother taps then the life-giving aspect of her departed mother and consequently emerges beautiful—as a rejuvenated mother—from the death-connoting cinders" (202). According to these folkloristic interpretations, then, beauty is an index of symbolic positioning within the narratives, disclosing important information about where the heroine is in a cycle of enchantment or disenchantment, which thus dictates her availability for courtship.

The notion that beauty indicates a woman's availability and attractiveness to men, however, is a deeply sexist and heterosexist view of the situation. It resonates unpleasantly with assessments from fields such as evolutionary psychology, wherein every facet of femininity and masculinity somehow must correspond to the ability to attract a viable heterosexual mate and thus pass on one's genetic material. Gottschall et al. summarizes the paradigm as such: "Men place great value on female physical attractiveness because it is a trustworthy indicator of relative fertility" (2008:176). They argue that in this conventional view, men's physical attractiveness is less important than women's because "male fertility is much less variable than female, and those variances are much more difficult to detect" and because of the difficulties inherent in raising human young: "women—unlike most female mammals—must balance preferences for physically attractive mates with preferences for parentally investing mates" (176). Despite the fact that this narrative is founded on a number of faulty assumptions—such as the supposed universality of monogamy in human societies, preoccupation with paternal investment, and selfishness lying at the heart of human inter-actions—those utilizing an evolutionary psychology or socio-biology paradigm project these assumptions onto everything and everyone. I find it striking that both Gottschall et al. and Cardigos, coming from different disciplinary perspectives, equate female beauty with fertility. Then again, if folklore is often a mirror of culture and we have wound up with a fairly sexist culture, is it any surprise if interpretations of that culture also appear fairly sexist? The next few sections of this article examine case studies that—fairly or not—link women's body parts with specific attributes.

Hair, Eyes, and Skin

If the feminist claims are to be believed, women's appear-ances in fairy tales are that much more important than men's appearances and thus get more descriptive time as well as descriptions that converge along culturally normative lines (e.g., reinforcing a narrow ideal of doll-like female beauty).

The phrase "golden hair," reputed to be stock in fairy tales, occurs 66 times, out of 73 total mentions of the adjective "gold-en." All but 14 of those "golden hair" phrases refer to women; of the 14 associations with boys/men, 5 apply to the supernat-urally enhanced golden hair of the boy in "Iron Hans" (ATU 502 in the Grimms) and 9 apply to the Devil's golden hairs, the object of a quest, in "The Devil with the Three Golden Hairs" (ATU 461 in the Grimms). Thus, men with golden hair get it from supernatural means (either by being supernatural crea-tures, as with the Devil, or by getting mixed up with supernat-ural creatures, as with the boy protagonist in "Iron Hans"). Women with golden hair, it is implied, are naturally that way, and moreover their golden hair is a special marker of beauty.

In two cases, the golden hair is incorporated into the protagonists' names: Beauty with the Golden Hair is sought after in
the tale titled "Beauty with the Golden Hair" by d'Aulnoy
(ATU 531), and "Golden Hair" is the female protagonist who
escapes a hostile donor figure in the style of "Rapunzel" and
later is turned into a frog in the tale collected by Massignon
titled "Golden Hair, or the Little Frog" (a blend of ATU 310
and 402).

An additional 30 tales mentioned women's hair that was
not blond or that did not have a specific color associated with
it, and 19 tales mentioned men's hair that was not color-speci-
fied. Comparatively, women were more likely to have golden
hair than men, but still, fewer than half of female characters
whose hair was mentioned have golden hair. Thus, golden
hair does not occur as the norm, though it is the most
commonly specified hair color on women. However, golden
hair does have some symbolic resonances in the world of
European folk belief: "Golden hair is of course a stable feature
of fairies" (Vaz da Silva 2002:203). Hair in general being more
associated with women than with men in fairy tales is indicative of the role hair plays in Western beauty standards, and
this gendered connotation possibly dovetails with the taboo
and ritual magic uses of hair (Holden 2000:116-7; Warner
1994:374).

In addition to golden hair, feminist scholars claim that
fairy-tale heroines are supposed to have blue eyes and pale,
perfect complexions (e.g., Warner 1994:362). In my data set,
there were in fact remarkably few descriptions of "blue eyes."
One occurred in Perrault's "Donkey Skin," which contains a
description of "Her blue eyes, so large and sweet" (Zipes
[1989] 2009:73). The other occurred in "The Blue Bird" by
d'Aulnoy, where an enterprising queen is described as

knowing "how to roll her large blue eyes" (321). It is, of course, significant that both of these mentions refer to women, but two instances out of 294 total eye mentions are not powerful indicators that blue eyes are popular in fairy tales. It is also important to note that both these tales were written by French intellectuals in the 1690s and that this movement represented a more complex, thickly descriptive strand of the literary fairy tale. Mentions of "eyes" did not significantly correlate to women, as eyes were mentioned 135 times with women and 145 times with men (the remaining 14 instances are gender-neutral). Beauty is not, according to my data set, the main reason for mentioning eyes, though there are occasional sentences such as "Then she turned her beautiful eyes to the captain of the guards" (in "The Ram" by d'Aulnoy, Zipes [1989] 2009:389). In "The Goose Girl at the Spring" in the Grimms' collection, the princess, when finally vindicated, "emerged with her golden hair and sparkling eyes" (2003:525). More frequently, however, eyes exist to be gouged out, to be rolled, to close (indicating sleep), to open (indicating wakefulness), to implore, to squint, to be filled with tears, to be dazzled by someone's beauty, to convey ill or good intent, or to be remarked upon (as in the famous exchange between Little Red Cap and the wolf in ATU 333 where she asks her "grandmother" about her large eyes). Thus, while eyes are a significant body part mentioned in fairy tales, their use does not conform to feminist claims about the specific kinds of eyes that are valued for women in Western culture.

There does seem to be a connection between women and the frequency of mentions of skin tone, especially paleness. There were 43 descriptions of men's skin and 78 descriptions of women's skin, displaying a clear pattern connecting women with pale skin. "White" was used to describe women's skin 19 times (men's 4 times), "pale" was used with women 15 times (with men 5 times), and other skin adjectives were used solely with women: "alabaster" (twice), "beautiful complexions" (twice), "ivory" (twice), "lovely" (thrice), "white and beautiful" (twice), and "whitened" (twice). These indicators of lightness and beauty were the most common types of skin words I documented; other words, describing darkness, redness, or goldness, were not used as much. Thus, it appears that the accusations by feminist critics that fairy tale heroines are often portrayed with white skin are accurate; paleness occupies a privileged place in Western conceptions of beauty that date back to the disparate places and periods from whence these fairy tales came. Skin tone is an internationally known folk narrative motif, cropping up in *The 1001 Nights/The Arabian Nights* as well as in contemporary body art practices such as skin lightening.

The contrast of these specific descriptive words with the overall importance of beauty for women in fairy tales is alarming, as it highlights the double bind of Western ideal femininity. Naomi Wolf describes this double bind in terms of the "beauty myth," arguing that the problem is not specific beauty standards (though the more unattainable they are, the more oppressive they are), but rather women's lack of choices ([1991] 2002:272). The double bind is that women who are not beautiful are punished for failing to adhere to the beauty myth, while those who try will inevitably fail once the standards shift, or they will fail once they are perceived to be trying in the first place. In Wolf's analysis of the beauty myth, beauty is seen to "objectively and universally exist," and the draw toward feminine beauty is "necessary and natural because it is biological, sexual, and evolutionary" (12). This language foreshadows Gottschall et al.'s work on gender in fairy tales and illustrates the need for nuanced attention to feminist criticism. While Gottschall et al. takes for granted the existence of an evolutionary reason for gender essentialism, Wolf interrogates it: "If the beauty myth is not based on evolution, sex, gender, aesthetics, or God, on what is it based?...The beauty myth is not about women at all. It is about men's institutions and institutional power" ([1991] 2002:13). Applied to my findings, the importance of beauty for women in fairy tales is concerning because of the very vagueness of beauty. This is yet one more impossible standard for women to strive to meet and to inexorably be punished for failing at. And as we will see below, the punishments women face in fairy tales can be quite dire.

Bodily Fluids

In my data set women are more associated with "blood" and "tears"—the only bodily fluids among the top ten body-part nouns, regardless of gender—than men. Cardigos and Vaz da Silva have both observed the significance of blood as a transformative substance in fairy tales. Cardigos, working primarily on Portuguese fairy tales, argues that women's "three bloods" (menstruation, defloration, and childbirth) influence both the plot structures of fairy tales and influence their content, as these bloody cycles "appear as both a curse and a source of wonder" (1996:47). Vaz da Silva takes Cardigos' arguments further, claiming that "the very process that constitutes disenchantment in fairy tales" involves a ritual period of three days (2002:179). Sometimes this disenchantment involves wounding a woman (symbolic defloration), or it can involve shedding animal skins or a loathly disguise (again, like Cinderella), which thematically parallels the shedding of blood of menstruation as the uterus sheds its lining. Because Cardigos and Vaz da Silva agree that women's bloody cycles provide the symbolic language of enchantment and disenchantment that fairy tales utilize, it makes sense from a folkloristic perspective that women would be linked with blood.

However, feminist scholars have also discussed the connections between women's bodies and fluids. Elizabeth Grosz summarizes this scholarship, moving from Mary Douglas on purity and pollution to Julia Kristeva and the abject, hypothesizing that "women's corporeality is inscribed as a mode of seepage" (1994:203). From this perspective, it makes sense that women more than men in fairy tales are associated with bodily fluids and moreover that these fluids would be charged with cultural meanings. Certain branches of feminism consider fluidity a central issue. As Margrit Shildrick and Janet Price note: "what is at issue for women specifically is that, supposedly, the female body is intrinsically unpredictable, leaky and disruptive," which has had the effect "that women remain rooted within their bodies, held back by their supposedly natural biological processes" (1999:2).

One of the feminist claims about women in fairy tales is that they are excluded from roles of power, sometimes violently, and for women who do seize power (e.g., evil stepmothers, witches, and crones) the punishments are quite dreadful. Dancing oneself to death in heated iron shoes and being devoured by reptiles in a vat are two of the punishments powerful women face in my data set (appearing in the Grimms' "Snow White" and Perrault's "The Sleeping Beauty in the Woods"). These certainly qualify as violent deaths. However, as Cardigos points out, despite the fact that women in fairy tales are associated with blood, there is an ambivalence surrounding blood symbolism and gender roles. Specifically, "the immediate association between blood and death is emphatically contradicted by the fact that in these cases [of

defloration and childbirth] it is the blood of fertility (or potential fertility)" (1996:47). Thus, mentions of women's blood do
not automatically connote violence against women as a theme
underlying the meanings of fairy tales. Rather, I have found
through exploring my data set that violence is associated more
with men than with women in fairy tales (Jorgensen forthcoming). Cardigos views narrative violence as a way for men to
symbolically wrest the power of procreation from women by
enacting bloody rites: "in typical hero tales the assertion of
phallic power is focused, precisely, on the shedding of blood
that is caused by male intervention" (1996:47), such as the
symbolic defloration of a maiden by slaying her serpentine
guardian.

Since blood and violence are not necessarily synonymous
in fairy tales, the depictions of women's bodies must be
considered multivalent. Lüthi believed that blood only rarely
appears in folktales: "Even when actual mutilations occur in
folktales we are not allowed to visualize the physical body of
the victim...we do not see blood flowing or a real wound
developing" (1986:12). However, blood appeared tenth among
the most frequent nouns in my entire data set, and as it is used
predominantly with one gender (appearing as the fifth most
commonly used body noun with women), it is not only a
stable feature of fairy tales, but also a significantly patterned
one. Blood does seem to indicate unsuitability or inappropri-
ateness when connected with women, as Cardigos and Vaz da
Silva have posited, but the meanings are social rather than (or
in addition to) symbolic. In the Grimms' "Cinderella" (ATU
510A), blood reveals that the stepsisters are false substitutes
for Cinderella. They are physically mutilated in a bid to be the
prince's bride, an act that limits their mobility and makes them
unsuitable for any future working life.

Suffering

Feminine patience and suffering is hinted at in the tales, too. The word "tears" appeared 75 times with women and 33 times with men, implying that women do a lot more crying in fairy tales than men do. Additionally, the phrase "bitter tears" appears, almost always in conjunction with women. There are seven mentions of "bitter tears" with women and only one with men, leading me to hypothesize that women's suffering is more emphasized in fairy tales than men's suffering. Female characters realize their helplessness in the world, such as in this description of the protagonist in "The Virgin Mary's Child" (ATU 710) in the Grimms' collection who is expelled from heaven: "But it was a miserable life, and whenever she thought about how beautiful it had been in heaven and how the angels had played with her, she shed bitter tears" (2003:9). Gretel in the Grimms' "Hansel and Gretel" (ATU 327A) spends quite a lot of time weeping; she sheds tears three times, and twice they are "bitter tears." First she weeps bitter tears when the children overhear their parents proposing to abandon them, then when they are captured by the witch and Gretel must do her bidding. It is notable that all the tales mentioning women's bitter tears, except one, appears in the Grimms' collection (the rest of these mentions are in "The Juniper Tree," "King Thrushbeard," and "One-Eye, Two-Eye, and Three-Eye"). This supports the hypothesis of several Grimms scholars, from Zipes and Haase to Tatar and Bottigheimer, that the Grimms were tailoring their tales to an agenda of not only civilizing and educating children, but also enforcing gender roles. The exception to all the female "bitter tears" occurring in the Grimms is in "The Ram" by d'Aulnoy, where the protagonist is exiled from her home and her companions are slain in order to protect the secret that she is still alive; then, she "wept such bitter tears over [them] that she became quite exhausted" (Zipes [1989] 2009:390).

Significantly, the one mention of a male's "bitter tears" also occurs in a tale by d'Aulnoy, "The Island of Happiness." The male figure who weeps bitter tears is not even a human or a main character, but rather Zephir, the West Wind, who has supported the hero in his quest to seek a princess. When the hero dies, Zephir weeps "bitter tears" over him, but the princess, upon losing her lover, "uttered such bitter cries that they could have moved the most insensitive heart" (Zipes [1989] 2009:308). This is one good example of a body-part mention that is not gendered. And this occurred after lamenting his long absence, during which she "added a flood of tears to the flow of the stream" (308). Thus, female tears, even when not described as "bitter," are prevalent in fairy tales and seem to suggest that women suffer disproportion- ately, whether they are represented as doing so in the fairy tales prescriptively (as with the Grimms) or descriptively (as with d'Aulnoy's tales, which provided social commentary on the gender roles of her day). This analysis directly contrasts with Lüthi's view that "Tears are shed only if this is important for the development of the plot" (1986:13). I argue that it is essential to read the body in fairy tales both in terms of what the bodies mean for the plots and in terms of how the bodies are shaped by cultural meanings and ideologies, which neces- sitates going deeper than superficial textual readings and determining the associations informing the uses of bodies in fairy tales.

Morality

Feminists have argued that women's bodies are inscribed with properly gendered behavior through the repetitive performances of identity that occur in fairy tales, especially when it comes to moral or "good" behavior. I found that moral evaluative words are frequently used with female characters. Of the times when "wicked" and "evil" appear, three-quarters are associated with female characters; when "wise" appears, 90% of the time it is associated with a woman. Despite the polarization of these terms, I would argue that they represent a thematic coherence whereby female figures in fairy tales, particularly those who are old (and "old" is used with women at least 60% of the time), tend to take on either the roles of donor figures or of antagonists/villains. As Scott Weingart and I noted in a previous article, when using not just word counts but also correlations and word co-occurrences, age figures prominently in relation to gender: "Old people and females were both described more than expected, given the distribution of nouns and adjectives. The most descriptions were attached to old females, and the least to young males" (Weingart and Jorgensen 2013:411). This type of language use Others older female bodies.

Measuring a character's kindness or goodness using body descriptors has proven challenging; fortunately, while coding the database I decided to cast a wide net by including words related to moral character, although this is not always precisely an embodied trait. It is telling that moral evaluative words like "wicked," "evil," and "wise" occur more with women than with men, indicating that female characters are polarized in terms of their goodness or badness. To study this, I used a "+/-" tag in the database to signify that a body mention or description had positive or negative moral connotations (what I call a moral evaluative tag, since there is an implicit or explicit moral evaluation happening at the textual level).

Since women characters in fairy tales tend to be split into

opposing categories of the good, kind protagonist or the evil, wicked antagonist, I had expected to find empirical evidence of some sort for this splitting phenomenon. Excepting five references that were to mixed-gender descriptions or gender-neutral bodies, there were 311 total moral evaluative tags, 237 applying to women and 73 to men. This was not a huge number, considering that there were 11,144 mentions in all, but it was patterned enough to be of interest. I found that while 76.21% of the moral evaluative references were to women and 23.79% to men—indicating that women were more likely than men to be assigned a moral evaluative phrase or function—the breakdown within the positive and negative tags was slightly different. 175 of the female references were negative and only 62 positive, while 47 of the male references were negative and 27 positive. That means that 73.84% of the moral evaluative references to women were negative and 26.16% positive, while 63.51% of the moral evaluative references to men were negative and 36.49% positive. Thus, women were more likely to be evaluated with negative words than men were, when men had a moral evaluation tacked on to them at all. This does not satisfy the challenges posed by feminists who claim that all fairy-tale heroines are saccharine-sweet and good, or if they are, those traits are established elsewhere than the body. Indeed, while other feminist scholars have observed the polarizing characterization of women in fairy tales, my analysis is unique for locating this judgmental process in descriptions adjacent to the body.

CONCLUSION

Discussions of beauty; hair, eyes, and skin; bodily fluids; suffering, and morality address the questions with which I began this article: does the depiction of women's bodies in fairy tales support feminist assertions about gendered bodies? Using simple statistical methods and a hand-coded data set derived from a canonical corpus of translated European fairy tales, I examined five main claims, finding that some claims were overstated (e.g., the relative unimportance of hair and eye color). However, a female fairy-tale character's beauty, and physical appearance in general, is in fact one of the most important features of her character. This pattern countermands Lüthi, who writes: "the popular idea that the folktale identifies the good with beauty and success and the bad with ugliness and failure cannot be accepted without qualification. Such correspondences frequently occur, but they are not indispensable; the folktale is not bound to actual ideals of such a kind" (1986:71, emphasis added). Clearly the folktale and fairy tale do not always portray beautiful characters as good, and wicked characters as ugly; there are plenty of counterexamples. However, because this connection has been widespread enough to be noticed by critics, and because my data shows that beauty is highly correlated with female characters, I reject Lüthi's idea that the correlation is not related to ideals from the real world. On the contrary, narrative ideals and real-world ideals are inextricably bound, whether the subject of the ideal is beauty, normative femininity, or gender identity.

The concept of gender performance ties in neatly to the emphasis on and artificiality of feminine beauty discussed above (Butler [1990] 1999). If femininity were a given, something that naturally and inherently existed inside all women, then there would not be so much narrative, rhetorical, or ideological labor invested in naturalizing women's beauty and acts of femininity. This labor is what the concept "gender performance" signifies at its heart. While gender performance has been theorized less in terms of narrative elements and more in terms of behaviors and acts (such as cross-dressing and drag), fairy tales provide excellent examples of gender performances, since they combine social meanings with structural and symbolic ones. Kimberly Lau has articulated the latter connection, commenting on "the unique melding of the structural and the symbolic aspects of fairy tales, for it is precisely after the hero wins access to the symbol, that is to say, when the hero symbolically deflowers the princess, that the disenchantment and subsequent wedding occurs" (1996:238). Although Lau does not mention the importance of social values in the equation of structure and symbol in the fairy tale in this quote, she connects society to this equation later in her paper, and if these three things are taken as a whole, they illuminate the performativity of gender in fairy tales. That is, because fairy tales present an abstract and artistic portrait of culture, they obscure the ideological underpinnings of the gendered inequalities evident in their structures, symbols, and social meanings. And because repetition occurs on various levels in fairy tales—including verbal formulas, repetitive episodes (things coming in threes), and reiterated versions and variants of tales—the genre of fairy tales is well-suited to analysis based on gender performance theory. As Cristina Bacchilega summarizes the issue: "Gender is performative. The authority of the performative depends on repetition, which requires multiple performances. In certain hyperbolic cases, however, this authority produces twisted effects which expose the norm as fantasy and compulsion" (1997:22). When laid bare, the norms in fairy tales appear fantastic in their twisted emphasis on beauty above all else as a defining factor of femininity.

The performance of femininity plays out in fairy tales through the body, through the associations between women and their bodies, and through the remarking of women's beauty. By highlighting the narrative creation and fetishization of the "passively beautiful female character with very limited options" (1997:29), Bacchilega illustrates how the iterative performance of gender works to enact certain ideologies in fairy tales. Similarly, in my data set, the emphasis on beauty for women and the importance of traits like hair, eyes, and skin all function to inscribe femininity on the body. These enchanting portraits of beautiful female characters are all the more dangerous because they appear so natural while supporting restrictive social norms.

The study of social norms (including those governing gender) offers an important reason to utilize quantitative methods. As Tangherlini reminds us, "we must recognize that computational approaches can help make sense of the often hidden patterns that characterize human expressive culture at scale…and provide us with tools to tackle research questions that previously may have seemed intractable" (2016b:10). These hidden patterns are present not only in the deep structures of expressive culture, but also in the social attitudes contained therein. Assembling the data on bodies from six collections' worth of fairy tales may not have been impossible without the aid of technology, but it would have been a long and challenging process, and I preferred to let the technology assist with locating patterns where it could. With the aid of quantitative methods, I have shown that in many cases, the feminists were right: fairy tales present an uneven view of the genders, representing femininity as morally polarized and imbricated with notions of beauty and with an emphasis on certain features such as hair, skin, blood, and eyes. This empirically disproves critics such as Bruno Bettelheim ([1975] 1989) who have claimed that gender in the fairy tale does not matter.

Not only does gender matter in terms of how it is inscribed on the body, it also matters in different ways for men and for women. This is a normative imposition, in the sense that feminists Shirley Castelnuovo and Sharon R. Guthrie explain it: "The 'normal' feminine body in contemporary Western societies is one that conveys vulnerability, accommodation, and seductiveness whether it be through gesture, movement, or occupation of space" (1998:137). The "normal" feminine body in fairy tales, with its emphasis on beauty, adjectival descriptors, and morality, imposes a whole set of normative values upon women, ones which, as Bacchilega has observed (1997) and I have substantiated, are often passed off as "natural" and desirable.

Quantitative approaches to fairy tales offer a corrective means to support the largely subjective methods folklorists use to interpret data and shore up comparative approaches (such as the historic-geographic method) that have long been significant in our discipline. Being attuned to tradition already keys us into social norms, and my analysis both legitimizes existing scholarship and points in new directions for merging feminist concerns with folkloristic ones. I have not confirmed every point that feminist scholars have made about women's bodies in fairy tales, but I have validated the general sense that women are portrayed in scripted ways. My research suggests that folk narratives model normative gendered bodies in ways that ultimately reinforce existing stereotypes and conform to patriarchal expectations (such as the double bind of femininity). With this understanding, we can continue to forge new models for understanding the interactions of gender, the body, and expressive culture.

REFERENCES:

Bacchilega, Cristina. 1997. *Postmodern Fairy Tales: Gender and Narrative Strategies.* Philadelphia: University of Pennsylvania Press.

Baker-Sperry, Lori, and Liz Grauerholz. 2003. The Pervasiveness and Persistence of the Feminine Beauty Ideal in Children's Fairy Tales. *Gender and Society* 17(5):711-26.

Bettelheim, Bruno. [1975] 1989. *The Uses of Enchantment: The Meaning and Importance of Fairy Tales.* New York: Vintage Books.

Bottigheimer, Ruth. 1986. Silenced Women in the Grimms' Tales: The "Fit" Between Fairy Tales and Society in Their Historical Context. In *Fairy Tales and Society: Illusion, Allusion, and Paradigm,* ed. Ruth Bottigheimer, pp. 115-31. Philadelphia: University of Pennsylvania Press.

_____. 2004. Fertility Control and the Birth of the Modern European Fairy-Tale Heroine. In *Fairy Tales and Feminism: New Approaches,* ed. Donald Haase, pp. 37-51. Detroit: Wayne State University Press.

_____. 2013. Geographical Translocations and Cultural Transformations. In *Marvelous Transformations: An Anthology of Fairy Tales and Contemporary Critical Perspectives,* ed. Christine A. Jones and Jennifer Schacker, pp. 555-9. Peterborough, ON: Broadview Press.

Broadwell, Peter M., and Timothy R. Tangherlini. 2016. Witch-

Hunter: Tools for the Geo-Semantic Exploration of a Danish Folklore Corpus. In "Big Folklore: A Special Issue on Computational Folkloristics," ed. Timothy R. Tangherlini. *Journal of American Folklore* 129(511):14-42.

Butler, Judith. [1990] 1999. *Gender Trouble: Feminism and the Subversion of Identity.* New York: Routledge.

Cardigos, Isabel. 1996. *In and Out of Enchantment: Blood Symbolism and Gender in Portuguese Fairytales.* Helsinki: Academia Scientiarum Fennica.

Castelnuovo, Shirley, and Sharon R. Guthrie. 1998. *Feminism and the Female Body: Liberating the Amazon Within.* Boulder and London: Lynne Rienner Publishers.

Crane, Thomas. [1885] 2001. *Italian Popular Tales.* Ed. Jack Zipes. Santa Barbara, CA: ABC-CLIO, Inc.

Dundes, Alan. 1989. The Psychoanalytic Study of the Grimms' Tales: "The Maiden Without Hands" (AT 706). In *Folklore Matters*, ed. Alan Dundes, pp. 112-50. Knoxville: University of Tennessee Press.

Falassi, Alessandro. 1980. *Folklore by the Fireside: Text and Context of the Tuscan Veglia.* Austin: University of Texas Press.

Finlayson, Mark Alan. 2016. Inferring Propp's Functions from Semantically Annotated Text. In "Big Folklore: A Special Issue on Computational Folkloristics," ed. Timothy R. Tangherlini. *Journal of American Folklore* 129(511):55-77.

Gottschall, Jonathan, et al. 2003. Patterns of Characterization in Folktales across Geographic Regions and Levels of Cultural Complexity: Literature as a Neglected Source of Quantitative Data. *Human Nature* 14(4):365-82.

_____, . et al. 2008. The "Beauty Myth" Is No Myth: Emphasis on Male-Female Attractiveness in World Folktales. *Human Nature* 19(2):174-88.

Grimm, Wilhelm, and Jacob Grimm. 2003. *The Collected Fairy Tales of the Brothers Grimm (3rd edition)*. Trans. Jack Zipes. New York: Bantam Books.

Grosz, Elizabeth. 1994. *Volatile Bodies: Toward a Corporeal Feminism*. Bloomington: Indiana University Press.

Haase, Donald. 2004. Feminist Fairy-Tale Scholarship. In *Fairy Tales and Feminism*, ed. Donald Haase, pp. 1-36. Detroit: Wayne State University Press.

_____. 2010. Decolonizing Fairy-Tale Studies. *Marvels & Tales: Journal of Fairy-Tale Studies* 24(1):17-38.

_____. 2016. Fairy Tale. In *Folktales and Fairy Tales: Traditions and Texts from around the World (2nd edition)*, ed. Donald Haase, Anne Duggan, and Helen Callow, pp. 319-22. Santa Barbara, CA: Greenwood.

Hannon, Patricia. 1998. *Fabulous Identities: Women's Fairy Tales in Seventeenth-Century France*. Amsterdam: Rodopi.

Holbek, Bengt. 1998. *Interpretation of Fairy Tales*. Folklore

Fellows Communications. Helsinki: Academia Scientiarum Fennica.

Holden, Lynn. 2000. *The Encyclopedia of Taboos*. Oxford, England: ABC-CLIO Ltd.

Hurley, Dorothy L. 2005. Seeing White: Children of Color and the Disney Fairy Tale Princess. *Journal of Negro Education* 74(3):221-32.

Jones, Christine A. 2016. *Mother Goose Refigured: A Critical Translation of Charles Perrault's Fairy Tales*. Detroit: Wayne State University Press.

Jones, Christine A., and Jennifer Schacker. 2013. *Marvelous Transformations: An Anthology of Fairy Tales and Contemporary Critical Perspectives*. Peterborough, ON: Broadview Press.

Joosen, Vanessa. 2011. *Critical and Creative Perspectives on Fairy Tales: An Intertextual Dialogue between Fairy-Tale Scholarship and Postmodern Retellings*. Detroit: Wayne State University Press.

Jorgensen, Jeana. 2007. A Wave of the Magic Wand: Fairy Godmothers in Contemporary American Media. *Marvels & Tales: Journal of Fairy-Tale Studies* 21(2):216-27.

_____. 2012. *Gender and the Body in Classical European Fairy Tales*. PhD diss., Indiana University.

_____. Forthcoming. Masculinity and Men's Bodies in Fairy Tales: Youth, Violence, and Transformation. *Marvels & Tales: Journal of Fairy-Tale Studies* 32(2).

Karsdorp, Folgert. 2016. *Retelling Stories: A Computational-Evolutionary Perspective*. PhD thesis, Radboud University.

Lau, Kimberly J. 1996. Structure, Society, and Symbolism: Toward a Holistic Interpretation of Fairy Tales. *Western Folklore* 55(3):233-43.

Lieberman, Marcia. 1972. "Some Day My Prince Will Come": Female Acculturation through the Fairy Tale. *College English* 34(3):383-95.

Lurie, Alison. 1970. Fairy Tale Liberation. *New York Review of Books* December 17:42-4.

Lüthi, Max. 1986. *The European Folktale: Form and Nature*. Trans. John D. Niles. Bloomington: Indiana University Press.

Malarte-Feldman, Claire-Lise. 1999. The Challenges of Translating Perrault's "Contes" into English. *Marvels & Tales: Journal of Fairy-Tale Studies* 13(2):184-98.

Massignon, Geneviève. 1968. *Folktales of France*. Trans. Jacqueline Hyland. Chicago: The University of Chicago Press.

Mulvey, Laura. 1999. Visual Pleasure and Narrative Cinema. In *Film Theory and Criticism: Introductory Readings*, ed. Leo Brady and Marshall Cohen, pp. 833-44. New York: Oxford University Press.

Munns, John. 2011. The eye of the beholder?: Beauty and ugliness in the crucifixion imagery of the late Middle Ages. *Theology* 114(6):419-26.

Nikolić, Davor, and Nikola Bakarić. 2016. What Makes Our Tongues Twist?: Computational Analysis of Croatian Tongue-Twisters. In "Big Folklore: A Special Issue on Computational Folkloristics," ed. Timothy R. Tangherlini. *Journal of American Folklore* 129(511):43-54.

Propp, Vladimir. 1968. *Morphology of the Folktale*. Trans. Laurence Scott. Austin: University of Texas Press.

Ragan, Kathleen. 2009. What Happened to the Heroines in Folktales?: An Analysis by Gender of a Multicultural Sample of Published Folktales Collected from Storytellers. *Marvels & Tales: Journal of Fairy-Tale Studies* 23(2):227–47.

Ranke, Kurt. 1966. *Folktales of Germany*. Trans. Lotte Baumann. Chicago: University of Chicago Press.

Schacker, Jennifer. 2003. *National Dreams: The Remaking of Fairy Tales in Nineteenth-Century England*. Philadelphia: University of Pennsylvania Press.

Schmiesing, Ann. 2014. *Disability, Deformity, and Disease in the Grimms' Fairy Tales*. Detroit: Wayne State University Press.

Seifert, Lewis C. 1996. *Fairy Tales, Sexuality, and Gender in France, 1690-1715: Nostalgic Utopias*. Cambridge, England: Cambridge University Press.

Shildrick, Margrit, and Janet Price. 1999. Openings on the Body: A Critical Introduction. In *Feminist Theory and the Body: A Reader*, ed. Janet Price and Margrit Shildrick, pp. 1-14. New York: Routledge.

Stone, Kay. 1985. The Misuses of Enchantment: Controversies on the Significance of Fairy Tales. In *Women's Folklore, Women's Culture*, ed. Rosan A. Jordan and Susan J. Kalčik, pp. 125-45. Philadelphia: University of Pennsylvania Press.

Sutton, Martin. 1996. *The Sin-Complex: A Critical Study of English Versions of the Grimms' Kinder- und Hausmärchen in the Nineteenth Century*. Kassel: Schriften der Brüder Grimm Gesellschaft.

Taggart, James M. 1990. *Enchanted Maidens: Gender Relations in Spanish Folktales of Courtship and Marriage*. Princeton, NJ: Princeton University Press.

_____. 1997. *The Bear and His Sons: Masculinity in Spanish and Mexican Folktales*. Austin: University of Texas Press.

Talairach-Vielmas, Laurence. 2007. *Moulding the Female Body in Victorian Fairy Tales and Sensation Novels*. Aldershot, England: Ashgate Publishing, Ltd.

Tangherlini, Timothy, ed. 2016a. Big Folklore: A Special Issue on Computational Folkloristics. Special issue, *Journal of American Folklore* 129(511).

_____. 2016b. Big Folklore: A Special Issue on Computational Folkloristics. In "Computational Folkloristics," ed. Timothy Tangherlini. *Journal of American Folklore* 129(511):5-13.

Tatar, Maria. 1992. *Off with their Heads! Fairy Tales and the Culture of Childhood*. 1987. Princeton, NJ: Princeton University Press.

_____. 2003. *The Hard Facts of the Grimms' Fairy Tales: Expanded Second Edition*. Princeton, NJ: Princeton University Press.

Tucker, Elizabeth. 2003. *Pregnant Fictions: Childbirth and the Fairy Tale in Early-Modern France*. Detroit: Wayne State University Press.

Turner, Kay, and Pauline Greenhill. 2012. Introduction: Once Upon a Queer Time. In *Transgressive Tales: Queering the Grimms*, ed. Kay Turner and Pauline Greenhill, pp. 1-24. Detroit: Wayne State University Press.

Vaz da Silva, Francisco. 2002. *Metamorphosis: The Dynamics of Symbolism in European Fairy Tales*. New York: Peter Lang.

_____. 2007. Red as Blood, White as Snow, Black as Crow: Chromatic Symbolism of Womanhood in Fairy Tales. *Marvels & Tales: Journal of Fairy-Tale Studies* 21(2):240-52.

Waelti-Walters, Jennifer. 1982. *Fairy Tales and the Female Imagination*. Montreal, Canada: Eden Press, Inc.

Warner, Marina. 1994. *From the Beast to the Blonde: On Fairy Tales and Their Tellers*. New York: Farrar, Straus and Giroux.

Weingart, Scott, and Jeana Jorgensen. 2013. Computational Analysis of the Body in European Fairy Tales. *Literary and Linguistic Computing* 28(3):404-16.

Wolf, Naomi. [1991] 2002. *The Beauty Myth: How Images of Beauty Are Used Against Women*. New York: Harper Perennial.

Yolen, Jane. 1988. America's Cinderella. In *Cinderella: A Casebook*, ed. Alan Dundes, pp. 294-306. Madison: University of Wisconsin Press.

Zipes, Jack. 2001. Preface to this Edition. In *Italian Popular Tales* by Thomas Crane, pp. vii-i. Santa Barbara, CA: ABC-CLIO, Inc.

_____. 2006. *Fairy Tales and the Art of Subversion* (2nd edition). New York: Routledge.

_____. trans. [1989] 2009. *Beauties, Beasts, and Enchantment: Classic French Fairy Tales*. Kent, UK: Crescent Moon Publishing.

_____. 2016. The Triumph of the Underdog: Cinderella's Legacy. In *Cinderella Across Cultures: New Directions and Interdisciplinary Perspectives*, ed. Martine Hennard Dutheil de la Rochère, Gillian Lathey, and Monika Woźniak, pp. 358-401. Detroit: Wayne State University Press.

MASCULINITY AND MEN'S BODIES IN FAIRY TALES: YOUTH, VIOLENCE, AND TRANSFORMATION

ORIGINALLY PUBLISHED IN *MARVELS & Tales: Journal of Fairy-Tale Studies* vol. 32, no. 2, 2018, 338-361.

THE STUDY OF MASCULINITY IN FOLKLORE AND FAIRY TALES, AND in Western scholarship in general, has lagged behind the study of femininity. Only recently emerging as a distinct academic focus, masculinity has long dominated scholarly viewpoints as the default or unmarked norm (as one would expect in patriarchal cultures). In fairy-tale scholarship, too, masculinity has often been treated as an after-thought, beyond the more general concern with topics like heroes. Here, I focus on masculinity not only as a contrasting element to femininity, but also as a complementary aspect of gender construction, in which masculinity and femininity together are viewed as co-constructed parts of a whole sex/gender system. Obviously this, too, is a cultural construction: Western ideas of masculinity and femininity are no more complementary (or dichotomous) than anything else in the world. In this article, I review what has been said about masculinity in Western folk-lore and fairy-tale studies, followed by an analysis of the descriptions of men's bodies in a digitized dataset of canonical fairy tales, and finally by a gender performance-based attempt to locate the gender in men's bodies. My combination of quantitative and qualitative methods, and of feminist theory with masculinity studies, allows for a novel approach to the topic. I posit that masculinity is constructed in fairy tales as contingent and vulnerable, with men susceptible to transformations and judged more by hierarchical values like stature and birth order than women, who tend to be judged by beauty.

The Construction of Masculinity

When feminist folklorists and fairy-tale scholars began investigating gender, they tended to focus on femininity. This was due in part to their sense that folklorists traditionally oriented their studies towards genres and themes that were relevant to men and they did so with the assumption that male was an unmarked category. In their introduction to *Women's Folklore, Women's Culture*, Rosan Jordan and Susan Kalčik criticize folklorists for concentrating on male-oriented public genres and thus ignoring domestic-sphere genres (1985, ix). Thus, feminist folklorists sought to draw scholarly attention to neglected women's genres as part of a corrective agenda. At the same time, feminist theory was introduced into folklore studies as not only a useful but also a transformative approach to studying expressive culture, ideology, and identity. The shift toward studying masculinity and men's folklore as its own subject, not merely as the default, occurred more recently in folkloristics. Joseph P. Goodwin's *More Man than You'll Ever Be: Gay Folklore and Acculturation in Middle America* is an early example (1989) of folklore scholarship on masculinity.

While feminism was beginning to reach folklore studies, masculinity studies was growing in adjacent parts of academia. As R. W. Connell and James W. Messerschmidt write of the field: "In the late 1980s and early 1990s, research on men and masculinity was being consolidated as an academic field" with the attendant publication of journals and textbooks to address this research agenda (2005, 833), all of which took cues and borrowed theories and vocabulary from feminism. Masculinity studies scholar Judith Kegan Gardiner has offered four points of consensus among feminist-inflected masculinity studies, which are helpful for evaluating what masculinity studies can offer folkloristic analyses of masculinity. These are that masculinity is a gender, not just an unmarked state; that masculinity is not a monolithic or static thing; that both/all genders should cooperate in political projects; and that essentialist views of genders should be challenged (2002, 11-12). This cultural constructionist view is largely compatible with that of folklore studies.

Simon Bronner, editor of and contributor to *Manly Traditions*, asserts that "this book is the first to focus on the problem of the construction of manliness in American folklife" (2005, xvi). Bronner disputes the claim of feminist folklorists that men's culture has been thoroughly documented and is correspondingly well understood, stating that the essays in *Manly Traditions* either document previously unnoticed men's cultures or shed new light on men's cultures using the construct of manliness as a critical focus. As might be expected, there is a lot less "feminist" in the version of masculinity studies done by folklorists like Bronner. For the most part, the contributors to *Manly Traditions* seemed to concur with Gardiner's cultural constructivist view of gender, but they are able to do so in a way that connects them to masculinity studies without necessitating an allegiance to feminism. What I perceive as the de-clawing of feminism in most essays in *Manly Traditions* tends to take a simplified view of feminism, which detracts from the important critical work feminism carries out within gender studies. The ways in which feminism gets posited in the book lead me to three specific problems with that volume as an example of masculinity studies: 1) whether masculinity studies is functioning as a backlash against feminism or as a critical enterprise unto itself; 2) whether masculinity studies can be successful without relying on divorcing men from masculinity; and 3) whether an activist dimension is central to masculinity studies. Bronner denies that the studies project is a backlash against feminism; instead, he affirms it is "progress toward fuller consideration of the way that gender is enacted, indeed embodied, in lived experience" (2005, xviii). There is danger, however, that enthusiasm for masculinity too easily slides into nostalgia for the way things were before feminism, as Gardiner asserts in her introduction to *Masculinity Studies & Feminist Theory* (2002, 10).

My goal, then, is to combine the insights from masculinity studies with the rigor of feminist analysis in order to decipher the meanings of masculinity in a folkloristic context, specifically the meanings of masculinity in fairy tales. Existing studies of masculinity in fairy tales fall into three categories: interpretations of these materials from outside an academic disciplinary perspective, observations made by feminist folklorists almost as an afterthought once they have discussed the construction of femininity in fairy tales, and dedicated works on masculinity in folk and fairy tales.

The most popular, and tellingly non-academic, study of masculinity in fairy tales is Robert Bly's *Iron John*, originally published in 1990. Utilizing a mythopoetic perspective, Bly interprets one version of ATU 502 from a particular translation of the Grimms to reveal a story supposedly about manhood and its tribulations. As an example of his universalizing approach, Bly writes about how "we hear from the Iron John story the importance of moving from the mother's realm to the father's realm" (2004, ix). Appropriating anthropological ideas about wounding as a part of initiation rites, Bly explores how the figure of Iron John helps young men navigate masculinity: "The young man investigates or experiences his wound—father wound, mother wound, or shaming-wound—in the presence of this independent, timeless, mythological initiatory being" (36). Lacking any sense of cultural context, Bly's work is nevertheless quite popular. As an example of the feminist response to Bly, Gardiner critiques his work as being "ahistorical, inaccurate, ethnocentric, racist, and sexist" (2002, 102).

And yet Gardiner's reading is more sympathetic than Jack Zipes's reading of Bly in "Spreading Myths about Iron John," in which Zipes provides a model for how folklorists can contribute unique insights to analyzing the men's movement (1994). Zipes's close textual reading of the Grimms' tale under-cuts much of Bly's attempt to claim this story for his purposes. And Zipes, unlike most of the folklorists who contributed to *Manly Traditions*, is explicitly concerned with women's welfare. Zipes reprimands Bly for his falsely homogenizing victimizing efforts, asking:

> But where in his treatise are all the wounds that men
> cause? There is no discussion of the manifold distur-
> bances in family and personal life caused by the devel-
> opment of capitalism; no class, gender, or racial
> distinctions made in Bly's diagnosis of the malaise
> affecting men; no consideration of the economic factors
> of unemployment and bureaucratization that cause
> violence in and outside the family...leaving women
> more victimized since the 1970s than ever before.
> (Ibid 117)

Both Zipes's and Gardiner's critiques of Bly situate the construction of masculinity within a much broader context of gender relations, rather than focusing on the isolated experience of the male character. Masculinity studies ought to examine the construction of male experiences and masculinity in relation to other subjects in order to avoid the misrepresentation of, in Bly's case, the "wounds" of the young man.

Feminist analyses of gender roles in fairy tales have tended to consider masculinity primarily in contrast to femininity, often as it relates to beauty, agency, and behavior. These analyses have also tended to emerge later, and in smaller numbers, than the examinations of femininity. As Ruth Bottigheimer believes: "Male tales...have received short scholarly shrift" (1993, 259). Kay Stone notes the traits of male heroes, who "can be slovenly, unattractive, and lazy, and their success will not be affected" (1975, 44). There is a consensus among critics that the attractiveness of heroes is not as important as the attractiveness of heroines. Maria Tatar writes in *The Hard Facts of the Grimms'*

Fairy Tales: "If the female protagonists of fairy tales are often as good as they are beautiful, their male counterparts generally appear to be as young and naïve as they are stupid" (2003, 87). Thus, physical attractiveness would not seem to be a defining trait in the success of male heroes.

There is also a sense that male characters in fairy tales are more active than female characters. Stone writes: "Heroes succeed because they act, not because they are. They are judged not by their appearance or inherent sweet nature but by their ability to overcome obstacles, even if these obstacles are defects in their own characters" (1975, 45). Marcia Lieberman concurs with the importance of being active for male characters, writing: "Girls win the prize if they are the fairest of them all; boys win if they are bold, active, and lucky" (1972, 385). Related to activity is aggression. Bottigheimer suggests in her study of the masculine tale "The Lazy Boy" that anger and aggressive actions belong solely to the masculine realm: "anger is the prerogative of authority figures, whose authority is often constituted by their maleness" (1993, 287).

Male characters are rewarded for acts of kindness, though the need to be polite and nice does not seem to be as ruthlessly enforced as it is with female characters. Additionally, these acts of kindness are possible because boys are active enough to seek out the opportunities to be kind in the first place. Lieberman notes: "The boy who sets out to seek his fortune ... is a stock figure and, provided that he has a kind heart, is assured of success" (1972, 392). The male protagonists in the Grimms, specifically, do possess compassion for their "natural allies and benefactors" (Tatar 2003, 88). But the compassion is only exerted in certain situations: "If the hero often distinguishes himself by showing mercy for animals, he remains singularly uncharitable when it comes to dealing with human rivals" (90). As with other scholars who discuss gender in fairy tales, Tatar's discussion of masculinity benefits from a comparison to femininity:

> In short, male heroes demonstrate from the start a meekness and humility that qualify them for an ascent to wealth, the exercise of power, and happiness crowned by wedded bliss; their female counterparts undergo a process of humiliation and defeat that ends with a rapid rise in social status through marriage but that also signals a loss of pride and the abdication of power. (94-95)

Male heroes, thus, seem to suffer less than their female counterparts, and their trajectory moves from lesser to greater agency, not necessarily the case in classic tales about heroines. These classic tales, of course, are not a universal set; tales written by women in seventeenth-century France and nineteenth-century Germany, for instance, vary in tone from those by the Grimm brothers, which Tatar is primarily focusing on here. Other male characters are not described in such charitable terms; Tatar notes "the ease with which men slip into the role of beasts ... the seeming interchangeability of man and beast" (ibid 170). As feminist scholar Susan Bordo has noted, tales of beastly bridegrooms contribute to the double bind of masculinity enforced for men: ideal men "have the sexual charisma of an untamed beast and are unbeatable in battle, but are intelligent, erudite, and gentle with women" (1999, 242).

Three works that specifically address masculinity in fairy tales from the perspective of culturally situated ethnography, disability, and symbolism are worth noting. One of the few works specifically on masculinity in folk and fairy tales is *The Bear and His Sons: Masculinity in Spanish and Mexican Folktales* by James Taggart. He utilizes folk narrative repertoires with life histories, ethnographic observations, and psychoanalytic theories to analyze how masculinity is represented in Spanish-language folktales. Taggart regards the stock protagonist Little John, as "obviously a symbol of manliness, and his story is a metaphor for the transformation of an unruly boy into a controlled man who is ready for marriage" (1997, 35). In *Disability, Deformity, and Disease in the Grimms' Fairy Tales*, Ann Schmiesing examines men's bodies in fairy tales specifically in the context of disability and disease in the Grimms' tales, combining theoretical tools from disability studies with folklore studies. She notes that many disabled male characters appear in the Grimms' collection, "in part because disability is a frequent attribute of male characters depicted as underdogs" (2014, 82). Examples include the Frog King, multiple instances of wounded soldiers, and monstrous births such as Hans My Hedgehog and characters who are reduced in physical stature (like Thumbling) or mental capacity (like Dummy characters). Notably, Schmiesing spends the most time scrutinizing men's bodies in the tales, bodies that are depicted in ableist terms both to inspire audience sympathy and to enforce a normalizing effect. Francisco Vaz da Silva, though he does not specifically discuss masculinity as a topic in *Metamorphosis: The Dynamics of Symbolism in European Fairy Tales*, has written much about the ways in which men's and women's bodies both undergo transformations in fairy tales. Vaz da Silva, like his feminist counterparts, has spent considerably more time discussing the constructions of feminine bodies. However, particular traits of male bodies emerge from Vaz da Silva's study. Men are more likely in European folk belief and folk narrative to turn into werewolves, and to require disenchantment by dismemberment, sacrifice, and bleeding (2002, 44). In Vaz da Silva's view, the werewolf is equivalent to the masculine body since a tail symbolizes a penis. Although Vaz da Silva spends far less time discussing male attractiveness than female attractiveness, he notes that golden hair, attractive attire, and recognizable markings, often on the legs or feet, are all part of the bundle of traits to be expected in European fairy-tale heroes.

Based on these scholarly explorations of male fairy-tale figures, one would expect to find male characters that are active, somewhat attractive (but with less of an emphasis on male attractiveness than on female attractiveness), and some combination of kind, simple, and humble. Yet male characters are also expected to be more aggressive than female characters, and perhaps more prone to violence. Some sorts of transformations, perhaps enabled by dismemberment or blood, would also be common. These traits, while contradictory, form the basis for the explorations of my dataset in the section following an explanation of my methods.

Men's Bodies in Digitized Dataset: Methods

My larger project utilizes 233 fairy tales, spanning 6 collections, to arrive at a sense of gendered bodies in fairy tales. The dataset I hand-coded into a spreadsheet consists of 11,144 entries, 5,453 of which describe female bodies, and 4,879 of which describe male bodies (the remaining 812 are either gender neutral or implicate both genders). Here, I address which nouns, adjectives, and actions or themes co-occur most with men's bodies, and I suggest what they mean in light of the criticism from feminists, folklorists, and masculinity studies scholars discussed above.

In order to get a representative sample of the way bodies appear in classical fairy tales, I chose to work with six tale collections, spanning the early modern and contemporary periods, and folk and literary sources. That said, this study can mostly account for these texts' contemporary translations, as translations are always a reflection of the period in which the text was translated; as a major example, the *Arabian Nights* reads quite differently depending on not only the era of its translation into French or English but also the individual translator, and the implications for depictions of gender and sexuality vary accordingly. The choice of texts to translate also has cultural, possibly exoticizing, connotations. Lawrence Venuti writes: "patterns of selecting texts for translation tend to be informed by literary canons in the receiving culture where the decision to translate is usually made" (163) and these decisions can lean towards texts that are foreign on the surface, but actually hew close to the receiving culture's values. Individual translators' choices to assimilate rather than exoticize a text thus come into play, making the task at hand one that requires some caveats.

My six chosen texts are: *Beauties, Beasts, and Enchantment: Classic French Fairy Tales* translated by Jack Zipes (covering the classical French tradition from the 1690s onward), *The Collected Fairy Tales of the Brothers Grimm* translated by Jack Zipes (based on the 1857 edition of the Grimms' tales), *Italian Popular Tales* compiled and translated by Thomas Crane and edited by Jack Zipes (spanning Italian literary and folk tales mostly from the 1800s), *Folktales of France* edited and translated by Geneviève Massignon (tales that she collected in the 1950s), *Folktales of Germany* edited and translated by Kurt Ranke (compiled from fieldwork collections from approximately 1850-1950), and *Folk-lore by the Fireside* by Alessandro Falassi (tales that he collected in Tuscany in the 1970s and translated). Keeping in mind Kathleen Ragan's admonition that any "study that attempts to draw conclusions about the folktale or culture from the folk-tale but does not consider gender in the compilation of the data set can also be considered compromised" (2009, 238), I chose my collections with an eye toward those that specified that they included female narrators when they were based on fieldwork, and also encoded data about the gender of the taleteller or author, collector, editor, and protagonist (though I do not utilize that contextual information in this article, instead focusing on the content of the tales).

While I attempted to prioritize collections that had been translated by folklorists, translation practices remain a complex and sometimes contentious topic. For example, Anne Duggan has stated that Zipes drew on Planché's much older translation of literary French fairy-tale texts into English for his *Beauties, Beasts, and Enchantments*, which complicates any uncritical use of these as English-language texts (2001; 2018). Christine Jones makes a compelling case for careful translation of canonical texts such as Charles Perrault's *Histoires ou Contes du tempes passé*, noting that every retelling of a tale also rein-vents the story: "Every time another teller, writer, or cine-matographer reimagines [Cinderella], it benefits from creative insight—they are all 'translators,' that is to say, writers of the tale" (2016, 19). My study relies on the status of translations as new versions of tales in order to link Anglophone versions of the tales with English-language visions of masculinity, though other studies might work closer with a given linguistic textu-ality or cultural context in order to derive different insights. In other words, English-language versions of classical fairy tales are already circulating and exerting an influence, and deserve to be understood based on their own language and merits, though I contend that they likely also share body-part motifs and descriptions with their analogues in other languages. Classical status is, of course, retrospectively bestowed, and thus this study makes no claims about tales that might have had classical status in their own time periods.

From each collection I worked with tales of magic, ATU types 300-749, extracting all descriptions of bodies and body parts to hand-code into my dataset for analysis. Similar to the word count method Ruth Bottigheimer used to ascertain who has access to speech (and hence power) in the Grimms collection (1986) and to the quantitative analysis of nouns and adjectives Alessandra Levorato used to reach ideological understandings of gender and power in a dozen English-language versions of "Little Red Riding Hood" (2003), this project represents a first step toward pairing feminist interpretative methods with empirical counts of gendered language in a large corpus of tales. While ever-more sophisticated computational methods of studying folkloric materials continue to evolve (see, for instance, Tangherlini 2016), I chose to focus on word counts. Like Bottigheimer and Levorato, I posit that the repetition of and associations with words (and the values implicitly assigned them) throughout a text can and will add up to an impression in the audience. I regard my study as a simple but necessary initial step in establishing empirical patterns in the descriptions of gendered bodies in fairy tales, and future research should of course move beyond this project's scope in terms of orientation to translation and cultural context, computational methods used, reader response data, and so on.

Quantitative Descriptions of Men's Bodies

This section deals primarily with nouns, adjectives, and themes (actions that happened to or with bodies, such as deaths or transformations, that did not fit easily into the category of either noun or adjective, but are still noteworthy) relating to men and masculinity. Of the nouns, some are used solely with men, and never with women. These include "beard" (56 mentions), "leg" (20), "dwarf" (16), "humpback" (11), "corpse" (6), "nails" (6), "tongues" (5), "spirits" (4), "chest" (4), "human" (4), "sockets" (14), "gut" (3), "souls" (3), "deformity" (3), "fist" (3), "cheek" (3), "organs," (3), "deformities" (2), "necks," (2), "nostrils" (2), "deaths" (2), "half" (2), "handful" (2), "hunger" (2), "mark" (2), "nostril" (2), and other words that only appear once. None of these words are sex-specific, including "organs," which in English vernacular can be used to refer to male genitals (but that is not the case with the usage in these texts). The appearance of the word "organs" here also comes with a caveat, as it only appears in one tale, "The Three Army Surgeons" (ATU 660) in the Grimms' collection. One could make the case that beards tend to occur more on men than on women, though it is not impossible for women—especially those who have a hormone imbalance—to grow beards. Here, though, it seems that beards are framed as culturally masculine.

Other nouns in my dataset appear with both women and men, but predominantly with men, so they are worth noting here. For the purposes of this investigation, I am considering words that appear with men at least 60% of the time to be a predominantly man-associated word. These words include: "head" (169 mentions, 66.80% with men), "death" (91, 61.49%), "youth" (81, 86.17%), "shoulders" (37, 71.15%), "back" (36, 76.60%), "form" (32, 64%), "body" (31, 68.89%), "legs" (29, 65.91%), "arm" (28, 68.29%), "knees" (22, 61.11%), "shoulder"

(22, 88%), "ear" (21, 84%), "bones" (20, 68.97%), "heads" (19, 73.08%), "ears" (16, 66.67%), "hairs" (13, 72.22%), "wounds" (10, 76.92%), "beating" (10, 76.92%), and others with fewer than 10 mentions each. The nouns in this group and the last group are the pillars of the body: people stand on their "leg"/ "legs," supported by joints like the "knees" and "shoulder"/ "shoulders," with their "head"/"heads" (centers of cognition) resting atop a "back," "chest," "necks," and "bones." The associative images are ones of strength and capability. These body parts also provide a three-dimensional image of men, suggesting that men are fleshed out, whole persons. At the same time, violated and disfigured bodies appear: men are more likely than women to have "wounds" or take a "beating" or to experience "death," while men exclusively have "deformity"/"deformities" or a "mark," and men are exclusively relegated to the status of "humpback," "corpse," and "dwarf" (at least, in the texts used here; bad women in other fairy-tale texts, such as those by d'Aulnoy, are given humpbacks and deformities). Body nouns that refer to men thus either uphold the ideal of normative masculinity—strong and capable—or point out its deficiencies and failings.

The adjectival descriptions connected with men in my database are also indicative of the construction of masculinity in fairy tales. There are 93 adjectives associated solely with men (and 88 adjectives shared between women and men, and 93 adjectives associated solely with women). Here I list those that occur more than twice. These adjectives include "gray-haired" (8 mentions), "handsomest" (7), "horrible" (5), "drunk" (4), "hoary" (3), "strongest," (3), "best-looking" (2), "crippled," (2), "curly" (2), "fiery" (2), "green" (2), "healthy" (2), "inhuman" (2), "kindhearted" (2), "poorer" (2), "sound" (2), "sturdy" (2), "swollen" (2), "tiny" (2), "vigorous" (2), and "wretched" (2). Only a few of these adjectives function to evaluate physical appearance; rather, they seem more concerned with health (or lack thereof) or moral evaluation.

The adjectives that appear predominantly with men—at least 60% of the time—are also worth noting. They include: "young" (326 mentions, 62.10% with men), "little" (262, 62.17%), "handsome" (114, 94.21%), "rich" (35, 83.33%), "human" (20, 60.61%), "strong" (19, 83.36%), "gray" (16, 94.12%), "fat" (14, 93.33%), "sick" (11, 61.11%), "right" (10, 83.33%), and others with fewer than 10 mentions each. There is only one subjective adjective in this bunch, "handsome;" the rest can be fairly objectively used to describe a person's state of being. This contrasts with the high number of physical evaluative words that were used exclusively or predominantly with women. Some of these words do correspond to a physical state, but they imply less judgment and more fact. There are also fewer moral evaluative words used with men than with women; women were more often than men described as "wicked," "wise," or "evil," while men are described as "kind-hearted" or "evil-hearted," descriptions that appear with men only twice and once respectively, as opposed to the higher numbers of "wicked," "wise," and "evil" descriptions of women. The implication is that men's moral status requires less qualification than that of women: men more than women can be assumed to be average in this area, since they do not require special descriptions to tell how exactly they deviate from the norm. This is another instance of the normalization of masculinity in fairy tales.

The adjectives that tend to cluster around men emphasize physical abilities and objectively assessable states of being. Strength and health appear to be important to masculinity, while being handsome is also an asset. However, while for women there are many adjectives assessing physical attractiveness, the list for men is limited to "handsome," "handsomest," "handsomer," "good-looking," and "best-looking" (the last three with less than five mentions each). Here, it is also important to note that English differentiates between "beautiful" and "handsome" in gendered ways, whereas in other languages (like French), the distinction is less important; this is another reason to take into account the nuances of working in translation. The first three of these adjectives are all variations on the same word, and the latter two are quite similar in structure. Men's stature is more likely to be commented on, as men are more than twice as likely to be described as "little" than as "handsome." The word "little" is used in different contexts, with various meanings. Sometimes "little" connotes extreme age or extreme youth, as with the many instances of little old men or little boys. In "The Seven-Headed Monster" in Massignon's collection, the protagonist is "a small boy all crippled and hunched" (1968, 34) who leaves home, and from then on is referred to as "the little cowman" since he herds the king's cows (ibid 35). In some cases, "little" helps reinforce the supernatural identity of a particular tale role as in the Grimms' tale "The Gnome" in which "a tiny little gnome" (2003, 308) is both antagonist and helper to the huntsman protagonist. This also holds true for supernaturally small protagonists, such as "Thumbling" in the Grimms, whose parents wished for a child "even if it were tiny and no bigger than my thumb" (ibid 132). "Little" is also used to describe relative age, as in "The Brother Who Was a Lamb" in Massignon's collection, where the girl is reluctant to leave her brother once a king offers to marry her: "I do not want to leave my little brother, the lamb" (1968, 143). Words relating to relative age within a family fittingly connect to one of the main themes of fairy tales, as the genre is concerned with the fragmentation and formation of families.

The preoccupation with size is peculiar, as it only extends to the diminutive end of the spectrum. Where "little" appears with gendered bodies 422 times in my dataset (262 with men, 160 with women), "big" appears only 26 times (15 with women, 11 with men). As discussed above, "little" is an efficient way of describing a protagonist, antagonist, or helper figure as notable due to age (its presence or lack) or supernaturally diminished stature. By the same token, one might expect that "big" would be used to differentiate characters occupying different roles, but this is not the case. Why does the adjective "small" appear so much more than "big," and why is it linked with men? I would argue that smallness, in addition to being a physical description linked to age and familial categories, is also a way to indicate powerlessness. Fairy tales are essentially about the transfer of power from old characters to the young. Many (male) protagonists begin as "little" boys or youths, and must make their way into the world and acquire power. Their lack of both stature and might is inscribed on their bodies with the adjective "little," in such a way that their physical beings are defined in relation to their quest for control and strength. Conversely, many of the (male) helpers and antagonists who are described as "little" display a disproportionate amount of strength and power, thus calling attention to the uneven distribution of power in fairy tales in translation.

Certain nouns and adjectives support the affiliation of men with violent acts. The nouns "wounds" and "beating" both appear more with men than with women, as they are each mentioned 10 times with men, and only 3 times with women. The noun "corpse," indicating that violence may have taken place, appears exclusively with men (six times total). Even words that only appear rarely, such as "cut" or "cuts" (one mention each), appear in connection with men. The adjective "wounded" is only used once, but with a man. The adjective "blind," appearing seven times with men and three times with women, often has overtones of violence, as in Massignon's "The Two Brothers" (ATU 613) in which one youth blinds the other so that they can both benefit from the money obtained from begging.

The other theme significantly associated with men is that of transformation. I had to treat this bodily happening as a theme, in addition to a noun in its own right, because not every description of a magical transformation included the word "transformation" (more often, a verb was used, such as "transformed," "became," or "turned into"). The theme "transformation" occurred with men 196 times (to women's 77 times), while the actual noun "transformation" was used with men 4 times and with women 3 times. Statistically, the theme "transformation" is very important for men: it occurs with men 71.79% out of all times it refers to a gendered body. Simply put, men are transformed into other shapes more than women are in this sample of fairy tales.

To summarize this exploration of male bodies in my dataset, physical stature and youth (or their lack) are two of the most frequently commented on traits of male bodies. As I posited above, the regularity of the adjective "little" may reinforce the scholarly notion that many male heroes are rewarded for being meek and mild at the tale's outset. Many of the adjectives applied to male bodies are less concerned with subjective evaluations of physical attractiveness than with establishing where a male body fits in relation to the norm: whether he is healthy or ill, hunch-backed, or strong (it is worth noting that these norms are sometimes applied to female characters too, as in Basile's and d'Aulnoy's tales). The lack of emphasis on beauty for men ("handsome" was mentioned as the top attractiveness adjective 114 times with men, compared with "beauty" as the top attractiveness adjective mentioned 418 times with women) corresponds to the scholarly hypothesis that physical appearance is less of an indicator of fairy-tale success for men than for women. One important point revealed by the empirical data is that violence, death, and transformation, significant factors in men's bodily experiences in fairy tales, are mentioned explicitly far less frequently in the tales' texts than beauty (the most significant theme for women) is. Violence (including death, dismemberment, and beatings) and transformations are themes that coalesce around male bodies in fairy tales, leading to the impression that the men's existence is contingent and fraught, a notion I investigate below.

Performance-based Analysis: Where is the Gender in Men's Bodies?

If one of the tenets of both feminist theory and masculinity studies is that men "have" gender as much as women do, then where is it located? How do men perform their gender? In this section, I analyze the constructions of masculinity in the tales in my dataset, applying insights from gender performance theory, other feminist theories, and masculinity studies, in an attempt to understand the conventions by which masculinity is normalized. The topics I explore in this section include the invisibility of masculinity, the anonymity that characterizes male fairy-tale characters, and the erasure of signs of male power.

One of the characteristics of idealized or hegemonic masculinity—the masculinity that men must try to live up to in their behaviors, even if attempting to enact a perfected ideal is doomed to fail—is that it is self-apparent, so obvious in its rightness as to be invisible. Of course, this rightness or natural- ness is not in fact natural at all, and must be brought about through cultural means. Where idealized femininity is natural- ized by symbolically becoming natural, idealized masculinity is naturalized by becoming transparent or undetectable. This strategy is reflected in how male bodies make up slightly less than half of the overall body count in the fairy tales in my dataset (even though the tales were evenly split between male and female protagonists according to my count). Also, as seen above, fewer words to evaluate physical attractiveness or morality are used with men than with women; this implies that there is less to think about regarding the male body. However, the above statements are the case when looking at the data set as a whole rather than breaking down materials according to national traditions; since masculinity is culturally constructed, it follows that it will be constructed differently in different social and historical contexts. On the whole, though, there is less to look at, less to judge, than with women's bodies. It is as though men simply are. This is reminiscent of Simone de Beauvoir's observation that women are the marked sex, the Other, in contrast to the normal, unmarked male iden- tity. As Elizabeth Grosz describes this phenomenon, "a corpo- real 'universal' has in fact functioned as a veiled representation and projection of a masculine which takes itself as the unquestioned norm, the ideal representative without any idea of the violence that this representational positioning does to others" (1994, 188). One of the cultural mechanisms by which this comes about, then, is the obscuring of male bodies in fairy tales: there are slightly fewer of them, and the descrip- tions attached to them seem more objective, requiring less evaluation.

Visibility and power have been linked in folklore and patri-archal culture more generally, so it is not surprising that masculinity is rendered less visible in many fairy tales. As Alan Dundes points out regarding American worldview, but with some references to Western worldview more generally, sight is the predominant sense referred to and respected within American folklore, conferring legitimacy and legibility (1980). Literary critic Peter Brooks discusses the importance of the gaze in structuring literary desire: "The relation to another body is repeatedly presented in visual terms, and the visual as applied to the body is often highly eroticized, a gaze subtended by desire" (1993, 11). Brooks goes on to write that paradoxically, in literature, history, and culture, the male body is both the norm and that which is veiled from inquiry. Brooks hypothesizes that the male nude body symbolizes the heroic, while the female nude "seems to be an object of male erotic looking from nearly the beginning" (ibid 17). As the female body is constructed as an object of male desire, the male body recedes farther from view. Being able to observe rather than be observed is thus an expression of (gendered) power in the West. More attention to cultural context and differences is, of course, needed; as Lewis Seifert observes in *Manning the Margins*, "men too can be and are 'marked'" (2009 17) in seventeenth-century French literature and culture. And, as Duggan notes in *Salonnières, Furies, and Fairies: The Politics of Gender and Cultural Change in Absolutist France*, d'Aulnoy's tales in particular posit that men and women can and should be intellectual equals (2005 chapter 6), and that men should beautify themselves for the pleasure of their female partners (Ibid 217-218).

Accompanying the pleasure and power inherent in being the gazer rather than the gazed-upon is the construction of the gazer as a whole, three-dimensional subject. As feminist film critic Laura Mulvey has observed: "In a world ordered by sexual imbalance, pleasure in looking has been split between active/male and passive/female" 1999, 838). In film, this happens through techniques such as camera angle and how much of the body is shown, as well as the conventions of identifying with characters in a film. Mulvey writes: "In contrast to woman as icon, the active male figure...demands a three-dimensional space" (ibid 838). While many of her observations in that essay are specific to the visual context of film, the mechanisms of identification and erotic power she describes are present in many expressive forms of Western culture including, I would contend, the fairy tale. This is especially evident in the body part nouns that cluster around men: they are the trunks and limbs, the substantial body parts that make characters seem three-dimensional, both metaphorically and literally. According to the size and allotment of body parts (limbs over extremities, for instance), male characters take up more space than female characters do. Their increased three-dimensionality is part of the construction of men as more substantial, more human, than women. However, as the three-dimensionality of male tale characters' bodies is not something that is obvious on the surface or in the texts of the tales, it is yet another example of the usefulness of empirical methods to get a more nuanced understanding of body parts in fairy tales.

In a related turn, masculinity is also more likely to be framed in such a way that male characters are idealized to the point of appearing anonymous or interchangeable with one another. Tatar writes: "Most people may be at a loss when it comes to naming fairy-tale heroes, but few have trouble characterizing them" (2003, 85). She goes on to list these characters as active, adventurous, and so on. However, she notices in the

Grimms collection, "If there is any attribute that these heroes share, it is naiveté" (ibid 86). These men, then, are literally a blank slate. Additionally, the male characters in tales with female protagonists are hardly described: Cinderella's prince "remains a colorless figure. The tale tells us nothing more about him than that he is the son of a king. Lacking a history, a story, and even a name, he is reduced to the function of prince-rescuer waiting in the wings for his cue" (ibid 92). With such blank male characters, they might as well be interchangeable, cogs in a happily-ever-after machine.

For all the male characters that appear to conform to an ideal and elude the gaze, there are male characters that are aberrations, drawing attention, and they also function to uphold a certain vision of masculinity. On the surface, many of the male bodies that appear deformed are that way in order to serve obvious narrative functions. Little gray old men and dwarves serve as clear-cut donor figures or villains, while being given a hump or a humpback is a punishment for an antagonist, as is the case in many of the Grimms' tales. Cristina Bacchilega, focusing on the female protagonists in various Bluebeard (ATU 312) retellings, notes that the villainous husband is often Othered through bodily means: "he is also a mysterious being who usually presents himself as a rich man with a beard, be it blue or green, or a silver nose in an Italian version, as the visible clue to his otherness" (1997, 109-110). In this case, the male character's body contains the markings that reveal his monstrous identity and hint at the danger he poses to the heroine and humankind. This follows Schmiesing's observation that "Disability and deformity are of course markers not only of the outcast underdog but also of wicked characters" (2014, 140) of both genders.

However, even where fairy-tale men are acknowledged to

be monstrous, as with Bluebeard, the focus is shifted away from the monstrosity of their actions, and onto other aspects of the narrative. Both critics of the tale "Bluebeard" (such as Bettelheim) and writers of certain versions of the tale (especially Perrault) shift the focus to judging the heroine's actions, namely her curiosity in violating the interdiction to open the forbidden chamber, resulting in what Bacchilega calls "an explicit condemnation of the heroine's curiosity, but total silence on the ethics of the husband's serial murders" (1997, 106). At the same time, certain versions of "Bluebeard" such as Perrault's implicitly critique Bluebeard's violence precisely by exaggerating the severity of his actions, compounded by Orientalized and feminized traits that attach to the body and behavior of Bluebeard himself (Duggan 2005, 156-163). In many versions of "Bluebeard" and the accompanying criticism, there are thus both textual and metatextual strategies for displacing the husband's transgressive behavior onto the wife, downplaying the threatening consequences of his masculinity.

Another of the ways in which the construction of fairy-tale masculinity is obscured is by divorcing monstrous behavior from monstrous bodies. Greenhill has observed of the antagonist Fitcher in the Grimms' "Fitcher's Bird" (ATU 311) that despite his being a serial murderer, "Fitcher's own body is unremarked and apparently unremarkable" (2008, 163). This is in contrast to the heroine and her dismembered (and then re-membered and revived) sisters: "Those who appear to inhabit the grotesque and the marvelous (the women) actually embody the non-monstrous, while those who appear ordinary (the men) are authentically fiendish" (ibid 163-164). The same principle applies in related tales with fiendish male characters whose bodily presence is downplayed. For instance, in the Grimms' "The Robber Bridegroom" (ATU 955), the cannibalistic bridegroom is obviously the antagonist of the tale, and yet one of the only mentions of his body—or any male body in the whole tale—is at the very end, when "he and his whole band were executed for their shameful crimes" (Grimm and Grimm 2003, 145). The other time a male body appears in the tale is when the old woman whose intervention saves the heroine says, "When they have you in their power, they'll chop you to pieces without mercy. Then they'll cook you and eat you, because they're cannibals" (ibid 143). The men are classified as cannibals, but that is all there is to them in terms of physical description. Instead, there are descriptions of the robbers giving a female victim wine until "her heart burst in two. Then they tore off her fine clothes, put her on a table, chopped her beautiful body to pieces, and sprinkled the pieces with salt" (ibid 143). Women's bodies are described in great detail in this tale, made into a gruesome spectacle, and yet the bodies inflicting the harm are hardly mentioned.

However, I believe the phenomenon of shifting the focus away from male bodies and male power also extends to tales with male characters that are less obviously monstrous. This occurs more subtly in one of the three Grimms' versions of "The Maiden Who Seeks Her Brothers" (ATU 451) titled "The Six Swans." When the heroine, who has taken a vow of silence while attempting to redeem her transformed brothers, is wedded to a king, the king's mother begins causing trouble for her. The king's body is only mentioned once, when the silent heroine's beauty "moved the king's heart, and he fell deeply in love with her" (2003, 170). Yet much is made of the king's "evil mother" (ibid 170), and her tactics to dishonor the heroine by stealing the children she gives birth to and smearing "the queen's mouth with blood while she was asleep" (ibid 170). Ultimately, the evil mother's ploy causes the king to be forced to send the heroine to a court, which condemns her to death. Throughout all of this, the person who is ostensibly the most powerful in the land—the king—is the least embodied narratively, while a spectacle is made of the powerless heroine. This may be a recent phenomenon; as Susan Bordo notes, "Modernity has been especially squeamish, it seems, about the male body" (1999, 26). The king, who should be able to protect his young wife, is instead rendered powerless by his "evil mother" (who is also repeatedly called an "old woman," conflating villainy with age). This is thus another instance in which a man whose actions (or in this case inaction) can harm women is not depicted as having a notable body or features; rather, the women are more embodied, more fully realized, almost as though to displace the blame for the harm onto them.

Displacing blame from men's actions and men's bodies occurs in many other tale types, and can be said to be a general pattern in classical Western fairy tales. In many French versions of "Beauty and the Beast" (ATU 425C), Jack Zipes notes: "The male protagonist is never responsible for the world being out of joint. Each tale depicts him as a victim (generally transfigured by a wicked female fairy)" (2006, 41). Maria Tatar has observed that generally in fairy tales "Even when they violate basic codes of morality and decency, fathers remain noble figures, who rarely commit premeditated acts of evil" (1992, 151). Some fathers do harm their daughters through their actions, but as Marina Warner argues, their influence has been lessened over time. Tracing the shifts in the Grimms' collection and others, Warner states: "Wicked fathers gradually drop from view in the fairytale tradition" (1994, 347). Warner attributes these changes to contextual shifts in what was deemed appropriate for fairy-tale audiences.

To return to the question with which I opened this section: where is the gender located in men's bodies? Only a handful of body part nouns or adjectives correspond specifically to men, such as "beard" and "handsome"; rather, a discursive field of forced objectification through violence and transformations seem to constitute masculinity. As Schmiesing observes in tales about transformed male characters, "transformation is a disabling deformation that circumscribes a character's agency" (2014, 100). However, gender plays a significant role in terms of how said agency is narrated. In contrast to often-passive female protagonists like the Maiden without Hands, the Frog King in the Grimms' collection

> grows more embodied, with far greater attention drawn to his experience of his body and his unwillingness to be stigmatized because of it. The frog is typical of male protagonists insofar as he is rewarded for pushing against adversity rather than silently and piously accepting it. (Schmiesing 2014, 108)

Violence against men follows narrative patterns, whereas the violence men do to women is practically obscured, which helps to conceal men's responsibility in perpetuating violence. Men's bodies are more three-dimensional than women's, filled out by the depiction of limbs rather than extremities, yet also more invisible in terms of their being the norm. Paradoxical though this sounds, this is often how culture works, depicting charged or contentious issues as refracted through an array of competing messages. This is certainly the case with femininity in different eras; the contradictory messages aimed at women have nonetheless expressed a unified ideology of oppression. Overall, the location of gender in men's bodies is slippery and fluid: men are not aligned with the body or nature in the same way that women are, though the size of their body (their "littleness" or lack thereof) defines their prospects of success. This can be attributed to the invisibility that masculinity and its position of power have occupied in the West. Initially, I was unsure whether this pattern would be replicated within fairy tales, as the more fantastic genres of expressive culture often express subversion and wish fulfillment, but now I feel confident that this is in fact the case with the translated tales I examined.

Perhaps more importantly, I have also found it nigh impossible to discuss the construction of masculinity without also discussing femininity. This situation may have emerged since prior feminist scholarship has paved the way for a nuanced dialogue about femininity while the dialogue on masculinity is still evolving; I believe this perceived complementarity is also caused by the inherent characteristics of the construction masculinity and femininity. Note that the inherent characteristics of the construction of masculinity and femininity differ from the inherent characteristics of masculinity and femininity themselves; I do not believe that the latter exists, as gender roles are culturally constructed. They may exhibit similarities over time and space, but these are due to contact and diffusion rather than sharing an essential, universal, unchanging identity (much the same way that there is little if any folklore that is universal or unchanging; rather, it spreads and adapts to local culture). As Bordo writes: "Our bodies, no less than anything else that is human, are constituted by culture" (2003, 142). Masculinity and femininity, as human constructs are interdependent concepts evident in this corpus of Western

European tales; it is difficult to refer to one without implicitly invoking the other. This, I would argue, is even more the case with masculinity than with femininity, for femininity is constructed as natural, contained within itself, having been marked in easily identified and signified ways. In contrast, masculinity is more likely to be constructed in relation to femininity, to constitute that which femininity lacks, which requires a reference to femininity as lack.

Conclusions

Hegemonic masculinity functions in part through establishing male bodies as the unmarked norm, the "normal" to which all bodies should aspire, and by which all bodies are measured. The male bodies explored in this article reveal a surprisingly contingent, vulnerable construction of masculinity. Men are subject to transformations (some voluntary, some involuntary), and death and violence of all kinds. More is said about the violence men receive than the violence men do to others—which is an inversion of the real world, where the bulk of violence is committed by men and masculine institutions.

In future research, finding ways to measure the violence done to and by bodies in fairy tales might prove fruitful. Based on what I was able to observe, however, these patterns in the representation of violence are congruent with larger social patterns: in eras when social change occurs, ruling classes lash out at those who appear to be eroding their privilege. In the same way, violence against women, both physical and discursive, increases when women gain more rights and freedoms. Bordo, along with other feminists, has suggested that anxiety over women's bodies and hungers "appears to peak, as well, during periods when women are becoming independent and are asserting themselves politically and socially" (2003, 161). I suggest that the same trend occurs in fairy tales, which began to crystallize as a genre around early modernity: the time of the Enlightenment, which transitioned to the Romantic era, the age of nationalism, and so on. These time periods witnessed heavy anxieties about the role of the person in society, especially if that person was perceived as gendered (i.e. feminine). Suzanne Magnanini is one of the authors to suggest that "The birth of the literary fairy tale was, then, a monstrous birth, and like all anomalous parturitions of that time, it was greeted with a combination of horror, pleasure, and repugnance" (2008, 6) and that the monstrous bodies in the fairy tales of Straparola and Basile – often gendered – function to create and uphold binaristic hierarchies.

However, this is not to suggest that patriarchal power was never disputed, or only disputed in recent movements that self-identified as feminist. Indeed, Duggan urges scholars to view gender politics according to the nuances of their respective time periods, such as situating the early modern French debate over the status of women in epistemologically appropriate terms (2018). Qualifying this statement as needed according to cultural context, I would suggest that men, whose power over women in early modern and modern Europe was significant, would narratively construct their power as contingent and themselves at risk, needing to justify their expansions of power (see Tucker 2003 for an account of such a struggle in early modern France). This was most likely not a conscious colonization of the fairy-tale or folktale genres, but rather a process whereby people were more likely to tell and retell those stories that narratively presented and solved conflicts that resonated with them. Women storytellers and authors, naturally, have pushed back against this dynamic in multiple ways, which is a topic to be considered in future research.

Another important facet of my research on fairy-tale masculinity was informed by taking a quantitative approach to the materials. The complementary nature of quantitative and qualitative methods is evident; for instance, in only counting explicitly-named body parts, I might have missed the importance of transformation and death to the construction of men's bodies in fairy tales. By putting quantitative and qualitative methods in dialogue, we can illuminate the implicit patterning of gender in folkloric materials such as fairy tales, and thus bring to light the hidden ways in which masculinity shapes lived experience and is expressed in folklore.

REFERENCES:

Bacchilega, Cristina. *Postmodern Fairy Tales*. Philadelphia: University of Pennsylvania Press, 1997.

Bly, Robert. *Iron John: A Book About Men*. 2nd edition. Cambridge, Massachusetts: De Capo Press, 2004.

Bordo, Susan. *Unbearable Weight: Feminism, Western Culture, and the Body*. Berkeley: University of California Press, 2003 [1993].

---. *The Male Body: A New Look at Men in Public and Private*. New York: Farrar, Straus and Giroux, 1999.

Bottigheimer, Ruth. "Silenced Women in the Grimms' Tales: The 'Fit' Between Fairy Tales and Society in Their Historical Context." *Fairy Tales and Society: Illusion, Allusion, and*

Paradigm. Ed. Ruth Bottigheimer. Philadelphia: U of Pennsylvania P, 1986. 115-131.

---. "Luckless, Witless, and Filthy-Footed: A Sociocultural
Study and Publishing History Analysis of 'The Lazy Boy.'" *The
Journal of American Folklore* 106.421 (1993): 259-84.

Bronner, Simon J. "Introduction." *Manly Traditions: The Folk
Roots of American Masculinities.* Ed. Simon J. Bronner. Bloomington: Indiana UP, 2005. xi-xxv.

Brooks, Peter. *Body Work: Objects of Desire in Modern Narrative.*
Cambridge, Massachusetts and London, England: Harvard UP,
1993.

Connell, R. W. and James W. Messerschmidt. "Hegemonic
Masculinity: Rethinking the Concept." *Gender and Society* 19.6
(2005): 829-859.

Crane, Thomas. *Italian Popular Tales.* Ed. and with an introduction by Jack Zipes. Santa Barbara, Denver, and Oxford: ABC-
CLIO, Inc, 2001 [1885].

Duggan, Anne. "Nature and Culture in the Fairy Tale of
Marie-Catherine d'Aulnoy." *Marvels & Tales* 15.2 (2001):
149-167.

---. *Salonnières, Furies, and Fairies: The Politics of Gender and
Cultural Change in Absolutist France.* Newark: University of
Delaware Press, 2005.

---. Personal communication with the author. 24 February

2018. E-mail.

Dundes, Alan. "Seeing is Believing." *Interpreting Folklore*. Bloomington: Indiana UP, 1980. 86-92.

Falassi, Alessandro. *Folklore by the Fireside: Text and Context of the Tuscan Veglia*. Austin: University of Texas Press, 1980.

Gardiner, Judith Kegan. "Introduction." *Masculinity Studies & Feminist Theory: New Directions*, Ed. Judith Kegan Gardiner. New York: Columbia University Press, 2002. 1-29.

---. "Theorizing Age and Gender: Bly's Boys, Feminism, and Maturity Masculinity." *Masculinity Studies & Feminist Theory: New Directions*. Ed. Judith Kegan Gardiner. New York: Columbia University Press, 2002. 90-118.

Goodwin, Joseph. *More Man than You'll Ever Be: Gay Folklore and Acculturation in Middle America*. Bloomington & Indianapolis: Indiana UP, 1989.

Greenhill, Pauline. "Fitcher's [Queer] Bird: A Fairy-Tale Heroine and Her Avatars." *Marvels & Tales* 22.1 (2008): 143-167.

Grimm, Wilhelm and Jacob Grimm. *The Collected Fairy Tales of the Brothers Grimm*. Third Edition. Trans. Jack Zipes. New York: Bantam Books, 2003.

Grosz, Elizabeth. *Volatile Bodies: Toward a Corporeal Feminism*. Bloomington and Indianapolis: Indiana UP, 1994.

Jones, Christine A. *Mother Goose Refigured: A Critical Translation of Charles Perrault's Fairy Tales*. Detroit: Wayne State UP, 2016.

Jordan, Rosan A., and Susan J. Kalčik. "Introduction." *Women's Folklore, Women's Culture*. Eds. Rosan A. Jordan and Susan J. Kalčik. Philadelphia: U of Pennsylvania P, 1985. ix-xiv.

Jorgensen, Jeana. *Gender and the Body in Classical European Fairy Tales*. Ph.D. diss., Indiana U, 2012.

Kimmel, Michael. "Foreword." *Masculinity Studies & Feminist Theory: New Directions*, Ed. Judith Kegan Gardiner. New York: Columbia UP, 2002. ix-xi.

Levorato, Alessandra. *Language and Gender in the Fairy Tale Tradition: A Linguistic Analysis of Old and New Story Telling*. New York: Palgrave Macmillan, 2003.

Lieberman, Marcia. "'Some Day My Prince Will Come': Female Acculturation through the Fairy Tale." *College English* 34.3 (1972):383-95.

Magnanini, Suzanne. *Fairy-Tale Science: Monstrous Generation in the Tales of Straparola and Basile*. Toronto: University of Toronto Press, 2008.

Massignon, Geneviève. *Folktales of France*. Trans. Jacqueline Hyland. Chicago: The U of Chicago P, 1968.

Mulvey, Laura. Visual Pleasure and Narrative Cinema. In *Film Theory and Criticism: Introductory Readings*. Eds. Leo Brady and Marshall Cohen. New York: Oxford UP, 1999. 833-44.

Propp, Vladimir. *Morphology of the Folktale*. Trans. Laurence Scott. Austin: U of Texas P, 1968 [1928].

Ragan, Kathleen. "What Happened to the Heroines in Folktales? An Analysis by Gender of a Multicultural Sample of Published Folktales Collected from Storytellers." *Marvels & Tales* 23.2 (2009):227–47.

Ranke, Kurt. *Folktales of Germany*. Trans. Lotte Baumann. Chicago: U of Chicago P, 1966.

Schmiesing, Ann. *Disability, Deformity, and Disease in the Grimms' Fairy Tales*. Detroit: Wayne State UP, 2014.

Seifert, Lewis. *Manning the Margins: Masculinity and Writing in Seventeenth-Century France*. Ann Arbor: The University of Michigan Press, 2009.

Stone, Kay. "The Misuses of Enchantment: Controversies on the Significance of Fairy Tales." *Women's Folklore, Women's Culture*. Eds. Rosan A. Jordan and Susan J. Kalčik. Philadelphia: U of Pennsylvania P, 1985. 125-145.

---. "Things Walt Disney Never Told Us." *Women and Folklore: Images and Genres*. Ed. by Claire R. Farrer. Prospect Heights, Illinois: Waveland Press, Inc., 1975. 42-50.

Taggart, James M. *The Bear and His Sons: Masculinity in Spanish and Mexican Folktales*. Austin: U of Texas P, 1997.

Tangherlini, Timothy. Big Folklore: A Special Issue on Computational Folkloristics. *Journal of American Folklore* 129.511 (2016): 5-13.

Tatar, Maria. *Off with their Heads! Fairy Tales and the Culture of Childhood*. Princeton, New Jersey: Princeton UP, 1992 [1987]

---. *The Hard Facts of the Grimms' Fairy Tales: Expanded Second Edition*. Princeton and Oxford: Princeton UP, 2003.

Thomas, Calvin. "Reenfleshing the Bright Boys; Or, How Male Bodies Matter to Feminist Theory." *Masculinity Studies & Feminist Theory*: New Directions. Ed. Judith Kegan Gardiner. New York: Columbia UP, 2002. 60-89.

Tucker, Holly. *Pregnant Fictions: Childbirth and the Fairy Tale in Early Modern France*. Detroit: Wayne State University Press, 2003.

Vaz da Silva, Francisco. *Metamorphosis: The Dynamics of Symbolism in European Fairy Tales*. New York: Peter Lang, 2002.

Venuti, Lawrence. *The Translator's Invisibility: A History of Translation*. Second edition. London and New York: Routledge, 2008 [1995].

Warner, Marina. *From the Beast to the Blonde: On Fairy Tales and Their Tellers*. New York: Farrar, Straus and Giroux, 1994.

Weingart, Scott, and Jeana Jorgensen. "Computational Analysis of the Body in European Fairy Tales." *Literary and Linguistic Computing* 28.3 (2013): 404–16.

---. "The Black and the White Bride: Dualism, Gender, and Bodies in European Fairy Tales." *The Journal of History and Cultures* 28.1 (2013): 49-71.

Zipes, Jack. *Fairy Tales and the Art of Subversion*, 2nd ed. New York: Routledge, 2006.

---, trans. *Beauties, Beasts, and Enchantment: Classic French Fairy Tales*. Kent, UK: Crescent Moon Publishing, 2009 [1989].

---. "Spreading Myths about Iron John." *Fairy Tale as Myth, Myth as Fairy Tale*. Lexington: The University Press of Kentucky, 1994. 96-118.

RESOURCES & RECOMMENDATIONS

HOW TO USE THIS RESOURCES & RECOMMENDATIONS SECTION

WHEN I FIRST CONCEPTUALIZED THIS book, I knew I wanted to share tons of knowledge with you, the reader...but I also knew that it would be all too easy to just info-dump a ton and overwhelm everyone (me included, probably). So to truly keep this book at the 101 level, and not have it run over into thousands of pages, I decided to create this resources and recommendations section in a very specific way. Hopefully this also makes it easy to navigate, no matter whether you're reading in print or digitally.

The idea is that I've provided curated lists with lots of granularity and description, and then you can flip to the giant bibliography to find the source and track it down on your own.

I ignored bibliographic principles the tiniest bit in listing online sources, going with the title of the website rather than the name of its author/curator/etc. as the first item in the citations. This is because within the annotated recommendations I talk about the site by its name, not the name of whomever created it, and I wanted to make it easy to find in the bibliography. Please don't tell my first-year writing students I broke the rules.

I've chosen to separate this into four sections: online resources, fave classical fairy-tale works (which includes tales from contemporary time periods circulating in oral tradition), fave fairy-tale retellings, and fave works of fairy-tale scholarship. That way, if you know you want something accessible online, you can start with the first section, whereas if you're trawling for some fun new twist on an old tale to read, you can go to the retellings section. And so on.

Mostly I assume everyone knows where/how to find Disney products if they so choose, so I don't mention them much. And I try to avoid spoilers when it comes to retellings, but it's hard sometimes. If something is over 20 years old I kinda feel like the cat's already out of the bag, you know? But rest assured, I made an effort!

These lists are as extensive as I can make them, but they're not exhaustive. With new fairy-tale retellings being filmed and penned and performed all the time, there's no way this list can be 100% comprehensive. But if nothing else, they're a great starting point!

BEST INTERNET RESOURCES

<u>Websites to get a general grasp on fairy tales:</u>
SurLaLune and Folktexts are where it's at if you want to poke
around and read and learn a lot. There's also a lot of good stuff
at Carterhaugh (especially if you want to take online classes),
Folklore & Fiction, and Professor of Words (also with the
online classes). *Once Upon a Blog* has lots of resources too.

<u>Websites containing essays on fairy-tale history and inter-</u>
<u>pretation:</u>
SurLaLune and Folktexts both have these kinds of essays,
often very insightful ones at that. You'll need to look around a
bit to find them though, as the sites contain both tale texts and
scholarly criticism. I trust both sources because Heidi Anne
Heiner of SurLaLune has educated herself on fairy-tale scholarship and D.L. Ashliman of Folktexts is a folklorist (I met him
once at a folklore conference and fan-girled over him a bit).

Online versions of the Motif-Index:
The two I'm aware of are Unpacking World Literature (hosted by the University of Alberta) and the Ruthenia site (hosted by Russian State University's Center for Typological and Semiotic Folklore Studies). These are both complete version of the Index, so while the Index itself is old and hasn't been updated in a few decades, you can at least explore what's there.

Online versions of the Tale Type Index:
Womp-womp, sad trombone noise, there is no fully digitized version of the Tale Type Index. The closest online version is the Multilingual Folk Tale Database (which is also now mirrored on the Alberta site mentioned above).

Repositories of lots of tales:
Folktexts and SurLaLune once again come in clutch. Folktexts is organized alphabetically by tale title, which may or may not correspond to the title of the version you're familiar with; between that and the fact that there's no search function, you may do a lot of scrolling around to find stuff. The site also includes other genres of folk narrative like myth and legend, but things are pretty clearly labeled, so you will know when you're encountering folktale and fairy tale and when you're in other territory. SurLaLune is also great, with lots of free-standing folktale and fairy-tale texts plus some annotated

versions. However, sometimes links are broken, and it too doesn't have a search function.

For Hans Christian Andersen specifically, I like the HCA Gilead site, which contains almost all of Andersen's 168 tales translated into English, along with other notes and articles about his life.

Next up is pretty much everything in public domain, but read at your own risk because depending on who translated a text and when, they may have gutted it.

Blogs and discussion boards:
A lot of the places where active fairy-tale discussions are happening are situated within Facebook groups (so I won't be linking to them, sorry). But if you take classes with Cartherhaugh or Professor of Words, they have private Facebook groups. Storied Imaginarium also offers classes, which revolve around creatively using fairy tales in retellings, and they tend to use Facebook groups for communication. Folklore & Fiction maintains a Facebook group for discussions too.

Sadly, not every digital fairy-tale resource is still active, though many that played a role in the development of discourse are still archived. These include Cabinet des Fées, which published some journal issues (and is obviously named after the volumes the *conteuses* published), and Tales of Faerie. SurLaLune also had an EZ Board but I think it's not the same after a 2005 data loss.

Podcasts:
For an awesome general folklore podcast that sometimes touches on fairy tales, listen to *The Folklore Podcast* hosted by Mark Norman. For a podcast that focuses on retelling fairy tales in a humorous way and discussing them, listen to *The Fairy Tellers* by Katrina Reinert and Geoff Insch. For a podcast that's about the history of fairy tales and their tellers, check out *Roots of Lore* by Caitlin Brehm.

Videos/streaming:
"The Hidden History of Little Red Riding Hood" by Magical Molly is a documentary on YouTube that I was interviewed on a few years ago. If you're on Twitch, check out the weekly show Folkwise, hosted by a variety of my folklore colleagues. Discussion topics vary, but fairy tales do come up every so often.

Not quite video, but rather *about* video: the International Fairy-Tale Filmography is a website hosted by the University of Winnipeg that lists pretty much every film that incorporates fairy-tale elements. It's very comprehensive.

FAVE CLASSICAL FAIRY-TALE WORKS

Overall classical collections:

These span a few time periods so bear with me. My top two picks for fairy-tale anthologies that focus on the traditional tales are Jennifer Schacker and Christine Jones's collection *Marvelous Transformations* and Maria Tatar's *The Classic Fairy Tales*. They're thorough, they're annotated with important contextual information, they're translated with an eye towards accuracy. Please note that there are two editions of Tatar's work out by Norton; the second edition is more thorough. And there's an annotated version with gorgeous illustrations too.

Jack Zipes has done some good work here too. His book *The Great Fairy Tale Tradition* provides a general overview, and I'll mention some of his subject-specific books below.

Andrew Lang's fairy tale books (*The Lilac Fairy Book*, and so on) are well-known collections of tales that Lang gathered from all over. His books helped popularize the notion of global fairy-tale collections.

For a (potentially) younger crowd, Kathleen Ragan's *Fearless Girls, Wise Women & Beloved Sisters* is a lovely collection of tales featuring strong heroines.

Italian collections:

You've gotta read Straparola and Basile to be versed in the classics, but there are a few other noteworthy collections as well. For Basile, Nancy Canepa's translation is the one I'd go with, under the title *Giambattista Basile's the Tale of Tales, or, Entertainment for Little Ones.*

For a general bunch of Italian tales, Thomas Crane's mid-nineteenth-century collection is good. It's called *Italian Popular Tales.*

Slightly offset from Italy, there were two really important collectors working in Sicily: Giuseppe Pitrè and Laura Gonzenbach. Pitrè's tales have been published in English, and Gonzenbach's tales were translated and published by Jack Zipes in two books: *Beautiful Angiola* and *The Robber with a Witch's Head.*

French collections:

Perrault's *Mother Goose Tales* is a necessary starting point to understand the French fairy-tale context. I'm a fan of the new translation by Christine A. Jones, and the introductory materials in it are quite good too. Definitely read some of the tales by conteuses like Madame d'Aulnoy; I don't really have a favorite book to recommend that contains all of them, but you can find a lot of them on the internet in public domain. For an overall taste of French fairy tales, I'd recommend *Beauties, Beasts and Enchantment: Classic French Fairy Tales* edited by Jack Zipes.

While the 1690s are generally considered the heyday of French fairy tales, they continued to be written throughout the 1700s (when significant versions of "Beauty and the Beast" appeared) and even the 1800s. Tales from this latter period appear in *Women Writing Wonder* (Koehler et al).

German collections:
Starting with the Grimms, I would again urge caution in regard to who the translator was/is. You'll find their works scattered all over the public domain repositories online, but if they were translated in the mid-to-late 1800s or the early-to-mid 1900s, there's a decent risk that the translator excluded and censored sexual, violent, and/or scatological elements. Zipes has translated both the 1812/1815 first edition and the 1857 final edition, so that's one good bet. That first edition is titled *The Original Folk and Fairy Tales of the Brothers Grimm: The Complete First Edition* and the 1857 edition is titled *The Complete Fairy Tales of the Brothers Grimm* (it has a very pretty pastel lavender cover).

In the 1850s, inspired by the Grimms, Franz Xaver von Schönwerth set out to collect tales from northern Bavaria. His manuscript was lost and then recovered, and it's been translated and published as *The Turnip Princess* by Maria Tatar. These tales are a treat to read. And some of the Grimms' female contemporaries were writing their own tales too; these haven't received a ton of critical attention, but some appear in *Women Writing Wonder* (Koehler et al).

This is slightly off topic since it's a book mostly of legends, not folktales/fairy tales, but I think *Sunken Castles, Evil Poodles: Commentaries on German Folklore* by Jürgen Hubert helps explain some of the major characters and motifs in German folk narrative. I believe the author's working on some new translations of German folktales too, so you can follow him on Twitter for updates (like I do).

British, Irish, and Scottish collections:
Joseph Jacobs was an Australian Jewish folklore collector who did a lot of work in England. His 1890s *English Fairy Tales* is pretty well known. W.B. Yeats (yes, that Yeats) also collected tales, but in Ireland. Donald Braid's *Scottish Traveller Tales: Lives Shaped through Stories* is a really delightful collection of stories that Braid collected from Scottish Travellers, along with some analysis from Braid (like me, he's an IU-trained folklorist). Additionally, there are some British women's nineteenth century literary tales in *Women Writing Wonder* (Koehler et al).

Romani/Gypsy collections:
Diane Tong's *Gypsy Folktales* is full of tales from all over the
European communities of Gypsy/Romani peoples.

Scandinavian collections:
For Hans Christian Andersen, I generally go with the translation by Erik Christian Haugaard. But I'd be remiss if I didn't
also mention that I wrote the introduction to a volume
published by Knickerbocker Classics.

There are more great folktales and fairy tales from the region,
though! Peter Asbjørnsen and Christian Moe were among the
earliest Scandinavian folktale collectors, and their Norwegian
tales (such as the beastly bridegroom story "East of the Sun
and West of the Moon") are pretty well known. And though I
tend to associate the Scandinavian scholars Reimund Kvideland and Henning Sehmsdorf with legend rather than folktale,
their book *All the World's Reward: Folktales Told by Five Scandinavian Storytellers* is a treasure.

The Danish collector Evald Tang Kristensen did pioneering
work, collecting not only the tales but also biographical information about their tellers. I don't think his entire corpus has
been translated into English, but you can find some of his tales
in the book *Danish Fairy and Folk Tale: A Collection of Popular
Stories and Fairy Tales*.

Slavic collections:

The classic Russian tale collector was Aleksander Afanas'ev, whose *Russian Fairy Tales* provided the basis for Vladimir Propp's pioneering structuralist work. Russian poets and authors also worked with folkloric materials, so you'll find both literary and folkloric tales in *Russian Magic Tales: From Pushkin to Platonov,* a wide-ranging anthology edited by Robert Chandler. Jack Haney's collection *Long, Long Tales from the Russian North* is full of tales from folk tradition that are also epically long.

Baltic collections:

There's always been a strong folklore-collecting impulse in the Baltic nations. Piret Päär's *Estonian Folktales* is a nice example of this, consisting mostly of tales from the Estonian Folklore Archives at the University of Tartu (I've been there!).

Middle Eastern collections:

The Arabian Nights/The Thousand and One Nights is the best-known manuscript from this region. You can find earlier English translations, like those by Richard Burton or Edward William Lane, for free online because they're in public domain, but they're also very quirky and influenced by their own biases.

I'm a fan of Yasmine Seale's recent translation, *The Annotated Arabian Nights: Tales from 1001 Nights,* in part since it also has gorgeous pictures. For a straight-up text, the translation by Husain Haddawy is also excellent.

There are a number of important historical Middle Eastern narrative texts (and criticism thereon) in Ulrich Marzolph's *101 Middle Eastern Tales and Their Impact on Western Oral Tradition*. I haven't been able to fully sink my teeth into the book yet but I'm looking forward to it, as Marzolph is an authority on the topic.

Contemporary European collections:
There are two great Italian collections I generally recommend: Alessandro Falassi's *Folklore by the Fireside*, stories that he collected in the 1970s in Tuscany, and Elizabeth Mathias and Richard Raspa's *Italian Folktales in America* (technically, these tales were collected in the U.S., but from a northern Italian immigrant woman).

Folklorist Richard Dorson edited an amazing book series called Folktales of the World, which I highly recommend. From it, I really like *Folktales of France*, (mostly) collected and edited by Geneviève Massignon and *Folktales of Germany*, edited by Kurt Ranke.

I was on the fence about where to put this one, but the texts have been modernized so I'm putting it here: Hungarian storyteller Csenge Zalka's book *Dancing on Blades: Rare and Exquisite Folktales from the Carpathian Mountains* mildly reinterprets Transcarpathian tales from one storyteller that are over one hundred years old. The collection takes its title from an intriguing version of "The Twelve Dancing Princesses" (ATU 306) wherein the princesses are cursed to dance every night upon blades.

Contemporary Middle Eastern collections:
There's been a fantastic emphasis on collecting folktales and fairy tales in contemporary Middle Eastern contexts. Some of my favorite collections are Monia Hejaiej's *Behind Closed Doors: Women's Oral Narratives in Tunis* and Ibrahim Muhawi and Sharif Kanaana's *Speak, Bird, Speak Again: Palestinian Arab Folktales* (this is a favorite, I teach it whenever I can).

I also recommend Hasan El-Shamy's *Folktales of Egypt* and Warren Walker and Ahmet Edip Uysal's *Tales Alive in Turkey*.

Dan Ben-Amos has done a lot of scholarship on folk narrative, and his *Folktales of the Jews* is one great example of this. Many of the stories within are not strictly fairy tales, but they're still interesting. And a lot of them come from the Israel Folktale Archives. For another collection featuring stories from that source, check out *The Power of a Tale: Stories from the Israel Folktale Archives*. Both books contain extensive annotations.

Contemporary Asian collections:
One of my favorite collections to teach is Kirin Narayan's *Mondays on the Dark Night of the Moon: Himalayan Foothill Folktales*, written in collaboration with storyteller Urmila Devi Sood. The collection is full of amazing stories as well as information about the times of year when they are told, and the role these stories serve in women's lives and rituals.

FAVE FAIRY-TALE RETELLINGS

The "Carter generation" aka the 1970s and 80s:
Angela Carter's tale collection *The Bloody Chamber* from 1979 is
really, truly iconic. She retells a number of well-known tales
("Sleeping Beauty," "Beauty and the Beast," "Little Red Riding
Hood") and some lesser-known ones ("Bluebeard," variants of
fairy kidnapping legends) with a glamorous gothic lens
heavily influenced by second-wave feminism.

Margaret Atwood wrote some of these too (ever think about
where the iconic red hoods in the sadly-always-relevant *Handmaid's Tale* come from?). Her short story "Bluebeard's Egg" is a
fascinating deconstruction of the gender politics of that tale in
a modern setting. It's available to read in the Zipes collection
Don't Bet on the Prince.

Feminist retellings:

Along with Carter's *The Bloody Chamber*, Barbara Walker's *Feminist Fairy Tales* retells fairy tales from, you guessed it, a feminist perspective. Her "The Frog Princess" adds an ecological twist and an unhappy ending to a gender-swapped "The Frog King."

Jack Zipes has collected a number of feminist retellings of fairy tales, some decades-old and some on the newer side, in *Don't Bet on the Prince: Contemporary Feminist Fairy Tales in North America and England*.

Robin McKinley has done a number of full-length novel retellings of fairy tales that are quite feminist. I love *Deerskin* since it reinterprets my adored tale type ATU 510B, but it needs a trigger warning or three. Newer to the scene, Alix Harrow's *A Spindle Splintered* reinterprets "Sleeping Beauty" through a modern lens of chronic illness and girl power.

Queer retellings:
For tale collections, Emma Donoghue's *Kissing the Witch: Old Tales in New Skins* is a classic. Not every tale in it is queer, but close, and they're all quite femme-centric. A couple of new collections have come along too, like Ana Mardoll's *Cinder the Fireplace Boy*, which retells many of the Grimms' tales with an emphasis on mixing up sexualities and genders while sticking close to their compact and direct storytelling style. Mardoll has also written *No Man of Woman Born*, which contains a genderqueer rendition of ATU 300, "The Dragonslayer," among other tales. The collaborative collection *Whispers Between Fairies* by Nathan Caro Fréchette and Derek

Newman-Stille contains some lovely tales, including striking queerings of "Beauty and the Beast" and "Cinderella." A few super-sexy collections get mentioned in the final category of this chapter.

In terms of standalone novel-length retellings, *Ash* by Malinda Lo and *Cinderella Is Dead* by Kalynn Bayron are both stellar (and both lesbian retellings of "Cinderella"). *Girl, Serpent, Thorn* by Melissa Bashardoust is a loose retelling of "Sleeping Beauty" but with mash-up elements from other fairy tales as well as Persian mythology. *Blanca y Roja* by Anna-Marie McLemore mixes "Snow White and Rose Red" with other elements, featuring a nonbinary main character among other not-quite-cis-het elements. S.T. Lynn has a series of short novels retelling fairy tales with trans characters; *Cinder Ella* features a Black trans woman as the main character.

In terms of graphic novels, *How to Be a Mermaid* by Maya Kern is a delight (and it's available to read for free online as of this writing). I'll talk about *The Magic Fish* by Trung Le Nguyen below, but it's also a delight, featuring a young coming-of-age and coming-out story all in one.

Super twisted/grim/"dark" tales:
I think the term "dark" is misleading, yes, but it's still pretty commonly used so we'll run with it. The vampire retellings below all count, as does the comic book series *Grimm Fairy Tales* published by Zenoscope, which is chock full of sex and violence. Stacy Jay's *Princess of Thorns* blends together a few fairy tales and contains literal torture. Sarah J. Maas's *A Court*

of Thorns and Roses (described in more detail below, under fantasy retellings) also depicts a lot of torture and trauma.

One of the best books to explore the dark side of fairy tales also leaves room for the light, or in this case, healing from child abuse. I cannot recommend luminary Terri Windling's edited collection *The Armless Maiden* highly enough, though it needs a hefty amount of trigger warnings too. Same with Robin McKinley's *Deerskin*.

If you like sex, blood, and violence, check out the Polish film *The Lure*. I want to assign it to my college students but I feel like it's just too disturbing.

Holocaust retellings:
Wow, yes indeed, this is a whole category of fairy-tale retellings. I really like the novel *Briar Rose* by Jane Yolen, which mixes "Sleeping Beauty" with a story of a Jewish family surviving World War II. But there's also *Gretel and the Dark* by Eliza Granville, which I haven't read but I've read an academic article about (this is common in my life).

Vampire retellings:
Same as above, yes, this is a thing. "The Lady in the House of Love" by Angela Carter (in *The Bloody Chamber*) is one classic; "Snow Glass Apples" by Neil Gaiman is another. Yet another is Tanith Lee's "Red as Blood." *Sunshine* by Robin McKinley puts "Beauty and the Beast" into a vampire-world setting.

And if you're game for considering any ol' human girl + vampire pairing as a "Beauty and the Beast" retelling, well, there's always *Twilight* (no, I'm not putting *Twilight* into my freakin' bibliography, you can find it if you want to).

Sci-fi retellings:
Cinder by Marissa Meyer is a retelling of "Cinderella" which features a protagonist with a cyborg foot, and it leads into a series with other fairy tales featured. *Beauty* by Sherri S. Tepper is a trippy futuristic look at "Sleeping Beauty."

Fantasy retellings:
These days, ACOTAR takes the cake for fairy-tale retellings set in a fantasy world. That's *A Court of Thorns and Roses* by Sarah J. Maas, which starts out "Beauty and the Beast" but opens up into a much more expansive fae-vs-human setting. It's inspired a lot of imitations in the fantasy romance genre.

Katherine Arden's trilogy, which begins with *The Bear and the Nightingale*, places Russian fairy tales into a somewhat historical setting. It's a wonderful read. Same with Naomi Novik's books: *Spinning Silver* juxtaposes "Rumpelstiltskin" with a Jewish family that faces unearthly beings, and *Uprooted* plays with "The Sorcerer and His Apprentice" tropes.

Horror retellings:

Not my wheelhouse (I have nightmares too easily to be a horror fan), but a few notable ones include *Snow White: A Tale of Terror* directed by Michael Cohn and *The Company of Wolves* directed by Neil Jordan, based on Angela Carter's werewolf tales from *The Bloody Chamber*.

Mash-up/postmodern retellings:

This is a bit of a catch-all category, but in case you haven't read the scholarship on postmodern fairy tales (like Cristina Bacchilega's book of that title) or fairy-tale pastiche (my article in *Marvels & Tales* on that subject), these are tales that aren't necessarily a retelling of a single tale-type. They also go beyond just being mash-ups that are easily recognizable; they're usually doing something new with fairy-tale motifs, themes, and plots, like throwing a bunch of them into the blender and seeing what comes out. Often (but not always) postmodern fairy tales criticize some aspect of modern-day society, like capitalism or strict gender roles. Heck, *Shrek* does both!

One of my favorites in this category is *Indexing* by Seanan McGuire. The premise is that the Tale Type Index documents a real phenomenon, tale types that exist in reality and try to make narrative incursions into our world. A needle in a vein could kick off a whole "Sleeping Beauty" incident that imperils entire towns, for example. A Snow-White-ish character works for the agency responsible for curtailing these narrative incursions. Chaos ensues.

In this vein, there's also *Fables* by Bill Willingham, which I'll discuss more extensively below in the graphic novels section, and *Once Upon a Time*, which have similar premises (fairy-tale characters exiled from their world, living in our world). Also the TV show *Grimm*, I guess. I never really got into either but my colleague Christy Williams has some brilliant analysis of *OUAT* in her book discussed in the next chapter.

Mercedes Lackey more than one fairy-tale retelling out there, but I think her novel *The Fairy Godmother* counts in this more postmodern vein because it starts with a Cinderella-ish character who doesn't really fit in with her happily-ever-after, and so she becomes a fairy godmother helping assorted other characters to their own HEAs.

Poems:

First, read *Transformations* by Anne Sexton and *Beginning with O* by Olga Broumas. Sexton's poetry is gorgeous and brutal, and she vividly illustrates human experience through the lens of fairy-tale, such as positing a Sleeping Beauty figure who, now awakened, has insomnia that veils a traumatic past. Broumas tackles myths as well as fairy tales in her book, and her "Rapunzel" is especially focused on women loving women with a shout-out to Sexton in the epigraph.

There are too many good fairy-tale poems out there for me to list them all, but luckily, you can find a lot of them online at the (sadly now defunct) magazine *Liminality*. I'll include a link to one of my faves in the bibliography, "Waking" by Sara Cleto and Brittany Warman, which puts the sleeping maidens from

"Snow White" and "Sleeping Beauty" into dialogue with one another.

Short story collections/venues:
Kissing the Witch by Emma Donoghue, which I mentioned above as highly queer, is one of my favorite fairy-tale short story collections of all time; same with Angela Carter's *The Bloody Chamber*.

But there's also Francesca Lia Block's *The Rose and the Beast*, which is set in a dreamy 1990s/2000s Los Angeles. She actually includes a "Bluebeard" retelling, which tends to be rare, so mad respect. Nalo Hopkinson's *Skin Folk* also includes a "Bluebeard," set in a Caribbean setting with the backdrop of colonialism and spirit beliefs. *Skin Folk* is a remarkable collection for its juxtaposition of classic fairy tales with Caribbean folklore, so it's a must-read in my opinion.

There are three more single-author collections I'd like to hype up. *The Merry Spinster* by Daniel M. Lavery (formerly Mallory Ortberg, in case you knew their brilliant writing on the website *The Toast*) delivers some of the most genderqueer tales I've ever encountered. *A Wild Swan: and Other Tales* by Michael Cunningham contains haunting twists on old tales, including an exploration of what one of the enchanted brothers from ATU 451 ("The Maiden Who Seeks Her Brothers," commonly seen in versions like the Grimms' "The Six Swans") experiences when he is transformed back to a human, but left with a swan wing. Finally, *Burning Girls and Other Stories* by Veronica Schanoes is just amazingly good; I really adore the two novellas in it, which look at certain antisemitic Grimms' tales from a Jewish lens.

For multi-author collections, I didn't know about *Beyond the Woods: Fairy Tales Retold* edited by Paula Guran til this past year, but now I'm really into it; it anthologizes some classic retellings but also contains lesser-known ones. And there's the more recent collection *Mothers of Enchantment*, edited by Kate Wolford, which contains various riffs on the fairy godmother character, which I really loved. Also recent, with a bit of scholarly framing to accompany the variety of tale texts, is *Inviting Interruptions*, edited by Cristina Bacchilega and Jennifer Orme. It has some new English translations and multimedia works you won't easily find elsewhere.

Kate Bernheimer has edited two stellar collections that are more essay-ish than retelling-ish, but I include them here because they're still on the creative end of the spectrum (rather than scholarly). *Mirror, Mirror on the Wall* features women's writing and *Brothers & Beasts* features men's writing.

A long-running classic series of fairy-tale retelling anthologies is of course the collaboration between Ellen Datlow and Terri Windling that produced a number of volumes. I'm just citing one here, *Snow White, Blood Red*, but they're all stellar.

Online, I like to read *Enchanted Conversation*, edited by Kate Wolford (you'll find short stories as well as blog posts and poems there, all centered around fairy tales). *Timeless Tales Magazine*, founded by Tahlia Kirk, has also published some lovely collections of retold tales.

Novels:

I haven't mentioned Donna Jo Napoli yet, so I'll do so here. She writes YA-ish fairy-tale retellings, which are always inventive and intriguing. *The Magic Circle* revisits "Hansel and Gretel" from the perspective of the witch (grounded in European folk belief), while *Beast* locates the cursed prince in Persia.

There are a couple of great takes on fairy tales in novel form by Catherynne M. Valente; *Six-Gun Snow White* sets the tale in the American Wild West (it is pretty violent though, just a heads-up), and *Deathless* places a variety of Russian fairy-tale figures in real-world Russian historical contexts like the Russian Revolution.

For yet another violent and disturbing "Snow White" retelling, check out *White as Snow* by Tanith Lee, which meshes the fairy tale with the myth of Persephone.

Gregory Maguire is, in my opinion, one of the writers who helped kick off the most recent fairy-tale vogue about twenty years ago. After the Carter generation, there were some retellings here and there, but I think they only really started getting trendy again in the early 2000s. Anyway, *Confessions of an Ugly Stepsister* both puts "Cinderella" in a specific historical setting (17th-century Holland) and switches to the perspective of a stepsister who's usually made out to be villainous.

YA/children's & illustrated books:
Ella Enchanted by Gail Carson Levine is a delightful book, which asks what happens if Cinderella had a fairy godmother's blessing that turned out to be a curse, wherein she is forced to literally interpret orders from anyone who speaks to her (the movie is not worth bothering with though).

The Sleeper and the Spindle, written by Neil Gaiman and illustrated by Chris Riddell, is a wonderful revision of multiple sleeping maiden stories at once.

Graphic novels and comics:
Stop what you're doing and read _The Magic Fish_ by Trung Le Nguyen if you haven't already. It's a gorgeous coming-of-age story featuring themes of identity (immigrant; LGBTQ+) with art that bridges Art Deco and manga elements.

Fables by Bill Willingham has the premise that a number of fairy-tale characters are exiled from their homeland and live secretly in an enclave in New York. Snow White and the Big Bad Wolf are two of the main characters. I just cite the first volume in my bibliography, but the series goes on for a good long while, including lots of spin-offs like a crossover with _The Thousand and One Nights_.

How to Become a Mermaid by Maya Kern is a web comic that is lovely and heartbreaking. It's available in print in _Inviting Interruptions_ too.

Stardust is a classic adventure story with a fairy tale twist;

while you can just pick up the text by Neil Gaiman, I really like the illustrations by Charles Vess (yes I know there's also a film; I don't think it's that great an adaptation).

The comic book series *Grimm Fairy Tales* is aimed at adults, with a lot of sex and violence on its pages.

Film/TV for adults:
Going old-school for a second, it's worth trying to watch some of the earliest fairy-tale films if you can: those by Georges Méliès (French, working in the early 1900s) and the animated ones by Walt Disney and also Tex Avery (who gave us a hyper-sexualized "Little Red Riding Hood" figure). While we're traveling in the wayback-when machine, I'd also highly recommend checking out French director Jean Cocteau's *Beauty and the Beast* which, while it's from the era before decent special effects, also provides some of the innovations that Disney would draw on in their animated version of the tale.

In addition to the spate of mediocre "Snow White" retellings that all inexplicably came out in 2012 (*Mirror, Mirror* and *Snow White and the Huntsman*), the 2000s have had a number of decent fairy-tale retellings in film and television. *Once Upon a Time* and *Grimm* both juxtaposed fairy-tale characters in the modern-day world, and both feature detective-like main characters (which is interesting, right?).

A lot of Guillermo del Toro's films are fairy-tale-related, such as *Pan's Labyrinth* and *The Shape of Water*. I'm a fan of the latter film because it's a rare mash-up of two tales, "Beauty and the Beast" and "The Little Mermaid," that I don't often see combined. Along similar lines, I love the violent Polish film *The Lure*, which is a surprisingly faithful retelling of Andersen's "The Little Mermaid" in tone if not in setting (which is modern). *And* it's a musical!

Oh, and watch David Kaplan's short film "Little Red Riding Hood" if you haven't already. If a young Christina Ricci as Little Red and a genderqueer ballerina wolf aren't enough to entice you into watching, I don't know what to tell you (you can usually find it online for free if you look).

Film/TV for children:
My college students tell me the Barbie Thumbelina films are good (this is not my wheelhouse, could you tell?).

Fairy-tale erotica/smut:
Oh, wow, did you even read my article "Innocent Initiations" in this volume? Joking. Mostly. Go raid its bibliography. More fairy-tale erotica has been published since then, a lot of it very easily found online. I've noticed a trend of eroticizing beastly men, maybe in part related to the explosion of vampire and/or werewolf romance and erotica lately. One example is *Depravity* by M.J. Haag, the first book in an erotic "Beauty and the Beast" retelling. Katee Robert publishes a series of novels titled Wicked Villains that makes the Disney film villains into the love interests; *Desperate Measures*, for

instance, explores a steamy dynamic between Jasmine and Jafar.

If you want raunchy tales straight from folk tradition (yes, it's totally a thing, though censorship has wiped a lot of it out of existence, sanitizing the tales at the level of the collector, the editor, the publisher, etc.), I recommend Afanas'ev's collection *Russian Secret Tales*. And for an American take on the same, there's Vance Randolph's *Pissing in the Snow and Other Ozark Folktales*.

FAVE WORKS OF FAIRY-TALE SCHOLARSHIP

Reference works on fairy tales:

There are two main reference works I reach for every time I'm doing research. The first is *The Oxford Companion to Fairy Tales* edited by Jack Zipes. It's pretty darn comprehensive. Next is *The Greenwood Encyclopedia of Folktales and Fairy Tales*, a three-volume work edited by Donald Haase. I refer to the 2008 version throughout this book since I like physically holding research books in my hands, but there's also a second edition from 2016 edited by Anne Duggan, Donald Haase, and Helen Callow that's been updated and expanded.

The *Enzyklopädie des Märchens* is a comprehensive collection of volumes of research on the folktale; I cite the online version in the bibliography, but there are physical book versions of it too. If you intend to do international, comparative work on fairy tales, it's a necessary starting point.

Additionally, D.L. Ashliman's *A Guide to Folktales in the English*

Language is based on the tale type system, and it tells you where to find variants of both common and lesser-known tales. I use it in my research often. My only gripe is that I'd love an updated version that uses the ATU system rather than the outdated AT system.

Academic journals you should know:
I'm not providing citations for these because they're whole journals, not individual articles therein. Everything mentioned here is peer reviewed, and if you're not affiliated with a university (which makes accessing these easy), you could see if your local public library will get you an issue on interlibrary loan. You can also, if you find a citation for an article that looks really interesting, email the author and ask if they'll share a draft of the piece with you.

The first one you should know about is *Fabula: Zeitschrift für Erzählforschung / Journal of Folktale Studies / Revue d'Etudes sur le Conte Populaire*. It's truly multilingual, like the whole of fairy tales studies, so you'll find articles in German, English, and French in it. The American counterpart to *Fabula* is *Marvels & Tales* which also publishes high-quality scholarship.

You'll also find some works on fairy tales in other academic folklore journals (and occasionally children's literature journals, though I don't know those as well). So it might be worth searching through issues of *The Journal of American Folklore, Western Folklore,* and *The Journal of Folklore Research,* which are three of the heavy-hitting U.S. journals.

Foundational works on folk narrative in general:
Okay, hear me out, neither of these is specifically about folk-tales or fairy tales but they do touch on them, and they talk about important theories (like structuralism and psychoanaly-sis) and important adjacent folk narrative genres (like myth).

Alan Dundes drew together documents from some of the founders of folklore studies in *International Folkloristics*, including household names like Jacob Grimm and Vladimir Propp, but also people you may have only encountered in this book, such as Kaarle Krohn (one of the creators of the Finnish/historic-geographic method) and Giuseppe Pitrè (an important collector of Sicilian tales). Also, Dundes provides informative introductions to every single chapter, putting the scholarship into broader context. If you want to get a sense of how folklore studies and fairy tale studies developed, this book is a must-read.

Second is *Sacred Narrative*, also edited by Dundes, and while it focuses on myth instead of fairy tale, it gives a really good run-down of the differences between the major folk narrative genres (folktale, myth, legend) and the various approaches (from anthropological to psychological to structural) to myth that also apply to folktale and fairy tale.

Works on the history of fairy tales:
Jack Zipes has amassed a lot of the history of fairy tales across a number of his books. *Fairy Tales and the Art of Subversion*

delivers some basic history of the genre, with chapters on Stra-parola and Basile, Perrault and the *conteuses*, the Grimms, Andersen, and children's literature authors who shaped the genre. *The Irresistible Fairy Tale* fills in some gaps in the canon-ical history, with chapters focusing on Giuseppe Pitrè and lesser-known female collectors like Laura Gonzenbach and Rachel Busk. And in two appendices, Zipes takes snarky swipes at the contested accounts of Ruth Bottigheimer and Willem de Blécourt, who are on the same page about the literary origins of fairy tales.

An important work of folktale history is Stith Thompson's *The Folktale.* Yes, the same Thompson who wrote the Motif Index and revised the Tale Type Index, so the guy clearly knew his stuff.

As noted in the history chapter, consume Bottigheimer's recent books with a grain of salt, but if you want a perspective that is ruthlessly sympathetic towards the literary tradition, you can read her *Fairy Tales: A New History.* You'll find a similar argument advanced (with a focus on the Grimms) in *Tales of Magic, Tales in Print* by Willem de Blécourt.

For a feminist take on fairy-tale history (including questions of what is even recognizable as a fairy tale; yes, we can blame the patriarchy for this in part) I really like *Twice Upon a Time: Women Writers and the History of the Fairy Tale* by Elizabeth Wanning Harries.

Works on German fairy tales:

If you're primarily reading in English, Maria Tatar's *The Hard Facts of the Grimms' Fairy Tales* is a great starting point. Jack Zipes's book *The Brothers Grimm: From Enchanted Forests to the Modern World* has a lot of useful biographical information about them too. Donald Haase's edited collection *The Reception of Grimms' Fairy Tales* also helps fill in a lot of the story of how the Grimms' tales were received and revised in the two hundred years since their publication.

I know I was a bit harsh on Bottigheimer above, but I don't dislike her or her scholarship. She has done some wonderful work on the Grimms' that stuns me with its eloquence and insightfulness every time I return to it. Her book *Grimms' Bad Girls & Bold Boys* is phenomenal, and one of her methods— counting the speech acts of male vs. female characters in that corpus—actually influenced my decision to do something similar in my dissertation.

Works on French fairy tales:
There are a few books I really like on the French fairy tale vogue of the late 1600s. Lewis Seifert did groundbreaking work in his book *Fairy Tales, Sexuality, and Gender in France, 1690-1715*. Anne Duggan followed up on it with her book *Salonnières, Furies, and Fairies: The Politics of Gender and Cultural Change in Absolutist France*. Keeping with the theme of gender (because it's impossible not to, with this particular context) is Patricia Hannon's *Fabulous Identities: Women's Fairy Tales in Seventeenth-Century France*.

And a special shout-out goes to Holly Tucker's *Pregnant*

Fictions: Childbirth and the Fairy Tale in Early-Modern France for so incisively drawing together French folk beliefs about conception, birth, and midwives with the content of the fairy tales being penned then.

Works on Italian fairy tales:
Nancy Canepa is my go-to scholar when it comes to Basile, one of the earliest originators of the Italian strand of the fairy-tale tradition. I like her book *From Court to Forest* on the topic.

I also really like Suzanne Magnanini's book *Fairy-Tale Science: Monstrous Generation in the Tales of Straparola and Basile* because it analyzes the tales in the context of magical and scientific beliefs of their time period.

Works on British fairy tales:
Jennifer Schacker's book *National Dreams: The Remaking of Fairy Tales in Nineteenth-Century England* is less about British fairy tales than about the translation and reinvention of fairy tales in Britain; nonetheless, it's fascinating stuff. Further, her recent book *Staging Fairyland* is about the role of fairy tales in British pantomime; if you're interested in the intersections of fairy tales and theater, this is the book to read.

Works on other European traditions:
I'd be remiss if I didn't talk about Linda Dégh's monumental

contribution to the discourse, *Folktales and Society: Story-Telling in a Hungarian Peasant Community*. What was unique at the time (this was first published in the late 1960s) was her focus on a female narrator, analyzing her repertoire both within its cultural context and within the context of the narrator's biography and values.

Bengt Holbek's *Interpretation of Fairy Tales* also gives an in-depth interpretation of Danish tales in their cultural context, but as I'll mention in subsequent headings, I think his work might actually be more useful for its take on structuralism.

James Taggart has done really interesting work on gender in Spanish tales, so check out *Enchanted Maidens* if that sounds interesting.

Works on Middle Eastern traditions:
There's obviously more to the tale tradition of an entire region than *The Thousand and One Nights/The Arabian Nights*, but I am gonna recommend Ulrich Marzolph's *The Arabian Nights Reader* anyway.

Hasan el-Shamy has done a lot of work in this area too, so I'd recommend his *Folk Traditions of the Arab World: A Guide to Motif Classification* as well as his *Tales Arab Women Tell* (though it gets kinda psychoanalytic, while simultaneously making a convincing argument about the centrality of the brother-sister relationship in Arab cultures).

Works on Asian traditions:

A couple of recent books have stolen my heart. They are Mayako Murai's *From Dog Bridegroom to Wolf Girl: Contemporary Japanese Fairy-Tale Adaptations in Conversation with the West* and Lucy Fraser's *The Pleasures of Metamorphosis: Japanese and English Fairy Tale Transformations of "the Little Mermaid"*.

Works on structure and structuralism:

Obviously you should read Vladimir Propp's *Morphology of the Folktale*, as it set the standards for how we now talk about syntagmatic (a.k.a. sequential) structure in folk and fairy tale. Bengt Holbek synthesizes structural and psychological approaches really usefully in *Interpretation of Fairy Tales*. Jessica Tiffin does some neat stuff with structure and pattern in her book *Marvelous Geometry*.

Freudian/psychoanalytic works:

If you want to make your college students cry, have them read Bruno Bettelheim's *The Uses of Enchantment*. It applies boilerplate Freudian theory to fairy tales with lots of cheerful asides about penises and vaginas. I don't understand the appeal but it's still on bookshelves today in all its gender essentializing glory.

And if you want to read some psychoanalytic interpretations of fairy tales that probably weren't plagiarized (cough Bettelheim cough; both Jack Zipes and Alan Dundes have written about this), I recommend Hungarian Géza Róheim's *Fire in the Dragon and Other Psychoanalytic Essays on Folklore.*

Bengt Holbek does a fantastic job of summarizing all the various psychoanalytic approaches to fairy tales in his *Interpretation of Fairy Tales* before settling on his own Freudian-lite methodology. This in turn has been roundly (but fairly) criticized by Portuguese scholar Vaz da Silva in his thoroughly intriguing book *Metamorphosis: The Dynamics of Symbolism in European Fairy Tales.*

Vanessa Joosen analyzes Bettelheim's influence on scholars and artists alike in her book *Critical and Creative Perspectives on Fairy Tales.*

Jungian/analytical psychology works:
I am super not into this line of inquiry, but from what I know, a good starting point would be Marie-Louise von Franz's book *The Feminine in Fairy Tales.*

Feminist works:
Oh, where to begin?! So many fantastic works.

Donald Haase's edited volume *Fairy Tales and Feminism: New Approaches* summarizes a lot of the trends in feminist fairy-tale scholarship. Cristina Bacchilega's *Postmodern Fairy Tales* applies feminist theory to a number of retellings. Many of Kay

Stone's pioneering essays are collected in her book *Some Day Your Witch Will Come*.

To get a chronology of certain developments in feminist theory and how they influenced trends among scholars and writers, I recommend Vanessa Joosen's book *Critical and Creative Perspectives on Fairy Tales*.

Maria Tatar's new book *The Heroine with 1,001 Faces* reinterprets a great deal of the folk narrative tradition (much of it, but not exclusively, fairy tales) as well as pop culture through a feminist lens, astutely investigating heroines bent on enacting social justice even in the face of massive patriarchal oppression.

Honestly, so much scholarship is infused with feminism these days, you could pick up almost any book published after 2010 and get a whiff of it. I am a fan of this trend, and you'll see it in my own works, too.

Queer works:
The landmark book in this area is *Transgressive Tales: Queering the Grimms* edited by Kay Turner and Pauline Greenhill. Most of the essays therein (including one by me!) focus on reading the Grimms' tales in a new and very queer light, but there are a handful of exceptions.

Unfortunately, that's kinda it. Numerous shorter works such as academic articles have taken up questions of queer theory in fairy tales, so I'd search for queer keywords in *Marvels & Tales*, for example.

Literary / literature-oriented works:
There are tons of great books investigating the overlap of folk-lore and literature and / or the literary characteristics of fairy tales. Max Lüthi's *The European Folktale: Form and Nature* lays out the basics of our modern understandings of fairy-tale style; I assign the first few chapters regularly in my college classes so I highly recommend picking it up.

Mentioned above, Cristina Bacchilega's work *Postmodern Fairy Tales* engages with a lot of literary theory. Stephen Benson's edited collection, *Contemporary Fiction and the Fairy Tale*, does similar, as does Susan Redington Bobby's edited collection *Fairy Tales Reimagined: Essays on New Retellings*.

Disability-centered works:
Two books take the cake: the very academic and narrowly Grimms-focused work of Ann Schmiesing and the broader, more memoir-like work of Amanda Leduc. Schmiesing's work, *Disability, Deformity, and Disease in the Grimms' Fairy Tales*, explains some basics of disability theory in order to analyze the Grimms' tales with it. But Schmiesing also uses the Grimms' biographies (which included elements of disability) to help understand their editorial choices better, which I think is neat. It's written in pretty accessible language for an academically-published book, in my

opinion. Leduc's *Disfigured* weaves autobiography in with fairy tales, asking who is the villain or the Other in these stories, and how that relates to real-world disability experiences.

Works on contemporary fairy tales:
Again I will sing the praises of Bacchilega's *Postmodern Fairy Tales*; it's especially good if you want to learn about the innovations of the Carter generation. Her more recent book *Fairy Tales Transformed?* is also quite good, and it covers a lot of the newer retellings that sprang up after the first book was published.

Christy Williams does interesting things with space and maps in fairy-tale retellings in her book *Mapping Fairy-Tale Space* (seeing her deliver a conference paper on the show *Once Upon A Time*, covered in the book, got me more interested in the show than watching the show did).

Jessica Tiffin interprets a number of retellings in her book *Marvelous Geometry*, with an emphasis on the self-aware playfulness we often see in postmodern retellings and what she terms metafiction (fiction about fiction).

Anna Kérchy's edited volume *Postmodern Reinterpretations of Fairy Tales* covers a wide range of media, from short stories to video games to books.

Works on fairy-tale film/TV:

Pauline Greenhill is a heavy-hitter here; not only is she one of the co-creators of the International Fairy-Tale Filmography, she also edited one of the first collections on the topic, *Fairy Tale Films: Visions of Ambiguity* (with Sidney Eve Matrix). Jack Zipes's book *The Enchanted Screen* has a ton of fairy-tale film history that's super fascinating.

More focused on TV, *Channeling Wonder* is a collection of essays edited by Pauline Greenhill and Jill Terry Rudy that focuses on the use of fairy tales in television contexts.

Claudia Schwabe's book *Craving Supernatural Creatures* analyzes German folklore critters in American pop culture, with a heavy emphasis on TV shows such as *Grimm*.

If you're into French film, Anne Duggan's book *Queer Enchantments* analyzes films by Jacques Demy.

Works on a single tale type:
Lucy Fraser's *The Pleasures of Metamorphosis: Japanese and English Fairy Tale Transformations of "The Little Mermaid"* focuses on precisely what the title says: versions of "The Little Mermaid" across East and West.

Alan Dundes has edited a *Cinderella* casebook under that name, and it collects a wide variety of scholarship on the tale type. If you want an updated take on "Cinderella," find *Cinderella Across Cultures*, a collection of essays edited by Martine Hennard Dutheil de la Rochère, Gillian Lathey, and Monika Woźniak.

Dundes also has a *Little Red Riding Hood* casebook full of essays interpreting the beloved tale. Sandra Beckett's book *Recycling Red Riding Hood* contains more interpretation than textual example, but she summarizes a broad range of LRRH texts that may be new to the reader. Jack Zipes's *The Trials & Tribulations of Little Red Riding Hood* contains both critical interpretation (from him) and a variety of versions of the tale type spanning centuries.

GLOSSARY

Allomotif: the range of motifs that a storyteller or writer might use to fill a motifemic slot (for example, a magical fish and a fairy godmother are both allomotifs that appear to fulfill the "donor figure" motifemic slot in "Cinderella" stories)

Arabian Nights: a large hybrid work of folk narrative scholarship and literature from the Arab Middle Ages; also called *The Thousand and One Nights*; prominently features a frame tale with the storyteller Scheherazade saving the day

Comparative Method: also called the Finnish method or the historic-geographic method, a scholarly method for seeking the origins and early forms of folk narrative texts

Contes des fees: the French term for fairy tales (literally, "tales of the fairies")

Donor Figure: the character in a fairy tale who tested the protagonist and rewards them with magical help

Finnish Method: also called the comparative method or the historic-geographic method, a scholarly method for seeking the origins and early forms of folk narrative texts

Folktale: a fictional, formulaic genre of folk narrative; folktales may or may not have magic in them; fairy tales are considered to be a subset of folktales

Frame Tale: a story that frames another story, like a series of nesting bowls or Russian dolls

Function: the ultimate "why" of a folklore text: why does it exist, what role/purpose does it serve in people's lives?

Genre: a category for classifying similar texts

Historic-Geographic Method: also called the Finnish method or the comparative method, a scholarly method for seeking the origins and early forms of folk narrative texts

Intertextuality: the idea that all texts are in dialogue with other texts, and all art thus informs other art (or literature, folklore, film, etc.)

Lays: a medieval genre of short narrative verse romances, thought to be a possible predecessor or near relative to fairy tales

Legend: a folk narrative genre based on belief; legends are generally told as though they actually did happen, or could have happened, often to a friend of a friend (or FOAF)

Magic Helper: a role in most fairy tales, occupied by a supernatural being that bestows help on the protagonist after they have been tested by the donor figure (sometimes the magic helper and donor figure are the same character; other times they are distinct)

Motif: a small unit of narrative detail that can transfer between stories; typically, motifs are events, objects, or characters

Motifeme: the structural slot in a tale where a storyteller or writer might slot in a variety of motifs (specifically called allot-motifs); so, the idea that someone needs to get Cinderella to the ball to meet the prince is the motifeme, and the variety of characters who might fulfill that role are allomotifs

Myth: a folk narrative genre that is based on sacred beliefs about the origins of people, deities, and the world; generally accepted as true by believers in a given religion

Nationalism: the belief that one's nation or ethnic group is deserving of autonomy and nationhood

Structuralism: an analytical approach to fairy tales that emphasizes the underlying plot structures in the stories rather than the superficial details such as character motifs

Tale type: the scholarly classification of tales by plot type by assigning numbers; often these are referred to as AT or ATU types based on the scholars who have created and refined the system: Aarne, then Thompson, then Uther.

THE GIANT BIBLIOGRAPHY

Afanas'ev, A. N, et al. *Russian Fairy Tales*. 2nd ed., Pantheon, 1973.

---, and Leon Kotkofsky. *Russian Secret Tales: Bawdy Folktales of Old Russia*. Clearfield, 1998.

Andersen, Christian Hans. *Hans Christian Andersen: The Complete Fairy Tales and Stories*. Translated by Erik Christian Haugaard. Anchor Books, 1983.

Arden, Katherine. *The Bear and the Nightingale: A Novel*. First ed., Del Rey, 2017.

Asbjørnsen, Peter Christen, and Jørgen Engebretsen Moe. *The Complete and Original Norwegian Folktales of Asbjørnsen and Moe*. Translated by Tiina Nunnally, University of Minnesota Press, 2019.

Ashliman, D. L. *A Guide to Folktales in the English Language: Based on the Aarne-Thompson Classification System*. Greenwood Press, 1987.

Bacchilega, Cristina. *Fairy Tales Transformed? : Twenty-First-Century Adaptations and the Politics of Wonder*. Wayne State University Press, 2013.

---. *Postmodern Fairy Tales: Gender and Narrative Strategies*. University of Pennsylvania Press, 1997.

Bar-Yitshak Ḥayah, and Idit Pintel-Ginsberg, editors. *The Power of a Tale: Stories from the Israel Folktale Archives*. Wayne State University Press, 2019.

Bashardoust, Melissa. *Girl, Serpent, Thorn*. First U.S. edition, First international ed., Flatiron Books, 2020.

Basile, Giambattista, and Nancy L Canepa. *Giambattista Basile's the Tale of Tales, or, Entertainment for Little Ones*. Wayne State University Press, 2007.

Bayron, Kalynn. *Cinderella Is Dead*. Bloomsbury, 2020.

Belle Et La Bête: Beauty and the Beast. Directed by Jean Cocteau. Criterion Collection, 2003.

Beckett, Sandra L. *Recycling Red Riding Hood*. Routledge, 2002.

Ben-Amos, Dan, et al. *Folktales of the Jews*. 1st ed., Jewish Publication Society, 2006.

Benson, Stephen editor. *Contemporary Fiction and the Fairy Tale.* Wayne State University Press, 2008.

Bernheimer, Kate, editor. *Brothers & Beasts: An Anthology of Men on Fairy Tales.* Wayne State University Press, 2007.

---, editor. *Mirror, Mirror on the Wall: Women Writers Explore Their Favorite Fairy Tales.* 1st Anchor Books ed., Anchor Books, 1998.

Bettelheim, Bruno. *The Uses of Enchantment: The Meaning and Importance of Fairy Tales.* 1st ed., Alfred A. Knopf, 1976.

Blécourt Willem de. *Tales of Magic, Tales in Print: On the Genealogy of Fairy Tales and the Brothers Grimm.* Manchester University Press, 2012.

Block, Francesca Lia. *The Rose and the Beast: Fairy Tales Retold.* HarperCollins, 2000.

Bobby, Susan Redington, editor. *Fairy Tales Reimagined: Essays on New Retellings.* McFarland & Company, 2009.

Bottigheimer, Ruth B. *Fairy Tales: A New History.* Excelsior Editions/State University of New York Press, 2009.

---. *Grimms' Bad Girls & Bold Boys: The Moral & Social Vision of the Tales.* Yale University Press, 1987.

Braid, Donald. *Scottish Traveller Tales: Lives Shaped through Stories.* University Press of Mississippi, 2002.

Broumas, Olga. *Beginning with O*. Yale University Press, 1977.

Cabinet des Fées. https://www.cabinetdesfees.com/

Canepa, Nancy L. *From Court to Forest: Giambattista Basile's Lo Cunto De Li Cunti and the Birth of the Literary Fairy Tale*. Wayne State University Press, 1999.

The Carterhaugh School of Folklore and the Fantastic. Created by Sara Cleto and Brittany Warman. https://carterhaugh-school.com/

Chandler, Robert, et al. *Russian Magic Tales from Pushkin to Platonov*. Penguin Books, 2012.

Cleto, Sara, and Brittany Warman. "Waking." *Liminality: A Magazine of Speculative Poetry*. http://www.liminalitypoetry.-com/issues/year-three/issue-10-winter-20162017/waking/

The Company of Wolves. Directed by Neil Jordan. Granada Ventures, 1984.

Crane, Thomas Frederick. *Italian Popular Tales*. ABC-CLIO, 2003.

Cunningham, Michael, and Yuko Shimizu. *A Wild Swan: And Other Tales*. First ed., Farrar, Straus and Giroux, 2015.

Datlow, Ellen, and Terri Windling. *Snow White, Blood Red*. Eos, 2000.

Dégh Linda. *Folktales and Society: Story-Telling in a Hungarian*

Peasant Community. Expanded Edition with a New Afterword. Translated by Emily M Schossberger, Indiana University Press, 1989.

Duggan, Anne E, et al., editors. *Folktales and Fairy Tales: Traditions and Texts from Around the World*. Second ed., Greenwood, an Imprint of ABC-CLIO, 2016.

---. *Queer Enchantments: Gender, Sexuality, and Class in the Fairy-Tale Cinema of Jacques Demy*. Wayne State University Press, 2013.

---. *Salonnières, Furies, and Fairies: The Politics of Gender and Cultural Change in Absolutist France*. University of Delaware Press, 2005.

Dundes, Alan, editor. *Cinderella: a Folklore Casebook*. Garland Pub, 1982.

---, editor. *International Folkloristics: Classic Contributions by the Founders of Folklore*. Rowman & Littlefield, 1999.

---, editor. *Little Red Riding Hood: A Casebook*. University of Wisconsin Press, 1989.

---, editor. *Sacred Narrative, Readings in the Theory of Myth*. University of California Press, 1984.

Dutheil de la Rochère, Martine Hennard, et al., editors. *Cinderella Across Cultures: New Directions and Interdisciplinary Perspectives*. Wayne State University Press, 2016.

El-Shamy, Hasan M. *Folktales of Egypt*. University of Chicago Press, 1980.

---. *Folk Traditions of the Arab World: A Guide to Motif Classification*. Indiana University Press, 1995.

---. *Tales Arab Women Tell: And the Behavioral Patterns They Portray*. Indiana University Press, 1999.

Enchanted Conversation. Created by Kate Wolford. https://www.fairytalemagazine.com/

The Fairy Tellers podcast. https://thefairytellers.podbean.com/

Falassi, Alessandro. *Folklore by the Fireside: Text and Context of the Tuscan Veglia*. University of Texas Press, 1980.

Folklore & Fiction. Created by Ceallaigh S. MacCath-Moran. https://csmaccath.com/blog

The Folklore Podcast. Hosted by Mark Norman. http://www.thefolklorepodcast.com/

FolkTexts. Created by D.L. Ashliman. https://sites.pitt.edu/~dash/folktexts.html

Folkwise Live on Twitch. https://linktr.ee/Folkwise

Franz, Marie-Louise von. *The Feminine in Fairy Tales*. Rev. ed., 1st Shambhala ed., Shambhala, 1993.

Fraser, Lucy. *The Pleasures of Metamorphosis: Japanese and*

English Fairy Tale Transformations of "the Little Mermaid". Wayne State University Press, 2017.

Fréchette, Nathan Caro, and Derek Newman-Stille. *Whispers Between Fairies*. Renaissance Press, 2020.

Gaiman, Neil, and Chris Riddell. *The Sleeper and the Spindle*. First U.S. ed., Harper, an Imprint of HarperCollins, 2015.

---. "Snow, Glass, Apples." In *Smoke and Mirrors: Short Fictions and Illusions*. Avon, 1998, pp. 331–46.

---, and Charles Vess. *Stardust*. Titan, 1999.

Gonzenbach, Laura, and Jack Zipes. *Beautiful Angiola: The Lost Sicilian Folk and Fairy Tales of Laura Gonzenbach*. Routledge, 2006.

Granville, Eliza. *Gretel and the Dark*. First American ed., Riverhead Books, a Member of Penguin Group (USA), 2014.

Greenhill, Pauline, and Jill Terry Rudy, editors. *Channeling Wonder: Fairy Tales on Television*. Wayne State University Press, 2014.

---, and Sidney Eve Matrix. *Fairy Tale Films: Visions of Ambiguity*. Utah State University Press, 2010.

Grimm, Jacob, et al. *The Complete Fairy Tales of the Brothers Grimm*. Bantam 3rd expanded ed., Bantam Books, 2003.

---. *The Original Folk and Fairy Tales of the Brothers Grimm: The Complete First Edition.* Princeton University Press, 2015.

Grundtvig, Sven, and Jens Christian Bay. *Danish Fairy and Folk Tale: A Collection of Popular Stories and Fairy Tales.* Nachdruck der Ausgabe von 1899, Nachdruck der Ausgabe von 1899 ed., Hansebooks GmbH, 2017.

Guran, Paula, editor. *Beyond the Woods: Fairy Tales Retold.* Night Shade Books, 2016.

Haag, M.J. *Depravity: A Beastly Tale Part 1.* 2016.

Haase, Donald, editor. *Fairy Tales and Feminism: New Approaches.* Wayne State University Press, 2004.

---, editor. *The Greenwood Encyclopedia of Folktales and Fairy Tales.* Greenwood Press, 2008.

---, editor. *The Reception of Grimms' Fairy Tales: Responses, Reactions, Revisions.* Wayne State University Press, 1993.

Haddawy, Husain, et al. *The Arabian Nights.* 1st ed., W.W. Norton, 2010.

Haney, Jack V, translator. *Long, Long Tales from the Russian North.* University Press of Mississippi, 2013.

Hannon, Patricia. *Fabulous Identities: Women's Fairy Tales in Seventeenth-Century France.* Rodopi, 1998.

Harries, Elizabeth Wanning. *Twice Upon a Time: Women Writers and the History of the Fairy Tale*. Princeton University Press, 2001.

Harrow, Alix E. *A Spindle Splintered*. Tom Doherty Associates, 2021.

HCA Gilead: Hans Christian Andersen's Fairy Tales and Stories. Created by Zvi Har'El. http://hca.gilead.org.il/

Hejaiej, Monia. *Behind Closed Doors: Women's Oral Narratives in Tunis*. Rutgers University Press, 1996.

Holbek, Bengt. Interpretation of *Fairy Tales: Danish Folklore in a European Perspective*. Suomalainen Tiedeakatemia, 1987.

Hopkinson, Nalo. *Skin Folk*. Warner Books, 2001.

Hubert, Jürgen. *Sunken Castles, Evil Poodles: Commentaries on German*. JürgenWerks, 2020.

The International Fairy-Tale Filmography. Created by Jack Zipes, Pauline Greenhill, and Kendra Magnus-Johnson. http://iftf.uwinnipeg.ca/

Jacobs, Joseph, et al. *English Fairy Tales and More English Fairy Tales*. Edited by Donald Haase, ABC-CLIO, 2002.

Jay, Stacey. *Princess of Thorns*. Random House Children's Books, 2014.

Jones, Christine A, and Charles Perrault. *Mother Goose Refig-*

ured: *A Critical Translation of Charles Perrault's Fairy Tales*. Wayne State University Press, 2016.

Joosen, Vanessa. *Critical and Creative Perspectives on Fairy Tales: An Intertextual Dialogue between Fairy-Tale Scholarship and Post-modern Retellings*. Wayne State University Press, 2011.

Kérchy Anna. *Postmodern Reinterpretations of Fairy Tales: How Applying New Methods Generates New Meanings*. Edwin Mellen Press, 2011.

Kern, Maya. *How to Be a Mermaid*. https://www.mayakern.-com/comics

Koehler, Julie L. J., et al., editors. *Women Writing Wonder: An Anthology of Subversive Nineteenth-Century British, French, and German Fairy Tales*. Wayne State University Press, 2021.

Kvideland, Reimund, et al. *All the World's Reward: Folktales Told by Five Scandinavian Storytellers*. University of Washington Press, 1999.

Lackey, Mercedes. *The Fairy Godmother*. 1st ed., Luna, 2004.

Lang, Andrew. *The Lilac Fairy Book*. Open Road Integrated Media, 1910.

Lavery, Daniel M. *The Merry Spinster: Tales of Everyday Horror*. First ed., Henry Holt and Company, 2018.

Lee, Tanith. "Red as Blood." In *Beyond the Woods: Fairy Tales*

Retold. Edited by Paula Guran. Night Shade Books, 2016, pp. 7–17.

---. *White As Snow.* 1st ed., Tor, 2000.

Levine, Gail Carson. *Ella Enchanted.* First ed., HarperCollins, 1997.

Likovich, Molly. "The Hidden History of Little Red Riding Hood." YouTube. https://youtu.be/LYQc8yv-8is

Little Red Riding Hood and Other Stories. Directed by David Kaplan. Malaprop Productions, 2009.

Lo, Malinda. *Ash.* Little, Brown, and Company, 2009.

The Lure (Córki Dancingu). Directed by Agnieszka Smoczynska. Criterion Collection, 2017.

Lüthi. Max. *The European Folktale: Form and Nature.* Translated by John D. Niles. Bloomington: Indiana University Press, 1982.

Lynn, S.T. *Cinder Ella.* Story Prism Studios, 2016.

Maas, Sarah J. *A Court of Thorns and Roses.* Bloomsbury Publishing, 2015.

Magnanini, Suzanne. *Fairy-Tale Science: Monstrous Generation in the Tales of Straparola and Basile.* University of Toronto Press, 2008.

Maguire, Gregory, et al. *Confessions of an Ugly Stepsister*. First paperback ed., Harper, 2000.

Mardoll, Ana. *Cinder the Fireplace Boy and Other Gayly Grimm Tales*. Acacia Moon Publishing, 2022.

---. *No Man of Woman Born*. Acacia Moon Publishing, 2018.

Marzolph, Ulrich. *101 Middle Eastern Tales and Their Impact on Western Oral Tradition*. Wayne State University Press, 2020.

---. *The Arabian Nights Reader*. Wayne State University Press, 2006.

Massignon Geneviève, and Richard M Dorson. *Folktales of France*. Translated by Jacqueline Hyland, University of Chicago Press, 1968.

Mathias, Elizabeth, et al. *Italian Folktales in America: The Verbal Art of an Immigrant Woman*. Wayne State University Press, 1988.

McGuire, Seanan. *Indexing*. 47North, 2013.

McKinley, Robin. *Deerskin*. Ace Books, 1993.

---. *Sunshine*. 1st ed., Berkley Books, 2003.

McLemore, Anna-Marie. *Blanca y Roja*. First ed., Feiwel and Friends, 2018.

Meyer, Marissa. *Cinder*. 1st ed., Feiwel and Friends, 2012.

Mirror Mirror. Directed by Tarsem Singh. 20th Century Fox Home Entertainment, 2012.

Muhawi, Ibrahim, and Kanaana Sharif. *Speak, Bird, Speak Again: Palestinian Arab Folktales*. University of California Press, 1988.

Multilingual Folk Tale Database. Created by Maarten Janssen. http://www.mftd.org/index.php?action=home

Murai, Mayako. *From Dog Bridegroom to Wolf Girl: Contemporary Japanese Fairy-Tale Adaptations in Conversation with the West*. Wayne State University Press, 2015.

Napoli, Donna Jo. *Beast*. 1st ed., Atheneum Books for Young Readers, 2000.

---. *The Magic Circle*. 1st ed., Dutton Children's Books, 1993.

Narayan, Kirin, and Urmila Devi Sood. *Mondays on the Dark Night of the Moon: Himalayan Foothill Folktales*. Oxford University Press, 1997.

Nguyen, Trung Le. *The Magic Fish*. First ed., RH Graphic, 2020.

Novik, Naomi. *Spinning Silver*. First ed., Del Rey, 2018.

---. *Uprooted*. Del Rey trade paperback ed., Del Rey, 2016.

Once Upon a Blog: Fairy Tale News. Created by Gypsy Thornton. http://fairytalenewsblog.blogspot.com/

Päär Piret, and Türnpu Anne. *Estonian Folktales: The Heavenly Wedding*. Varrak, 2005.

Pan's Labyrinth. Directed by Guillermo del Toro. New Line Home Entertainment, 2006.

Pitrè Giuseppe, et al. *The Collected Sicilian Folk and Fairy Tales of Giuseppe Pitrè*. Routledge, 2009.

Professor of Words. Created by Susan Redington Bobby. http://professorofwords.com/

Ragan, Kathleen, and Jane Yolen. *Fearless Girls, Wise Women, and Beloved Sisters : Heroines in Folktales from Around the World*. 1st ed., W.W. Norton, 1998.

Randolph, Vance. *Pissing in the Snow and Other Ozark Folktales*. University of Illinois Press, 1976.

Ranke, Kurt, editor. *Enzyklopädie des Märchens Online*. https://www.degruyter.com/database/emo/html?lang=en

---. editor. *Folktales of Germany*. Translated by Lotte Simon-Baumann, University of Chicago Press, 1966.

Robert, Katee. *Desperate Measures (Wicked Villains)*. Trinkets and Tales LLC, 2019.

Róheim Géza, and Alan Dundes. *Fire in the Dragon and Other Psychoanalytic Essays on Folklore*. Princeton University Press, 1992.

Roots of Lore podcast. Hosted by Caitlin Brehm. http://caitlin-brehm.com/podcast/

Ruthenia's Motif-Index of Folk Literature. On the Ruthenia site (hosted by Russian State University's Center for Typological and Semiotic Folklore Studies). https://www.rutheni-a.ru/folklore/thompson/

Schacker, Jennifer. *Staging Fairyland: Folklore, Children's Entertainment, and Nineteenth-Century Pantomime.* Wayne State University Press, 2018.

---, and Christine A Jones, editors. *Marvelous Transformations : An Anthology of Fairy Tales and Contemporary Critical Perspectives.* Broadview Press, 2013.

---. *National Dreams: The Remaking of Fairy Tales in Nineteenth-Century England.* University of Pennsylvania Press, 2003.

Schanoes, Veronica, and Jane Yolen. *Burning Girls and Other Stories.* First ed., Tordotcom, a Tom Doherty Associates Book, 2021.

Schönwerth Franz Xaver von. *The Turnip Princess: And Other Newly Discovered Fairy Tales.* Edited by Erika Eichenseer. Translated by Maria Tatar, Penguin Books, 2015.

Schwabe, Claudia. *Craving Supernatural Creatures: German Fairy-Tale Figures in American Pop Culture.* Wayne State University Press, 2019.

Seale, Yasmine, translator. *The Annotated Arabian Nights: Tales from 1001 Nights.* Edited by Paulo Lemos Horta, First ed., Liveright Publishing Corporation, a Division of W. W. Norton & Company, 2021.

Seifert, Lewis Carl. *Fairy Tales, Sexuality, and Gender in France, 1690-1715: Nostalgic Utopias.* Cambridge University Press, 1996.

Sexton, Anne. *Transformations.* Houghton Mifflin, 1971.

Shrek. Directed by Andrew Adamson. DreamWorks Home Entertainment, 2001.

The Shape of Water. Directed by Guillermo del Toro. 20th Century Fox Home Entertainment, 2018.

Snow White and the Huntsman. Directed by Rupert Sanders. Universal Studios Home Entertainment, 2012.

Snow White: A Tale of Terror. Directed by Michael Cohn. Universal, 2002.

Stone, Kay F. *Some Day Your Witch Will Come.* Wayne State University Press, 2008.

Storied Imaginarium. Created by Carina Bissett. https://thestoriedimaginarium.com/

SurLaLune Fairy Tales. Created by Heidi Anne Heiner. https://www.surlalunefairytales.com/

SurLaLune Fairy Tales Discussion Board. https://www.-

surlalunefairytales.com/oldsite/board-archives/2005/may2005/index.html

Taggart, James M. *Enchanted Maidens: Gender Relations in Spanish Folktales of Courtship and Marriage.* Princeton University Press, 1990.

Tales of Faerie. http://talesoffaerie.blogspot.com/

Tatar, Maria. *The Annotated Classic Fairy Tales.* 1st ed., Norton, 2002.

---, editor. *The Classic Fairy Tales : Texts, Criticism.* Second ed., W.W. Norton & Company, 2017.

---. *The Hard Facts of the Grimms' Fairy Tales.* Princeton University Press, 1987.

---. *The Heroine with 1,001 Faces.* First ed., Liveright Publishing Corporation, a Division of W. W. Norton & Company, 2021.

Tepper, Sheri S. *Beauty.* Grafton, 1993.

Thompson, Stith. *The Folktale.* University of California Press, 1977 (1946).

Tiffin, Jessica. *Marvelous Geometry: Narrative and Metafiction in Modern Fairy Tale.* Wayne State University Press, 2009.

Timeless Tales Magazine. Created by Tahlia Kirk. https://www.timelesstalesmagazine.com/

Tong, Diane. *Gypsy Folktales*. 1st ed., Harcourt Brace Jovanovich, 1989.

Tucker, Holly. *Pregnant Fictions: Childbirth and the Fairy Tale in Early-Modern France*. Wayne State University Press, 2003.

Turner, Kay, and Pauline Greenhill, eds. *Transgressive Tales: Queering the Grimms*. Wayne State University Press, 2012.

Tyler, Joseph, et al. *Grimm Fairy Tales Volume 1*. Zenoscope Entertainment, 2006.

Unpacking World Literature: Thompson's Motif Index. https://sites.ualberta.ca/~urban/Projects/English/Motif_Index.htm

Vaz da Silva, Francisco. *Metamorphosis: The Dynamics of Symbolism in European Fairy Tales*. P. Lang, 2002.

Walker, Barbara G. *Feminist Fairy Tales*. 1st ed., Harper Collins, 1996.

Walker, Warren S, and Ahmet Edip Uysal. *Tales Alive in Turkey*. Harvard University Press, 1966.

Williams, Christy. *Mapping Fairy-Tale Space: Pastiche and Metafiction in Borderless Tales*. Wayne State University Press, 2021.

Willingham, Bill, and Lan Medina. *Fables: Legends in Exile*. DC Comics, 2002.

Windling, Terri, editor. *The Armless Maiden and Other Tales for Childhood's Survivors*. First ed., Tor, 1995.

Yeats, W. B, and Paul Muldoon. *Irish Fairy and Folk Tales*. Modern Library, 2003.

Yolen, Jane. *Briar Rose*. Tor Books, 1992.

Zalka, Csenge Virág. *Dancing on Blades: Rare and Exquisite Folktales from the Carpathian Mountains*. First ed., Parkhurst Brothers, 2018.

Zipes, Jack, translator. *Beauties, Beasts and Enchantment: Classic French Fairy Tales*. New American Library, 1989.

---. *The Brothers Grimm: From Enchanted Forests to the Modern World*. Routledge, 1988.

---. *Don't Bet on the Prince: Contemporary Feminist Fairy Tales in North America and England*. Methuen, 1986.

---. *The Enchanted Screen: The Unknown History of Fairy-Tale Films*. Routledge, 2011.

---. *Fairy Tales and the Art of Subversion: The Classical Genre for Children and the Process of Civilization*. 2nd ed., Routledge, 2006.

---. *The Great Fairy Tale Tradition: From Straparola and Basile to the Brothers Grimm : Texts, Criticism*. W.W. Norton, 2001.

---. *The Irresistible Fairy Tale: The Cultural and Social History of a Genre*. Princeton University Press, 2012.

---. *The Oxford Companion to Fairy Tales*. Oxford University Press, 2000.

-- and Laura Gonzenbach. *The Robber with a Witch's Head: More Stories from the Great Treasury of Sicilian Folk and Fairy Tales Collected by Laura Gonzenbach*. Routledge, 2005.

---. *The Trials &Tribulations of Little Red Riding Hood*. 2nd ed., Routledge, 1993.

INDEX

ACKNOWLEDGMENTS

Thanks, first, to Wayne State University Press and the University of Illinois Press and the editors I've worked with there, for nurturing my writing and allowing me to reprint some of the articles of mine you've published.

My cover designer, Cover Villain, and my editor, Donna Martz, have both done wonderful jobs in helping my book find its way into the world. Find them at CoverVillain.com and MartzProofing.com. My indexer, Susan Redington Bobby, also pulled off a massive feat in indexing this monster of a book. You can find her at ProfessorOfWords.com

My friends in the writing community have come through with encouragement and assistance, as well as humor and levity, as needed. My academic colleagues have shared their enthusiasm for my work, which bolstered me through many solitary bouts of writing angst.

ABOUT THE AUTHOR

Dr. Jeana Jorgensen studied folklore at the University of California, Berkeley under Alan Dundes and went on to earn a PhD in folklore from Indiana University. She has authored nearly 30 academic articles and book chapters in addition to blog posts, poems, stories, and rants. She spends entirely too much time on Twitter (@foxyfolklorist), dances, and plays with her sourdough starter.

To learn more about her upcoming books and sign up for her newsletter, you can go to: www.folklore101.com

www.ingramcontent.com/pod-product-compliance
Lightning Source LLC
Chambersburg PA
CBHW030353130626
46549CB00004B/1481